Domain Object Assembler (227)

Populates, persists, and deletes domain objects using a u

Paging Iterator (253)

Iterates efficiently through a collection of domain objects that represents query results.

CACHE PATTERNS

Cache Accessor (271)

Decouples caching logic from the data model and data access details.

Demand Cache (281)

Populates a cache lazily as applications request data. A demand cache is useful for data that is read frequently but unpredictably.

Primed Cache (291)

Explicitly primes a cache with a predicted set of data. A primed cache is useful for data that is read frequently and predictably.

Cache Search Sequence (305)

Inserts shortcut entries into a cache to optimize the number of operations that future searches require.

Cache Collector (325)

Purges entries whose presence in the cache no longer provides any performance benefit.

Cache Replicator (345)

Replicates operations across multiple caches.

Cache Statistics (361)

Record and publish cache and pool statistics using a consistent structure for uniform presentation.

CONCURRENCY PATTERNS

Transaction (379)

Executes concurrent units of work in an atomic, consistent, isolated, and durable manner. Nearly every database platform supports native transactions.

Optimistic Lock (395)

Maintains version information to prevent missing database updates. Optimistic locking uses application semantics to validate a working copy's version before updating the database.

Pessimistic Lock (405)

Attaches lock information to data to prevent missing database updates. Explicit pessimistic locking often offers better application diagnostics than analogous native transaction support.

Compensating Transaction (417)

Defines explicit compensating operations to roll back units of work that are not part of a native database transaction.

Data Access Patterns

Database Interactions in Object-Oriented Applications

The Software Patterns Series

Series Editor: John M. Vlissides

The Software Patterns Series (SPS) comprises pattern literature of lasting significance to software developers. Software patterns document general solutions to recurring problems in all software-related spheres, from the technology itself, to the organizations that develop and distribute it, to the people who use it. Books in the series distill experience from one or more of these areas into a form that software professionals can apply immediately.

Relevance and *impact* are the tenets of the SPS. Relevance means each book presents patterns that solve real problems. Patterns worthy of the name are intrinsically relevant; they are borne of practitioners' experiences, not theory or speculation. Patterns have impact when they change how people work for the better. A book becomes a part of the series not just because it embraces these tenets, but because it has demonstrated it fulfills them for its audience.

Titles in the series:

Data Access Patterns: Database Interactions in Object-Oriented Applications, Clifton Nock

Design Patterns Explained: A New Perspective on Object-Oriented Design, Alan Shalloway/ James R. Trott

Design Patterns Java™ Workbook, Steven John Metsker

The Design Patterns Smalltalk Companion, Sherman Alpert/Kyle Brown/Bobby Woolf

The Joy of Patterns: Using Patterns for Enterprise Development, Brandon Goldfedder

The Manager Pool: Patterns for Radical Leadership, Don Olson/Carol Stimmel

.NET Patterns: Architecture, Design, and Process, Christian Thilmany

Pattern Hatching: Design Patterns Applied, John Vlissides

Pattern Languages of Program Design, edited by James O. Coplien/Douglas C. Schmidt

Pattern Languages of Program Design 2, edited by John M. Vlissides/James O. Coplien/ Norman L. Kerth

Pattern Languages of Program Design 3, edited by Robert Martin/Dirk Riehle/ Frank Buschmann

Small Memory Software, James Noble/Charles Weir

Software Configuration Management Patterns, Stephen P. Berczuk/Brad Appleton

For more information, check out the series web site at www.awprofessional.com/series/swpatterns

Data Access Patterns

Database Interactions in Object-Oriented Applications

Clifton Nock

✦Addison-Wesley

Boston • San Francisco • New York • Toronto • Montreal
London • Munich • Paris • Madrid
Capetown • Sydney • Tokyo • Singapore • Mexico City

The publisher offers discounts on this book when ordered in quantity for bulk purchases and special sales. For more information, please contact:

U.S. Corporate and Government Sales
(800) 382-3419
corpsales@pearsontechgroup.com

For sales outside of the U.S., please contact:

International Sales
(317) 581-3793
international@pearsontechgroup.com

Visit Addison-Wesley on the Web: www.awprofessional.com

Library of Congress Cataloging-in-Publication Data
Nock, Clifton.

Data access patterns: database interations in object-oriented applications / Clifton Nock.
    p. cm. -- (Software patterns series)
Includes index.
ISBN 0-13-140157-2
    1. Software patterns. 2. Computer software--Development. 3. Relational databases. 4. Object-oriented programming (Computer science) I. Title. II. Series.

QA76.76.P37N63 2003
0005.1--dc22   2003060021

The art displayed on chapter opening pages is used with the permission of M. C. Escher, "Development I" © 2003 Cordon Art B. V. - Baarn - Holland. All rights reserved.

ISBN: 0-13-140157-2

Text printed on recycled paper
First printing

To Angie

Contents

Preface

Data is a major element in the foundation of any enterprise. Accountants make and defend decisions using financial data. Manufacturers and purchasers rely on stock and order data to temper inventory. Salespeople study customer history data. Executive management depends on data to examine company controls.

Enterprise software enables these key decision-makers to read, write, and organize data. Data access facilities within business applications play an important role in their quality and usability. Developers must exert considerable effort to design efficient data access code, otherwise an entire application may appear to be slow or prone to defects.

DATA ACCESS PATTERNS

Enterprise software developers tackle the same data access problems regardless of their application domain. These are some examples of common issues that arise when designing data access components:

- Applications need to work with multiple database products.

- User interfaces need to hide obscure database semantics.

- Database resource initialization is slow.

- Data access details make application code difficult to develop and maintain.

- Applications need to cache data that they access frequently.

- Multiple users need to access the same data concurrently.

There are common solutions to these problems. Some of these solutions are intuitive and have been discovered independently by literally thousands of developers. Others are more obscure, and have been solved in only the most robust data access solutions.

Data access patterns describe generic strategies for solving common design problems like these. A pattern does not necessarily dictate a particular implementation. Instead, it describes an effective design and structure that form the basis for a solution.

This book describes patterns that apply specifically to relational data access. Relational databases are by far the most prevalent and proven data storage mechanism that enterprise software uses today. Other persistence technologies, like object-oriented and hierarchical databases, are gaining in popularity. These alternative databases store data closer to its runtime object form, so conventional object-oriented design patterns and techniques apply more readily.

WHO SHOULD READ THIS BOOK?

This book is intended for software architects, designers, and engineers who are responsible for building data access software components. In addition, the material in this book is also appropriate for students who wish to understand common data access problems and solutions.

This book describes data access patterns using common database and object-oriented concepts and terminology. It is expected that the reader has a basic familiarity with both of these. If you run across a term that is not familiar to you, please consult the glossary at the end of the book.

The patterns in this book apply to many platforms, programming languages, and databases. The sample code for each pattern is written using the Java 2 Standard Edition (J2SE), Java 2 Enterprise Edition (J2EE), and Java Database Connectivity (JDBC) APIs. The sample code expresses database operations using Structured Query Language (SQL). A basic understanding of Java and JDBC is helpful when studying this sample code, but it is not essential. Comments and explanations accompany any code that is not straightforward.

HOW THIS BOOK IS ORGANIZED

This book is a pattern catalog. It describes a set of data access patterns in detail. The parts of the book group multiple patterns based on their applicability. Since it is a catalog, do not feel compelled to read the pattern descriptions in order. If a pattern depends on concepts that another pattern defines, it clearly states this fact.

Patterns are identified by concise, descriptive, and familiar names. Pattern names are significant because you can use them in conversation and documentation. It is much more effective to describe a set of interacting classes as an instance of Resource Decorator than to repeatedly describe each element of a pattern in detail.

This book's **"Introduction"** presents the motivation for studying and applying data access patterns. It briefly introduces each pattern. This chapter also defines the form that subsequent chapters use for describing pattern details.

The remainder of the book is the pattern catalog, divided into parts for each pattern category:

- **Part 1, "Decoupling Patterns,"** describes patterns that decouple data access code from other application logic, resulting in cleaner application code that is less susceptible to defects caused by changes that relate only to data access details.

- **Part 2, "Resource Patterns,"** describes patterns for efficient database resource management.

- **Part 3, "Input/Output Patterns,"** describes patterns that simplify data input and output operations using consistent translations between relational data in its physical form and domain object representations.

- **Part 4, "Cache Patterns,"** describes patterns that enable strategic data caching and address the tradeoffs between data access optimization and cache overhead.

- **Part 5, "Concurrency Patterns,"** describes patterns that implement concurrency strategies.

The inside front cover provides a reference listing of the patterns in this book and their descriptions. As you become familiar with the book's structure and the pattern form, you may find this listing convenient for identifying and quickly locating a specific pattern.

SUMMARY

Like any other pattern catalog, this book is not exhaustive. You are encouraged to tweak the solutions to fit your applications and discover new data access patterns along the way. Using and identifying patterns is beneficial, even if you do not document them as formally as those in this book.

I am genuinely interested in any feedback and insight that you have regarding the patterns described here. You can write me in care of Addison-Wesley or send e-mail to dataaccesspatterns@awl.com.

Acknowledgments

First and foremost, I thank my mentor and friend, Paul Monday, for inspiring me to write and advising me throughout the process. Paul's technical expertise and drive are an invaluable resource for me and many others. His ideas have made a significant impact on the content and final form of this book.

I offer my sincere gratitude to Bill Giovinazzo, Neil Harrison, Ralph Johnson, John Neidhart, Clark Scholten, John Vlissides, and Rebecca Wirfs-Brock for their thoughtful and constructive suggestions regarding the technical content of this book.

Many current and former colleagues of mine deserve my genuine appreciation as well. Some directly influenced my personal understanding of the concepts that this book describes, and others directed my career path toward opportunities where I could explore and learn freely: Axel Allgeier, John Broich, Mike Gorman, Gary Grieshaber, Maneesh Gupta, Wray Johnson, Mark Madsen, David Misheski,

Bob Nelson, Lynn Nelson, Scott O'Bryan, Schuman Shao, David Wall, and Bill Wiktor.

My six-year-old son, Dylan, and I shared an "office" while I wrote a lot of this book. He perfected the science of stapler bookbinding and made his way through an astounding amount of printer paper along the way. He wrote several of his own books in the time it took me to write this one. Dylan, Liam, Ethan, and Angie: You have given me unconditional patience, encouragement, and adoration. I am blessed to share my life and work with you.

Introduction

Nearly every enterprise application is backed by persistent data. An application's data is often worth considerably more to its users than the application itself. The majority of many systems' resources are dedicated to implementing and managing data access details and logistics. For this reason, it is important to understand both your data's structure and application's interactions with it in detail so you can tune both for efficiency and maintainability.

A thoughtfully designed data model is the best foundation for efficient data access. Normalized databases with properly defined indices result in more efficient queries and updates. More often than not, programmers and designers are not at liberty to alter or redefine existing data models. Changing an aspect of a data model from one software release to the next might require complicated table conversion processes that disrupt an enterprise's computing environment during an upgrade. In addition, your customers are likely to have built their own custom applications or reports using the data. Changing the data model forces your customers to upgrade these as well. This is likely to deter them from upgrading at all.

Optimizations to data access code are a much more feasible approach, since implementation changes require only the installation of new software. Operations associated with data access can easily be the most expensive in an entire enterprise system. Naive or inefficient data access code makes the difference between streamlined, transparent throughput and slow response times. It follows, then, that data access code is a perfect candidate to target when investigating major optimizations.

Another area to consider where data access strategies pervade is maintenance. Data access code that is spread across many components is difficult to change and optimize, let alone comprehend. Data access code is best left encapsulated within a small number of components so that it is more maintenance-friendly.

The same data access issues tend to arise across a wide variety of application domains. Financial, human resource management, inventory, and customer tracking software can have vastly diverse data models and user interfaces, but still suffer from common data access bottlenecks such as connection overhead, superfluous queries, and concurrency problems.

Just as the same issues appear in many types of applications, developers have solved these problems with common strategies. For example, numerous applications incorporate connection pooling as a mechanism for reducing connection initialization overhead. As this practice became more prevalent and publicized, developers utilized it to improve a growing number of software products. Ultimately, connection pooling has become a common data access optimization strategy supported by many commercial middleware products and defined by standards.

Resource Pool (117) is an example of a data access pattern that has been identified through the abstraction and refactoring of multiple, independent connection pool implementations. Like most of the patterns in this book, it applies to many application domains and platforms. This chapter illustrates how to identify and apply data access patterns and introduces the data access patterns described in the remainder of this book.

APPLICATIONS AND MIDDLEWARE

Creating enterprise software requires two distinct types of expertise. First, developers must be intimately acquainted with the application domain. An *application domain* includes objects and logic that accurately model business concepts and processes. Creating an effective business application requires you to understand what data is involved, the relationships among the data, and what expert users expect to do with it. It is painfully obvious when an application is not designed by domain experts because it forces users into unnatural paradigms.

The second expertise required to develop enterprise software is the ability to write efficient and transparent middleware. The term "*middleware*" refers to the plumbing between application code and the system. Examples of middleware are system resource libraries, prefabricated graphical user interface (GUI) components, and database drivers. In addition, you can consider any code that you write that acts as a conduit between an application and these libraries to be middleware as well. Writing efficient, maintainable middleware code requires extensive knowledge of database resources and libraries.

These specialties differ in a few regards. Developers with application domain expertise usually attain their skill through industrial experience, while middleware experts learn from professional training and documentation. It is uncommon to find programmers with both skill sets. Most middleware programmers are not able to design a truly marketable business application. Conversely, many business application developers do not write efficient middleware code.

Another difference between applications and middleware is marketability. From the perspective of an application development company, applications generate revenue while middleware does not. Customers purchase applications based on the business processes they implement, so domain features are what makes an application marketable. On the other hand, business customers are less interested in middleware features other than expecting the middleware to be fast and robust. Application vendors invest more in application development than middleware for this reason.

Finally, business functionality is unique among applications. An application's features often focus on processes that are specific to a vertical industry. As a result, application domain code varies significantly. By contrast, middleware code can usually be consistent across all application domains, since all applications require similar middleware functionality.

As middleware developers gain experience working on multiple applications, they understand the common features and add them to their personal bag of tricks. Certain techniques apply to nearly every application domain. Developers refine and reuse these techniques, ultimately abstracting them in the form of reusable code or designs. This makes middleware code cheaper and more efficient for each project. As middleware code gets cheaper to develop, software companies can increase their investment in application development, which can in turn lead to higher revenues.

SOFTWARE ABSTRACTIONS

Beginning programmers tend to tackle concrete problems with specific solutions. The resulting code precisely addresses the immediate needs of their customers and requirements. As projects progress and programmers gain experience, they learn how to factor common code and designs into modules.

Modules are a form of *software abstraction*. Software abstraction is the process of making a solution to a specific problem useful in a broader scope. As you abstract a specific solution, you focus on the solution's distinctive characteristics while decoupling it from other components in the system [Booch 1994]. This concentrated focus simplifies complex solutions because it deemphasizes the interactions with other objects. Software abstraction usually leads to more effective and reusable designs and code. Done well, abstractions and reuse significantly reduce overall software development and maintenance costs.

Suppose you have been handed a requirement to cache account information for the purpose of improving a shopping cart application's performance. You start with an empty cache object and add an entry to it every time the application references a new account. Subsequent account references are faster since their information is already available in the cache.

You can approach this problem at any of the following levels:

1. *Hardwiring* is a brute-force approach that solves only the specific problem. You change every aspect of your application code that requires account information to first check the cache and, if necessary, query the database.

2. *Modularizing* involves solving the problem once and utilizing the solution multiple times. You create a common subroutine to check the cache and query the database, if required. Application code calls this subroutine whenever it needs account information.

3. *Generalizing* means designing modules to solve a broader problem set than your specific requirements dictate. In this example, you can define a common cache

lookup subroutine that works with any table and cache, not just those for account data.

4. *Patterns* address design problems across multiple application domains and programming environments. Demand Cache (281) describes a common solution for a class of similar caching problems. The account information cache is a specific instance of Demand Cache.

This list forms a progression of software abstractions. Each abstraction level is potentially more reusable than the previous ones. However, development of abstractions requires a broader understanding of problem domains and predictions of other problems and requirements that are likely to arise in future iterations.

DESIGN PATTERNS

Design patterns provide generic, reusable designs that solve problems at the design level. A design pattern does not define code and is not specific to a given programming domain. Instead, it provides a proven, tested solution for a class of similar design problems. Design patterns also lend common terminology that you can use to make your own designs easier to document and understand [Gamma 1995].

Patterns describe techniques that experts have abstracted from multiple specific solutions. Identifying and understanding patterns provide two essential benefits. First, they introduce effective design strategies to less experienced designers, alleviating them from rediscovering these patterns using trial and error. Second, they attach common names to ideas that you can readily use in conversation, design meetings, and documentation.

Design patterns are not created from theoretical examples. Experienced object-oriented designers recognize that certain object structures and interactions lend themselves more readily to maintenance and reusability than others. Just like architects and civil engineers define broad building concepts that apply at many levels, software designers assemble a set of patterns that they can apply to a variety of domains.

Many seasoned designers have taken the initiative to identify and document patterns. Design pattern catalogs consolidate related patterns in a single reference collection. The most influential design pattern catalog is the book *Design Patterns: Elements of Reusable Object-Oriented Software* by Erich Gamma, Richard Helm, Ralph Johnson, and John Vlissides [Gamma 1995]. It identifies and describes patterns that solve broad object-oriented design problems. Many other more special-ized catalogs exist, targeting domains such as enterprise application architecture [Fowler 2002], J2EE applications [Alur 2001, Marinescu 2002], business software [Carey 2000], embedded systems [Pont 2001], and testing [Binder 1999].

DATA ACCESS PATTERNS

Just as design patterns document solutions to common design problems, data access patterns have a similar role within the field of data access. The data access patterns in this book describe common abstractions for solutions that you can apply directly within your own applications. Some data access patterns are so uni-versally applicable that many commercial products implement them by default. Resource Pool (117) and Object/Relational Map (53) are two such examples. Application servers or plumbing platforms that implement patterns like these save you from building the same infrastructure on your own.

Other data access patterns are less pervasive, but still apply across many appli-cation domains. For example, data caching is a common optimization, but you must implement it carefully so that you do not impose more overhead than the physical database operations you are trying to avoid issuing do. In this respect, you must consider specific usage patterns and the nature of the data to be cached. These are characteristics to which a more generic product might have a difficult time adapting.

THE PATTERN CATALOG

This book is a catalog of data access patterns. Each chapter describes a pattern in full and related patterns are grouped into parts. This is only an organizational cat-egorization and has little bearing on the application and interactions of the pat-terns themselves.

Since it is a catalog, you can read this book in any order. The patterns do relate to each other, and these relations are documented in the "Related Patterns and Technology" section for each pattern. However, these relations do not necessarily act as prerequisites.

Here is a preview of the catalog's organization and its patterns:

Decoupling Patterns

Decoupling patterns describe strategies for decoupling data access components from other parts of an application. This decoupling allows flexibility when choosing an underlying data model, as well as when making changes to the overall data access strategies for a system.

Another essential aspect to decoupling patterns is the data access abstraction they expose to the rest of the system. This abstraction must be sufficiently versatile to expose the appropriate level of data access capabilities. However, it must also be broad enough to make it feasible to plug in alternate data sources and algorithms. All of the patterns in **Part 1, "Decoupling Patterns,"** work toward these goals.

- **Data Accessor** (9)—Encapsulates physical data access details in a single component, exposing only logical operations. Application code maintains knowledge about the underlying data model, but is decoupled from data access responsibilities.

- **Active domain object** (33)—Encapsulates the data model and data access details within relevant domain object implementations. Active domain objects relieve application code of any direct database interaction.

- **Object/relational map** (53)—Encapsulates the mapping between domain objects and relational data in a single component. An object/relational map decouples both application code and domain objects from the underlying data model and data access details.

- **Layers** (75)—Stack orthogonal application features that address data access issues with increasing levels of abstraction.

Resource Patterns

Resource patterns describe strategies for managing the objects involved in relational database access. A substantial amount of relational database access code today employs a standard call-level interface like Open Database Connectivity (ODBC), Object Linking and Embedding Database (OLE DB), and JDBC. Interface standards have matured in recent years, but most retain well-known concepts like database connections, statement handles, and operation processing. The patterns in **Part 2, "Resource Patterns,"** address performance and semantic issues that frequently arise when accessing relational data using a call-level interface.

- **Resource Decorator** (103)—Dynamically attaches additional behavior to an existing resource with minimal disruption to application code. A resource decorator enables the extension of a resource's functionality without subclassing or changing its implementation.

- **Resource Pool** (117)—Recycles resources to minimize resource initialization overhead. A resource pool manages resources efficiently while allowing application code to freely allocate them.

- **Resource Timer** (137)—Automatically releases inactive resources. A resource timer alleviates the effect of applications or users that allocate resources indefinitely.

- **Resource Descriptor** (159)—Isolates platform- and data source-dependent behavior within a single component. A resource descriptor exposes specific platform idiosyncrasies that relate to particular database resources as generic, logical operations, and enables the majority of data access code to remain independent of its physical environment.

- **Retryer** (171)—Automatically retries operations whose failure is expected under certain defined conditions. This pattern enables fault tolerance for data access operations.

Input/Output Patterns

Part 3, "Input/Output Patterns," describes patterns that simplify data input and output operations using consistent translations between relational data in its physical form and domain object representations.

- **Selection Factory** (191)—Generates query selections based on identity object attributes.

- **Domain Object Factory** (203)—Populates domain objects based on query result data.

- **Update Factory** (215)—Generates update operations based on modified domain object attributes.

- **Domain Object Assembler** (227)—Populates, persists, and deletes domain objects using a uniform factory framework.

- **Paging Iterator** (253)—Iterates efficiently through a collection of domain objects that represent query results.

Cache Patterns

Cache patterns address solutions that reduce the frequency of data access operations by storing common data in a cache. These patterns usually cache domain objects rather than physical data. This is an important design point because it optimizes the cached form that the caller requires. The patterns in **Part 4, "Cache Patterns,"** provide structures for generic, efficient, and extensible caching.

- **Cache Accessor** (271)—Decouples caching logic from the data model and data access details.

- **Demand Cache** (281)—Populates a cache lazily as applications request data. A demand cache is useful for data that is read frequently but unpredictably.

- **Primed Cache** (291)—Explicitly primes a cache with a predicted set of data. A primed cache is useful for data that is read frequently and predictably.

- **Cache Search Sequence** (305)—Inserts shortcut entries into a cache to optimize the number of operations that future searches require.

- **Cache Collector** (325)—Purges entries whose presence in the cache no longer provides any performance benefit.

- **Cache Replicator** (345)—Replicates operations across multiple caches.

- **Cache Statistics** (361)—Record and publish cache and pool statistics using a consistent structure for uniform presentation.

Concurrency Patterns

Concurrency patterns address what happens when multiple users issue concurrent database operations that involve common data. Most databases include locking features to help with this class of problem, but customized, application-level solutions can be tuned for specific application semantics and providing better feedback to end-users. The patterns in **Part 5, "Concurrency Patterns,"** describe strategies for robust, concurrent data access with data integrity preservation being the prime motivating factor.

- **Transaction** (379)—Executes concurrent units of work in an atomic, consistent, isolated, and durable manner. Nearly every database platform supports native transactions.

- **Optimistic Lock** (395)—Maintains version information to prevent missing database updates. Optimistic locking uses application semantics to validate a working copy's version before updating the database.

- **Pessimistic Lock** (405)—Attaches lock information to data to prevent missing database updates. Explicit pessimistic locking often offers better application diagnostics than analogous native transaction support.

- **Compensating Transaction** (417)—Defines explicit compensating operations to roll back units of work that are not part of a native database transaction.

THE PATTERN FORM

Each pattern chapter in this book follows a consistent form. The form serves to formalize various aspects of each pattern's analysis. Every chapter is divided into the following sections, each of which addresses a particular pattern characteristic.

Pattern Name

A pattern's name serves as its most recognizable identifier. You can refer to pattern names in conversation and design documentation to explain which patterns you have employed without requiring a great deal of additional explanation. The convention in this book is to name patterns with short and unambiguous noun phrases. As a quick reference tool, any time a pattern name is mentioned outside its own chapter, it is followed by its page number in parentheses. An example of this is Optimistic Lock (405).

Description

The "Description" section is a sentence or short paragraph that succinctly explains the solution that a data access pattern provides. Use a pattern's description to quickly gauge its relevance to a particular design problem. The inside front cover of this book lists each data access pattern by name and gives its description as a quick reference.

Context

Engineers do not identify patterns from scratch. A pattern's originators have solved the same problem several times before coming up with a general solution. A pattern's context is a characterization of the problem or class of problems that it solves. This section also includes an illustrative example of the problem.

Applicability

A pattern's applicability is a list of conditions that indicate when its integration into a design is likely to be beneficial. Do not view these items as prerequisites, but rather as general guidelines.

Structure

The static structure of a pattern is illustrated using one or more Unified Modeling Language (UML) class diagrams. The interfaces, classes, and relationships in the diagram represent the pattern's fundamental concepts in broad terms. By no means should you feel obligated to use the precise entity names and relationships that this section defines. They intentionally use generic names to form the basis for subsequent discussion. It is anticipated that you will customize these entities as you apply them to a particular problem.

These terms make up a small naming convention for some of the patterns' structural entities:

- *Client*—The application or caller that consumes the pattern's implementation.

- *Data*—Data in its physical form, as stored in the database.

- *Domain object*—A domain-specific object representation of data.

- *Accessor*—An object whose role within a pattern is to encapsulate data access.

- *Base*—A generic, base implementation of an interface.

- *Concrete*—A specific, concrete implementation of an interface.

- *Factory*—An object whose primary role is to create or resolve implementation instances.

The "Structure" section also describes the role of each participant entity within the context of the pattern.

Interactions

This section describes the interactions among a pattern's participants. In essence, these interactions define how a pattern solves a problem. In some cases, the interactions are illustrated by one or more UML sequence diagrams. Sequence diagrams show the operational flow between participants as they carry out their individual roles. In other cases, this section describes interactions using only text, when that is more succinct than a sequence diagram.

Consequences

The consequences of a pattern describe the positive and negative effects that it can have on the overall system or application. This section contains one or more of each of these consequence types:

- *Benefits*—A pattern's benefits are its positive effects on the overall system. These usually line up with a pattern's description and embody the reason you employ the pattern in the first place.

- *Drawbacks*—A pattern's drawbacks describe its potentially degrading effects on the overall system. Not all drawbacks occur along with every application of a pattern, but they are conditions to keep in mind as you employ it.

- *Tradeoffs*—A pattern's tradeoffs describe considerations involving balancing mutually exclusive benefits and liabilities.

Strategies

This section describes useful techniques for implementing a pattern. It addresses the less obvious aspects of implementation details and offers suggestions for overcoming common problems.

Sample Code

The "Sample Code" section contains examples that usually implement the example scenario presented in the "Context" section. These are not full applications, but rather code blocks that focus directly on illustrating the pattern's key features.

All of the examples in this book use Java, and most of them use JDBC and SQL. JDBC is the standard relational data access interface for Java code, and SQL is the most common language for expressing relational database operations. The patterns in this book are by no means limited to Java, JDBC, and SQL. However, these technologies are widely understood and lend themselves to concise examples. I have made every effort to keep the sample code simple and clearly documented. As a result, you do not need to understand Java syntax details and semantics fluently to read the sample code.

Sample code intentionally omits necessary but uninteresting code details like import statements and connection uniform resource locators (URLs). These omissions are for the sake of brevity and retaining focus on the implementation aspects that relate to the pattern.

Related Patterns and Technology

Every data access pattern relates to other patterns, standards, or products in some way. This section cross-references these relationships. Examples of pattern relationships are:

- *Usage*—One pattern uses another if it builds on its foundation. For example, Domain Object Assembler (227) depends on implementations of Selection Factory (191), Domain Object Factory (203), and Update Factory (215). In a few cases, usage relationships extend across multiple levels. This section only describes direct relationships.

- *Instantiation*—One pattern is an instance of another if it refines its structure. For example, Resource Decorator (103) is an instance of the Decorator pattern described in [Gamma 1995] because it defines an application of it that is geared specifically to database resources.

- *Alternative*—Patterns are alternatives of each other if their solutions can be interchanged with similar results. Demand Cache (281) and Primed Cache (291) are examples of alternatives that can be applied to the same class of caching problems.

- *Cooperation*—Patterns cooperate when they can be applied together to form a comprehensive solution. For example, Cache Collector (325) can cooperate with Cache Accessor (271) to implement a robust caching solution.

APPLYING DATA ACCESS PATTERNS

Reading and understanding patterns exposes you to ideas that may find a place in your own software designs. Applying data access patterns involves several skills. The most important skill is being able to identify an appropriate pattern when an applicable problem arises. In some cases, problems match pattern descriptions exactly and obviously. Others require a certain amount of creativity to notice that a pattern may be specialized in ways other than what the examples in the text describe. Nearly as important is being able to identify when a chosen pattern does not apply to a given design problem. Inappropriate patterns can convolute your design and might force you to build awkward constructs that compromise your design goals.

Practice and a willingness to try and discard solutions are the best ways to attain these skills. Here are some general items to consider as you apply patterns:

- *Be familiar with the patterns*—Read the pattern descriptions enough to understand what each pattern offers. You will not be able to apply a pattern with just this information. However, having a basic familiarity may remind you to investigate certain patterns in more detail when an applicable design or optimization problem presents itself.

- *Refer to patterns in design and code documentation*—A great advantage of documenting patterns is defining reusable nomenclature. Documented patterns give names to general and proven ideas. Refer to any patterns that you apply in your design and code documentation. This gives the reader a place to look to understand your design at a broader level and also saves you from explaining your design in detail.

- *Change entity names to match your domain*—Consider the class, interface, and operation names that patterns describe to be placeholders rather than final names. As you apply a pattern, replace its entity names with those that match your domain. Your code will make more sense to casual readers who are unfamiliar with the pattern.

- *Take liberties with the patterns*—Patterns describe abstract design ideas that have broad application. If a pattern solves a particular problem for you, but does not directly fit into your existing design, then change it. Even if you use parts of a pattern or change its structure or interaction, it still adds value to your application, and it is still worth documenting. It is always better to keep your design clean than to strictly adhere to a pattern.

- *Do not constrain your design*—Patterns are not a panacea for software design. Pattern catalogs collect and document related patterns, but they are by no means a totality of all solutions. Use patterns when they benefit your design, but do not constrain your design to the exclusive use of patterns.

- *Invent your own patterns*—As you practice applying patterns to design and optimization problems, you may also begin to identify abstract solutions of your own. Take the time to document these as patterns using a form of your choice and refer to them in your design documentation. You can expand on your own patterns in one place and refer to them elsewhere. When you only have one place to document patterns, you are more likely to take the time to explain their concepts in detail.

SUMMARY

Expertise in database technology is diverse because it encompasses data modelling, database administration, interaction with programming interfaces, and understanding many competing technologies. It is rare for a single engineer to specialize in all of these aspects, but it often happens that development organizations grant certain lucky individuals all of these responsibilities.

Database technology changes frequently. Manufacturers of database products face tough competition, and vendors deliver new programming interfaces and features regularly as a means to differentiate their products from others. As a "database expert," you may be expected to keep up on these products and incorporate them into your software when applicable.

One approach you can take to meet this grand expectation is to thoroughly research current technology, choose what works best for your software, and design your software around it. This strategy is effective for your current software release, but it may lead you to make assumptions based on the chosen technology that contradict the incorporation of additional features in subsequent releases of your software. A better strategy is to build your software to be agile. *Agile software* adapts readily and transparently to new requirements and new technology. Even when you cannot predict how rapid technology changes will affect your architecture, you can isolate design decisions based on current technology so that they can be changed with minimal effect on the rest of the system. This approach is commonly known as future-proofing. The faster you are able to incorporate new, useful database features into your software, the more you can differentiate the software against your competitors.

This book serves as an illustration of this concept. It does not directly depend on the use of any specific, current database technology. Instead, the patterns and code in this book are intentionally generic. The concepts apply across many relational database technologies, because most of these technologies exhibit common characteristics. Consequently, the patterns in this book and other sources enable you to isolate specific design decisions so that you can future-proof the software that you build.

Part 1

Decoupling Patterns

The previous chapter introduced the differences between application and middleware code. Developing application code requires extensive domain knowledge and experience with the business objects and processes that the software is supposed to model. On the other hand, middleware code consists of more technical details, for which programmers who are used to working with system-level resources and libraries are more qualified. Even small application development groups can benefit by dividing software into layers that separate application and middleware code. With a clean separation, application code deals exclusively with business objects and logic while middleware code handles system and database details.

Defining the exact nature of this separation requires you to consider the types of maintenance and enhancements that you expect to address in future releases. Ask these questions as you evaluate a potential architectural solution:

- *What features were dropped to meet schedules?*—Even if you do not have time to implement these features, you should consider building isolated placeholders that facilitate their future incorporation.

- *What additional features do you expect your customers to request?*—This is hard to predict and requires research and imagination. Consider meeting with potential customers for brainstorming sessions or usability testing. They can decide how to use your application in their environment and can help you determine what features are important.

- *Do you expect the underlying data model to change?*—Will you be modifying the data model in future releases? Do you need to adapt to variations in the data model for different customer environments?

- *Do you expect to support new database platforms?*—As you expand your customer base, you may be forced to support additional database platforms that partnerships and contracts dictate.

- *Do you plan to take advantage of advances in database technology?*—If it is important for your application to utilize cutting-edge database technology, then consider which components need to adapt when something new comes along.

- *Are you dependent on third-party components?*—When you find defects in your code, you have complete control of the debugging and repair process. However, if you identify a defect in a third-party component on which you depend, you have to wait for a fix from its vendor. In addition, it is not uncommon for professional partnerships to dissolve. In these cases, you may find yourself incorporating some competing technology in place of another vendor's component.

- *Do you expect performance problems to occur?*—Many best practices recommend designing your software with a focus on structure and maintainability first, and fixing performance problems later. Even when you follow this good advice, you can still predict and isolate likely bottlenecks.

Decoupling patterns describe strategies for accommodating the issues that you raise when you answer these questions. The primary, common goal of these patterns is to decouple orthogonal software components. The extent to which you decouple components depends on how much you expect them to vary independently. For instance, if you expect to support additional database platforms in future releases, then it is a good idea to isolate all the code that is specific to a particular database in a separate, swappable component.

Another common example of decoupling is defining the line between applications and middleware. If you plan to expand your application or build new, similar applications, it is beneficial to decouple them from middleware code. This allows you to reuse the same middleware components and develop new applications more quickly.

THE DATA MODEL AND DATA ACCESS

An application's *data model* is the static structure of its data. It encompasses one or more tables, any associated indices, views, and triggers, plus any referential integrity features defined between tables. The term "data model" also refers to an application's understanding of this static structure, whether it is hardwired or discovered dynamically using metadata.

In most cases, you define a data model with data that is intended to be used exclusively by your applications. From your customer's perspective, you encapsulate the specifics of the data model within your applications. This grants you leeway to change or add to the data model, since you can change the applications at the same time.

In some cases, you may publish your data model so that customers or consultants can integrate your applications' data into those from other vendors. A common example of this is a generic reporting tool that analyzes arbitrary data models and graphically summarizes their data. Another scenario is when a customer integrates your applications with others using an enterprise application integration (EAI) framework. If you support or encourage these scenarios, you are more limited to the types of changes that you can make to your applications' data models. For instance, you can add columns to a table, but you cannot remove columns without the risk of breaking dependent applications.

A final scenario is when your customers define their own data models. You can design your application to work explicitly with their legacy data. This degree of agility can be a significant selling feature, but your application must readily adapt to a variety of table configurations.

In contrast to its data model, an application's *data access* refers to its dynamic mechanism for reading and writing data. Data access code involves implementing direct database operations using commercial drivers or libraries.

You can choose to combine the notions of the data model and data access in your application. Combining them results in one or more cohesive database components that can take advantage of their data model knowledge to optimize data access operations. For example, this can allow a database component to form queries that explicitly take advantage of known table indices, an optimization that substantially improves query performance. On the other hand, separating an application's data model and data access enables you to change or more readily adapt to changes in the data model.

DOMAIN OBJECTS AND RELATIONAL DATA

A primary benefit of object-oriented programming is the ability to model your application domain directly in software. Writing application code that manipulates Customer and Account objects is more straightforward and less error-prone than computing offsets, passing large structures, and mapping all data to primitive types.

True domain objects model application concepts, not necessarily those imposed by the data model. This means that you should not always define objects based on the layout of tables and columns. Doing so binds your domain objects to the data model and forces applications to understand these details. Suppose you have CUSTOMERS and EMPLOYEES tables that, for historical reasons, include similar but not identical address columns. The column names and types may be inconsistent in the data model, but you can define Customer and Employee domain objects that expose the same Address object type. This consistency can lead to common address processing code that handles both customer and employee addresses identically.

Well-defined domain objects lead to cleaner application code, but present a problem for middleware. Object-oriented programming and relational databases are significantly different paradigms. Any software that utilizes both of these concepts must translate between them at some point. Mapping relational data to domain objects requires you to process query results and create analogous objects based on the application's data. Conversely, the other direction requires you to generate database operations that make changes to persistent relational data that corresponds to domain object changes. Figure P1.1 illustrates a mapping that translates between Customer, Employee, and Address domain objects and the corresponding relational data:

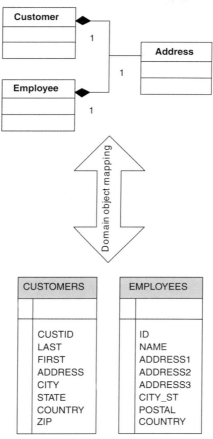

FIGURE P1.1: A domain object mapping translates between domain objects and relational data.

Object-oriented databases that serialize and store objects directly in their runtime form provide one solution. They eliminate the need for extra domain object mapping altogether. However, object-oriented databases are not commonly used in enterprise software because they make it harder to integrate with other products that depend heavily on relational data models. In addition, most major database vendors do not provide object-oriented database engines.

Many applications therefore provide their own domain object mapping, intentionally or not. Even the most basic applications tend to tackle this problem on their own. In its simplest form, solving this problem requires an application to issue explicit database operations and manipulate corresponding domain objects with brute force.

This strategy gets unwieldy when many tables and objects are involved. As the magnitude of the mapping problems increases, you can address the problems with increasingly robust designs. One solution is to define a set of common operations or a framework that populates and persists domain objects in a uniform, consistent manner. Part 3, "Input/Output Patterns," describes some patterns that can help you build these types of structures.

You can also consider building or buying a full-fledged object/relational mapping tool. Object/relational mapping formalizes the process of mapping domain objects to and from relational data. Object/Relational Map (53) describes this strategy in detail.

DECOUPLING PATTERNS

Decoupling patterns define how application code relates to its data model and data access code. As you decide on an application architecture, you need to consider how much cohesion you want between orthogonal components based on how much you expect them to vary independently. Decoupling components also makes it easier to build and maintain them concurrently.

Another essential aspect of applying a decoupling pattern is defining the data access abstraction that it exposes to the rest of the system. This abstraction must be sufficiently versatile to expose the appropriate level of data access capabilities. On the other hand, it must also be broad enough to make it feasible to plug in alternate data sources and algorithms if required.

This part of the book contains chapters for each of the following patterns:

- **Data Accessor** (9)—Encapsulates physical data access details in a single component, exposing only logical operations. Application code maintains knowledge about the underlying data model, but is decoupled from data access responsibilities.

- **Active Domain Object** (33)—Encapsulates the data model and data access details within relevant domain object implementations. Active domain objects relieve application code of any direct database interaction.

- **Object/Relational Map** (53)—Encapsulate the mapping between domain objects and relational data in a single component. An object/relational map decouples both application code and domain objects from the underlying data model and data access details.

- **Layers** (75)—Stack orthogonal application features that address data access issues with increasing levels of abstraction.

These patterns differ in the level of database abstraction they expose to application code as well as the organization of data model awareness and data access within the architecture. These differences do not make them mutually exclusive. Layers (75) describes some examples of how you might combine these patterns to build a solution that completely separates an application's data model, data access, and domain object mapping. Extensive decoupling allows you to vary each of these components independently and leads to agile and adaptable software designs.

Data Accessor

DESCRIPTION

Encapsulates physical data access details in a single component, exposing only logical operations. Application code maintains knowledge about the underlying data model, but is decoupled from data access responsibilities.

CONTEXT

Developing enterprise software requires a rich mix of programming and business experience. Application logic must accurately reflect business processes within its domain as well as utilize data access and system resources efficiently.

Take an employee payroll system as an example. Consider a simple batch process that issues reimbursement checks for employee expenses. This process requires the following database operations:

1. Get a list of all employees for whom expense reimbursements are due.

2. For each employee in this list, get a list of active expenses reported.

3. Issue the employee a check for the total.

4. Reset the employee's expense status.

5. Delete the employee's active expense records.

The application logic for this process is straightforward. It does not stray much from the steps listed here. However, its code has the potential to be the opposite. The database code for each of these steps requires multiple physical database operations and management of the corresponding resources. If you mix this code within the application logic, it quickly becomes convoluted.

The following code block illustrates this phenomenon. It implements the employee expense reimbursement process using Java, JDBC, and SQL. Notice the mix of database, technology, and domain details.

```java
Connection connection
    = DriverManager.getConnection(...);

// Get a list of employees that need to be
// reimbursed for expenses.
PreparedStatement employeesStatement
    = connection.prepareStatement(
    "SELECT EMPLOYEE_ID FROM P_EMPLOYEES "
    + "WHERE EXPENSE_FLAG = ?");
employeesStatement.setString(1, "Reimburse");

ResultSet employeesResultSet
    = employeesStatement.executeQuery();

while(employeesResultSet.next())
{
    int employeeID = employeesResultSet.getInt(1);

    // Get a list of expense records for the employee.
    PreparedStatement expensesStatement
        = connection.prepareStatement(
        "SELECT AMOUNT FROM A_EXPENSES "
        + "WHERE EMPLOYEE_ID = ?");
    expensesStatement.setInt(1, employeeID);

    ResultSet expensesResultSet
        = expensesStatement.executeQuery();
```

```
    // Total the expense records.
    long totalExpense = 0;
    while(expensesResultSet.next()) {
        long amount = expensesResultSet.getLong(1);
        totalExpense += amount;
    }

    // Issue the employee a check for the sum.
    issueEmployeeCheck(employeeID, totalExpense);

    // Update the employee's expense status to none.
    PreparedStatement updateExpenseStatus
        = connection.prepareStatement(
        "UPDATE P_EMPLOYEES SET EXPENSE_FLAG = ? "
        + "WHERE EMPLOYEE_ID = ?");
    updateExpenseStatus.setString(1, "None");
    updateExpenseStatus.setInt(2, employeeID);
    updateExpenseStatus.executeUpdate();
    updateExpenseStatus.close();

    // Delete all of the employee's expense records.
    PreparedStatement deleteExpenseRecords
        = connection.prepareStatement(
        "DELETE FROM A_EXPENSES WHERE EMPLOYEE_ID = ?");
    deleteExpenseRecords.setInt(1, employeeID);
    deleteExpenseRecords.executeUpdate();
    deleteExpenseRecords.close();

    expensesStatement.close();
    expensesResultSet.close();
}

employeesResultSet.close();
employeesStatement.close();
```

Now, scale this implementation style to an entire suite of applications. Having database access code sprinkled throughout application logic makes it especially hard to maintain. One reason is that developers who support and enhance this code must be intimately familiar with both the application logic and data access details. Bigger problems arise when you need to support additional database plat-forms or incorporate optimizations such as a connection pool. With data access code spread throughout an entire product, these enhancements become major engineering projects that span a majority of the product's source files.

The Data Accessor pattern addresses this problem. Its primary objective is to build an abstraction that hides low-level data access details from the rest of the application code. This abstraction exposes only high-level, logical operations. With a robust abstraction in place, application code focuses on operations from the domain point of view. This focus results in clean, maintainable application logic. Figure 1.1 illustrates how the data accessor abstraction and implementation decouple the application logic from the physical database driver:

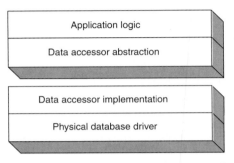

FIGURE 1.1: The Data Accessor pattern decouples application logic from the physical data access implementation by defining an abstraction that exposes only logical operations to the application code.

The data accessor implementation handles all the physical data access details on behalf of the application code. This isolation makes it possible to fix database access defects and incorporate new features in a single component and affect the entire system's operation.

The logical operations that you expose depend on your application's data access requirements. In the employee expense process described earlier, it might be helpful to define logical read and write operations in terms of table and column names without requiring the application code to issue SQL statements or directly manage prepared statements or result sets. The "Sample Code" section in this chapter contains an example of some simple logical database operations.

You can also use a data accessor to hide a database's semantic details as well as constraints that your system's architecture imposes. Here are some ideas for encapsulating physical data access details:

- *Expose logical operations; encapsulate physical operations*—The data accessor abstraction can expose logical database operations such as read, insert, update, and delete, instead of requiring application code to issue SQL statements or something at a similar, lower level. The data accessor implementation generates efficient SQL statements on the application's behalf. This is beneficial because it saves application developers from learning the intricacies of SQL and also allows you to change your strategies for issuing these operations without affecting application code.

- *Expose logical resources; encapsulate physical resources*—The more details you hide from application code, the more you are at liberty to change. One example of this is database resource management. If you let applications manage their own database connections, it is hard to incorporate enhancements like connection pooling, statement caching, or data distribution later on.

  You may find it convenient to provide logical connection handles to applications. Applications can use these handles to associate operations with physical connection pools and physical connection mapping strategies. The data accessor implementation is responsible for resolving exact table locations and physical connections at runtime. This is especially convenient when data is distributed across multiple databases.

- *Normalize and format data*—The physical format of data is not necessarily the most convenient form for applications to work with, especially if the format varies across multiple database platforms. For example, databases often store and return binary large object (BLOB) data as an array or stream of raw bytes. The data accessor implementation can be responsible for deserializing these bytes and handing an object representation to the application.

- *Encapsulate platform details*—Business relationships change frequently. If your company initiates a new partnership that requires your application to support additional database products, encapsulating any database platform details within a data accessor implementation facilitates the enhancements. If you take this as far as to hide any particular technology, such as SQL, then you can more readily support non-SQL databases as well, all without extensive application code changes.

- *Encapsulate optimization details*—Application behavior should not directly depend on optimizations like pools and caches because that hinders your ability to change these optimizations in the future. If you only allow application code to allocate logical resources and issue logical operations, then you retain the freedom to implement these logical operations within the data accessor implementation with whatever optimized strategies are at your disposal.

The Data Accessor pattern makes application code more amenable to enhancement and optimization. In addition, it defines a clear separation between application domain code and data access details. Besides the maintenance issues described throughout this chapter, this separation benefits engineering teams as well, since you can divide the development of different components among multiple programmers with diverse skills and experience.

APPLICABILITY

Use the Data Accessor pattern when:

- You want to hide physical data access complexity and platform issues from application logic. Doing so keeps application logic cleaner and more focused on the business objects and processes that it models.

- You want to manage additional semantics over and above those that the underlying physical database driver provides. Database drivers do not normally handle data distribution or application-level locking mechanisms because the implementation of these features depends heavily on an application's topological and semantic architecture.

- You want to define multiple data access implementations and choose between them at runtime. Different implementations might accommodate multiple database platforms or even completely new database technology, such as extensible markup language (XML) queries or an object-oriented database.

STRUCTURE

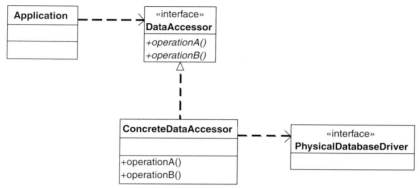

FIGURE 1.2: The static structure of the Data Accessor pattern.

Figure 1.2 illustrates the static structure of the Data Accessor pattern. The DataAccessor interface defines the data access abstraction in terms of logical operations that the application code uses. You must define these operations to be extensive enough so that applications can do useful work without forcing applications to use unnatural constructs or workarounds. You can tailor the exact logical operation semantics to keep application code as straightforward as possible. You must also be careful not to expose any physical semantics in these logical operations. Doing so enables application code to depend on exposed physical features, making it difficult to change later. Also be mindful that you do not need to define the entire set of logical operations in a single interface as Figure 1.2 shows. It is common to separate logical query, update, result set, and transaction operations into multiple interfaces.

ConcreteDataAccessor provides the implementation of logical operations in terms of physical database operations. This class depends directly on specific database technology. You may define more than one concrete implementation if you need to support different physical database interfaces or technologies.

Notice that this pattern encapsulates an application's data access, but it does not encapsulate its data model.

INTERACTIONS

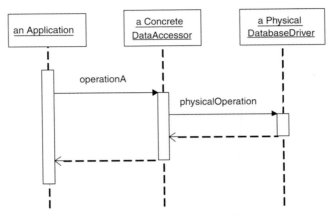

FIGURE 1.3: An application invokes operationA on a ConcreteDataAccessor.

Figure 1.3 portrays what happens when an application invokes operationA on a ConcreteDataAccessor. The ConcreteDataAccessor implements the logical operation in terms of one or more physical operations. It is also likely to interpret or convert the input and output data as well as handle physical resource management on the application's behalf.

CONSEQUENCES

The Data Accessor pattern has the following consequences:

Benefits

- *Clean application code*—Application code that is replete with data access details is difficult to read and maintain. Application logic tends to become obscured by the many calls necessary to do even simple database calls. When an application uses a well-designed data accessor abstraction that exposes logical database operations, its code can focus more on its own business logic.

- *Adoption of new database features or platforms*—When physical data access code is spread throughout a system, it is hard to add support for new features or platforms because it involves searching the entire code base and replacing or adding new calls where necessary. This process is tedious and error-prone. When a data accessor implementation encapsulates physical data access code, you only have one isolated component to enhance.

- *Incorporation of optimization strategies*—Data access code usually is a primary analysis focal point when tuning an application's performance. Data access code is a common bottleneck source and simple optimizations often have significant effects. When data access code is spread across a system, it requires much more effort to apply and measure optimizations because you must repeat their implementations multiple times. When you encapsulate all physical data access code within a data accessor implementation, you can incorporate an optimization strategy once and it immediately applies across the entire system.

- *Swappable physical data access implementations*—You can swap among multiple data accessor implementations without changing application code. This enables you to conveniently support multiple, diverse database platforms and technologies.

Drawback

- *Limits application control of data access*—Application code is limited to the logical operations defined by a data accessor abstraction. When a data accessor abstraction is not well-designed or versatile enough for an application's data access requirements, the application code may resort to unnatural or awkward workarounds that ultimately lead to unexpected results.

STRATEGIES

Consider these strategies when designing a data accessor abstraction:

- *Define versatile logical operations*—Keep in mind that while a data accessor abstraction hides many data access details from application code, the logical operations that it defines must not unnecessarily limit it. A truly useful data accessor abstraction exposes simple, common database operations, but also allows versatility. If the abstraction does not provide all the logical database operations that applications require, then applications need to use the operations that it does define in unexpected or inefficient combinations. This can lead to more convoluted code than if it handles data access directly.

For example, the data accessor abstraction defined in the "Sample Code" section allows the client to designate a selection row when it issues a read operation. A selection row is roughly analogous to a partial or full primary key value. This feature works fine for the sample client application, but suppose another application needed to read a range of employee identifiers. The abstraction does not expose any support for this type of query, so the application would need to read all records and explicitly filter them. In this case, the data accessor abstraction's semantics have caused the application code to be less efficient and more complex.

One strategy for avoiding this scenario is to research application use cases before designing a data accessor abstraction. Writing prototype or hypothetical application code helps you understand what features application developers need and what semantics keep their code clean.

On the other hand, be wary of designing data accessor abstractions too heavily. Adding operations for speculated scenarios may impose a significant development burden and unnecessary complexity on data accessor implementations.

- *Incorporate enhancement and optimization points*—A common development tradeoff is to remove features to meet schedule. While architects and developers can plan full-featured, highly scalable applications, they may not be successful if they take years to develop. The Data Accessor pattern enables you to design applications so that you can readily incorporate additional database features and optimizations in subsequent product releases. Even if you do not have enough development resources to incorporate all of an application's desired data access features, you should consider them and determine where and how you will implement them.

  A common example involves database platform support. In the first product release, you can deliver a data accessor implementation that supports a single database product using SQL access. If you hide all platform and SQL details within the data accessor implementation, you can add other platforms and database support in later releases without requiring changes to application code.

  You can also approach optimizations such as connection pools with a similar strategy. Hiding connection management within a data accessor implementation enables you to conveniently integrate optimizations like these in a single component, again affecting the entire system's performance characteristics without requiring any application code to change.

- *Guard against inefficient application usage*—It is common for application code to employ physical database access code inefficiently. This can have significant negative effects on overall system performance. One example is an application that prepares the same statement multiple times. This application's data access code is likely to be measurably slower than the code of an application that reuses statement handles where possible. However, recycling statement handles adds complexity to application code, making them good candidates for encapsulation within a data accessor implementation.

  Design your data accessor abstraction so that it is impossible or improbable that application usage will have a significant effect on performance or storage overhead. For example, if you expose the notion of a database connection, make it a logical connection that does not directly incur physical database connection overhead. This way, if an application opens and closes logical connections repeatedly, it will not affect overall system resource overhead.

  The data accessor abstraction offers a point where you can bridge the gap between a robust, application-friendly interface and a highly optimized, full-featured implementation.

To completely insulate applications from changes to a particular data accessor implementation, you should minimize all direct references to it. Instead, write application code exclusively in terms of the data accessor abstraction.

However, you need to instantiate data accessor implementation objects at some point. These are three alternatives for centralizing this instantiation so that it is easier to alter in the future:

- *Singleton data accessor implementation*—Define a global, singleton instance of a data accessor implementation that any application code can access. The singleton instance initializes itself only once and isolates its initialization details.

- *Initialization and parameter passing*—You can instantiate a single data accessor implementation object in your application's initialization code and pass it to any other application code that needs it. This strategy isolates initialization code to a single component, but it requires that many of the application classes' constructors and operations define an extra parameter.

- *Data accessor factory*—You can define a globally accessible factory class to instantiate new data accessor implementation instances. You still encapsulate the data accessor initialization within a single module, the factory returns new data accessor implementation instances whenever an application requests them.

SAMPLE CODE

This code example illustrates a data accessor abstraction that defines logical database access operations for reading, inserting, updating, and deleting data. Notice that this interface's callers do not need to manage database resources, issue SQL statements, or make direct JDBC calls. The logical operations define the data they are accessing, but do not disclose any underlying implementation.

```
public interface DataAccessor {

    /**
    Reads data from a table.

    @param table        The table.
    @param columns       The columns to read, or null to read
                         all the columns in the table.
    @param selectionRow A set of filter columns and values
                         used to subset the rows, or null to
                         read all the rows in the table.
    @param sortColumns   The columns to sort, or null to read
                         without sorting.

    @return             The list of rows.
    **/
    List read(String table,
              String[] columns,
              Row selectionRow,
              String[] sortColumns) throws DataException;

    /**
    Inserts data into a table.

    @param table        The table.
    @param rows          The rows to insert.
    **/
    void insert(String table, List rows) throws DataException;
```

```
/**
Updates data in a table.

@param table         The table.
@param selectionRow  A set of filter columns and values
                     used to subset the rows, or null to
                     update all of the rows in the table.
@param updateRow     A set of update columns and values.
**/
void update(String table,
            Row selectionRow,
            Row updateRow) throws DataException;

/**
Deletes data from a table.

@param table         The table.
@param selectionRow  A set of filter columns and values
                     used to subset the rows, or null to
                     delete all of the rows in the table.
**/
void delete(String table, Row selectionRow)
    throws DataException;
}
```

ConcreteDataAccessor is a DataAccessor implementation that operates in terms of multiple JDBC connections. This class is responsible for:

- Managing database resources such as connections, statement handles, and result sets.

- Generating and issuing SQL statements.

- Resolving qualified table names and physical database connections. For the sake of this example, suppose that this application accesses accounting and payroll data on different systems. ConcreteDataAccessor maps logical operations to databases based on the format of the table name provided by the client. This rule is an arbitrary constraint that is part of this particular application's design. However, you can implement more robust, directory-based distribution mechanisms the same way.

As you read through this example, consider some other data access details that you could implement within a concrete data accessor implementation, such as customized data conversion, user-based authorization, and logical operation logging.

```java
public class ConcreteDataAccessor
implements DataAccessor {

    private Connection accountingConnection;
    private Connection payrollConnection;
    private Connection otherConnection;

    /**
    Constructs a ConcreteDataAccessor object.
    */
    public ConcreteDataAccessor() throws DataException {
        try {
            accountingConnection
                = DriverManager.getConnection(...);
            payrollConnection
                = DriverManager.getConnection(...);
            otherConnection
                = DriverManager.getConnection(...);
        }
        catch(SQLException e) {
            throw new DataException(
                "Unable to construct DataAccessor", e);
        }
    }

    /**
    Reads data from a table.

    @param table        The table.
    @param columns      The columns to read, or null to read
                        all the columns in the table.
    @param selectionRow A set of filter columns and values
                        used to subset the rows, or null to
                        read all the rows in the table.
    @param sortColumns  The columns to sort, or null to read
                        without sorting.

    @return             The list of rows.
    **/
    public List read(String table,
                     String[] columns,
                     Row selectionRow,
                     String[] sortColumns)
                        throws DataException {
```

```
try {
    // Generate the SQL SELECT statement based on
    // the caller's input.
    StringBuffer buffer = new StringBuffer();
    buffer.append("SELECT ");

    // List the columns if the caller specified any.
    if (columns != null) {
        for(int i = 0; i < columns.length; ++i) {
            if (i > 0)
                buffer.append(", ");
            buffer.append(columns[i]);
        }
    }
    else
        buffer.append(" * ");

    // Include the resolved qualified table name.
    buffer.append(" FROM ");
    buffer.append(resolveQualifiedTable(table));

    // Generate the WHERE clause if the caller
    // specified a selection row.
    if (selectionRow != null) {
        buffer.append(
            generateWhereClause(selectionRow));
    }

    // Generate the ORDER BY clause if the caller
    // specified sort columns.
    if (sortColumns != null) {
        buffer.append(" ORDER BY ");
        for(int i = 0; i < sortColumns.length; ++i) {
            if (i > 0)
                buffer.append(", ");
            buffer.append(sortColumns[i]);
            buffer.append(" ASC");
        }
    }

    // Resolve the appropriate connection for this
    // table.
    Connection connection = resolveConnection(table);
    synchronized(connection) {
        // Execute the query.
        Statement statement
            = connection.createStatement();
        ResultSet resultSet
            = statement.executeQuery(
```

```
                             buffer.toString());
                 ResultSetMetaData rsmd
                     = resultSet.getMetaData();
                 int columnCount = rsmd.getColumnCount();

                 // Create a list of result rows based on the
                 // contents of the result set.
                 List resultRows = new LinkedList();
                 while(resultSet.next()) {
                     Row resultRow = new Row();
                     for(int i = 1; i <= columnCount; ++i) {
                         resultRow.addColumn(
                             rsmd.getColumnName(i),
                             resultSet.getObject(i));
                     }
                     resultRows.add(resultRow);
                 }

                 // Release database resources and return.
                 resultSet.close();
                 statement.close();
                 return resultRows;
             }
         }
         catch(SQLException e) {
             throw new DataException("Unable to read table "
                 + table, e);
         }
     }

     /**
     Inserts data into a table.

     @param table        The table.
     @param rows         The rows to insert.
     **/
     public void insert(String table,
                     List rows) throws DataException {
         try {
             for(Iterator i = rows.iterator(); i.hasNext(); ) {
                 Row row = (Row)i.next();

                 // Generate the SQL INSERT statement based on
                 // the caller's input.
                 StringBuffer buffer = new StringBuffer();
                 buffer.append("INSERT INTO ");
                 buffer.append(resolveQualifiedTable(table));

                 // List the column names.
```

```
                buffer.append(" (");
                boolean firstColumn = true;
                for(Iterator j = row.columns(); j.hasNext();){
                    if (!firstColumn)
                        buffer.append(", ");
                    else
                        firstColumn = false;
                    buffer.append(j.next());
                }

                // List the column values.
                buffer.append(") VALUES (");
                firstColumn = true;
                for(Iterator j = row.columns(); j.hasNext();){
                    if (!firstColumn)
                        buffer.append(", ");
                    else
                        firstColumn = false;

                    String column = (String)j.next();
                    Object columnValue
                        = row.getColumnValue(column);
                    buffer.append(
                        generateLiteralValue(columnValue));
                }

                // Resolve the appropriate connection for
                // this table.
                Connection connection
                    = resolveConnection(table);
                synchronized(connection) {
                    // Execute the insert.
                    Statement statement
                        = connection.createStatement();
                    statement.executeUpdate(
                        buffer.toString());
                    statement.close();
                }
            }
        }
        catch(SQLException e) {
            throw new DataException(
                "Unable to insert into table " + table, e);
        }
    }

    /**
    Updates data in a table.
```

```
@param table        The table.
@param selectionRow A set of filter columns and values
                    used to subset the rows, or null to
                    update all the rows in the table.
@param updateRow    A set of update columns and values.
**/
public void update(String table,
                   Row selectionRow,
                   Row updateRow) throws DataException {
    try {
        // Generate the SQL UPDATE statement based on the
        // caller's input.
        StringBuffer buffer = new StringBuffer();
        buffer.append("UPDATE ");
        buffer.append(resolveQualifiedTable(table));

        // Generate the SET clause.
        buffer.append(" SET ");
        boolean firstColumn = true;
        for(Iterator i=updateRow.columns(); i.hasNext();){
            if (!firstColumn)
                buffer.append(", ");
            else
                firstColumn = false;
            String column = (String)i.next();
            buffer.append(column);
            buffer.append(" = ");
            Object columnValue
                = updateRow.getColumnValue(column);
            buffer.append(
                generateLiteralValue(columnValue));
        }

        // Generate the WHERE clause if the caller
        // specified a selection row.
        if (selectionRow != null) {
            buffer.append(
                generateWhereClause(selectionRow));
        }

        // Resolve the appropriate connection for this
        // table.
        Connection connection = resolveConnection(table);
        synchronized(connection) {
            // Execute the update.
            Statement statement
                = connection.createStatement();
            statement.executeUpdate(
                buffer.toString());
```

```
                statement.close();
            }
        }
        catch(SQLException e) {
            throw new DataException(
                "Unable to update table " + table, e);
        }
    }


    /**
    Deletes data from a table.

    @param table        The table.
    @param selectionRow A set of filter columns and values
                        used to subset the rows, or null to
                        delete all the rows from the table.
    **/
    public void delete(String table,
                        Row selectionRow) throws DataException{
        try  {
            // Generate the SQL DELETE statement based on the
            // caller's input.
            StringBuffer buffer = new StringBuffer();
            buffer.append("DELETE FROM ");
            buffer.append(resolveQualifiedTable(table));

            // Generate the WHERE clause if the caller
            // specified a selection row.
            if (selectionRow != null) {
               buffer.append(
                   generateWhereClause(selectionRow));
            }

            // Resolve the appropriate connection for
            // this table.
            Connection connection = resolveConnection(table);
            synchronized(connection) {
                // Execute the delete.
                Statement statement
                    = connection.createStatement();
                statement.executeUpdate(buffer.toString());
                statement.close();
            }
        }
        catch(SQLException e) {
            throw new DataException(
                "Unable to delete from table " + table, e);
        }
    }
}
```

```java
/**
Resolves the connection based on the table name.
*/
private Connection resolveConnection(String table) {
    // These are just arbitrary rules for the sake
    // of this example.
    if (table.startsWith("A"))
        return accountingConnection;
    else if (table.startsWith("P"))
        return payrollConnection;
    else
        return otherConnection;
}


/**
Resolves the qualified table name.
*/
private String resolveQualifiedTable(String table) {
    // These are just arbitrary rules for the sake
    // of this example.
    if (table.startsWith("A"))
        return "ACCTDATA." + table;
    else if (table.startsWith("P"))
        return "PAYROLL." + table;
    else
        return table;
}

/**
Generates a SQL literal string.
*/
private String generateLiteralValue(Object literalValue) {
    StringBuffer buffer = new StringBuffer();
    if (!(literalValue instanceof Number))
        buffer.append("'");
    buffer.append(literalValue);
    if (!(literalValue instanceof Number))
        buffer.append("'");
    return buffer.toString();
}

/**
Generates a SQL WHERE clause based on a selection row.
*/
private String generateWhereClause(Row selectionRow)  {
    StringBuffer buffer = new StringBuffer();
    buffer.append(" WHERE ");
```

```
            boolean firstColumn = true;
            for(Iterator i=selectionRow.columns(); i.hasNext();){
                if (!firstColumn)
                    buffer.append(" AND ");
                else
                    firstColumn = false;
                String column = (String)i.next();
                buffer.append(column);
                buffer.append(" = ");
                Object columnValue
                    = selectionRow.getColumnValue(column);
                buffer.append(
                    generateLiteralValue(columnValue));
            }
            return buffer.toString();
        }
    }
```

Row is a simple helper class that DataAccessor uses to represent logical input and output data. Keep in mind that if you had chosen to return a java.sql.ResultSet instead, you would have immediately coupled your application directly to JDBC technology, preventing future, transparent moves to non-JDBC databases in the future.

```
public class Row {

    private Map contents = new HashMap();

    public Row() {
    }

    public Row(String column, Object columnValue) {
        contents.put(column, columnValue);
    }

    public void addColumn(String column, Object columnValue) {
        contents.put(column, columnValue);
    }

    public Object getColumnValue(String column) {
        return contents.get(column);
    }

    public Iterator columns() {
        return contents.keySet().iterator();
    }
}
```

DataException represents any exception that is thrown within the context of a data accessor implementation. This exception class wraps concrete exceptions like java.sql.SQLExceptions. This is another step toward decoupling consuming application code from the ConcreteDataAccessor's underlying JDBC implementation.

```java
public class DataException
extends Exception {

    DataException(String message, Throwable cause) {
        super(message, cause);
    }
}
```

Next is an example of a client that uses a data accessor abstraction to implement the employee expense reimbursement check process described in the "Context" section. Notice how there is no JDBC or SQL code. Instead, the example does all its data access using the logical operations provided by the data accessor abstraction.

```java
// Get a list of employees that need to be
// reimbursed for expenses.
List employeeRows
    = dataAccessor.read("P_EMPLOYEES",
                        null,
                        new Row("EXPENSE_FLAG", "Reimburse"),
                        null);

for(Iterator i = employeeRows.iterator(); i.hasNext(); ) {

    Row employeeRow = (Row)i.next();
    Integer employeeID
        = (Integer)employeeRow.getColumnValue("EMPLOYEE_ID");
    Row employeeSelectionRow
        = new Row("EMPLOYEE_ID", employeeID);

    // Get a list of expense records for the employee.
    List expenseRows
        = dataAccessor.read("A_EXPENSES",
                            new String[] { "AMOUNT" },
                            employeeSelectionRow,
                            null);

    // Total the expense records.
    long totalExpense = 0;
    for(Iterator j = expenseRows.iterator(); j.hasNext(); ) {
        Row expenseRow = (Row)j.next();
        long amount
```

```
                = ((Long)expenseRow.getColumnValue("AMOUNT"))
                    .longValue();
            totalExpense += amount;
        }

        // Issue the employee a check for the sum.
        issueEmployeeCheck(employeeID, totalExpense);

        // Update the employee's expense status to none.
        dataAccessor.update("P_EMPLOYEES",
                        employeeSelectionRow,
                        new Row("EXPENSE_FLAG", "None"));

        // Delete all the employee's expense records.
        dataAccessor.delete("A_EXPENSES",
                        employeeSelectionRow);
    }
```

RELATED PATTERNS AND TECHNOLOGY

- Data Accessor is also known as Data Access Object [Alur 2001] and Logical Connection.

- A data accessor implementation is an instance of Adapter [Gamma 1995] since it adapts an abstraction that is convenient for application usage to a particular physical database driver.

- Singleton [Gamma 1995] and Abstract Factory [Gamma 1995] describe strategies for isolating a data accessor instantiation within a single component that is conveniently accessible throughout an application.

- [Marinescu 2002] and [Matena 2003] describe an alternate approach to encapsulating physical data access operations called Data Access Command Beans. Data Access Command Beans define logical database operations using Command [Gamma 1995] semantics.

- Consider using Data Accessor to abstract the data access portion of an Active Domain Object (33) or Object/Relational Map (53).

- One or more data accessor abstractions can make up layers, as described in Layers (75). You can also define multiple data accessor abstractions for different layers. Each abstraction might address a different aspect or level of data access functionality.

Active Domain Object

DESCRIPTION

Encapsulates the data model and data access details within relevant domain object implementations. Active domain objects relieve application code of any direct database interaction.

CONTEXT

Applications that manipulate rows of physical data directly from a database lend themselves to several potential problems. First, application code is directly coupled with a data model. It can discover the details of the model at runtime using metadata, but it is more likely that a programmer has hardwired them within the application code. Second, data model changes or upgrades to new database products often cause incompatibilities for code that relies on specific data type charac-

33

teristics. Finally, when a programmer mixes application domain code with data access code, its readability and meaning tend to become obscured and ultimately more difficult to maintain and enhance. The Active Domain Object pattern addresses this issue by encapsulating a data model within a set of domain objects that are specifically designed for application use.

Recall the example described in Part 1, "Decoupling Patterns." In the example, two tables, CUSTOMERS and EMPLOYEES, store contact information for customers and employees, respectively. Figure 2.1 shows the column definitions for both tables. They store similar name and address data, but their representation of this data is inconsistent. This lack of consistency may be intentional, but more likely it stems from a history of unrelated, legacy design decisions. Updating the data model would require you to create a table conversion utility that existing customers would need to run when they upgraded to your latest software release. Another reason why you might not want to change the data model is that it forces customers to alter other software, such as reporting tools, that depend on the model as it currently exists. If the model's inconsistencies are just a cosmetic problem and the tables are not lacking any functional or relational information, then changing the data model may not be the best decision.

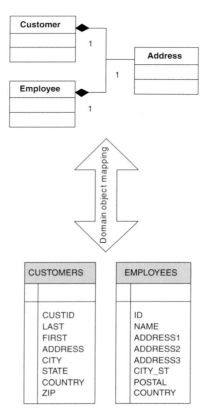

FIGURE 2.1: The CUSTOMERS and EMPLOYEES tables and the domain objects that model them.

You can choose to access these tables directly within application code whenever application logic dictates a need for them. However, the data model's inconsistencies will quickly spread throughout the application code. As an application developer, you must remember the two different forms of name and address data as well as which form applies to CUSTOMERS and which form applies to EMPLOYEES. Not only is this confusing and arbitrary, but it forces you to write redundant code. For example, when you render a name and address on a mailing label or Web page, you may need to write the rendering code twice: once for each form. Even worse, there is a chance that the two rendering implementations will diverge and expose the data model's inconsistency to end-users.

Figure 2.1 also shows three domain classes: Customer, Employee, and Address. Each models a domain concept and is easy for applications to create and manipulate. Notice that Customer and Employee reference the same Address class. This adds a level of consistency that does not exist in the data model.

The Active Domain Object pattern alleviates this problem by hiding details of the data model within relevant domain objects. Active domain objects take responsibility for their own domain object mapping. For example, a Customer object initializes itself by reading and mapping relevant data from the CUSTOMERS table. Likewise, an Employee object is responsible for reading and mapping its contents from the EMPLOYEES table. Figure 2.2 illustrates how active domain objects decouple application logic from physical data access and data model details:

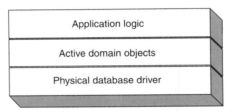

FIGURE 2.2: The Active Domain Object pattern decouples application logic from the physical data model and access implementation by encapsulating the logic within relevant domain objects.

The term "*active*" refers to domain objects that do more than simply represent data. They expose logical operations that take care of most of the relevant database interaction for their data. Some examples of logical operations that an active domain object can define include:

- *Initialize*—Initialize the domain object's contents by reading data from one or more tables.

- *Refresh*—Refresh the domain object's contents from the database to ensure that it is consistent with any changes that have been made since it was initialized.

- *Save*—Save changes to the domain object's contents by inserting or updating data in the database.

- *List*—Issue a query and return a collection of domain objects that represents the query's results.

Notice how these operations are named using domain terminology and not necessarily data access terminology. This helps to further mask the data access details, ensuring a more complete decoupling of application code from direct data access. You may find it convenient to use even more specific domain terminology, such as processChangeOfAddress or enrollCustomer.

Active domain objects enable you to describe the concepts that a relational data model represents using robust domain objects. At the implementation level, they define a straightforward grouping for related data access operations. You can encapsulate details such as data distribution, table relationships, and data conversion within domain objects. If applications use only the domain objects that you define to access physical data, then you have more freedom to update the data model since you can mask data model changes within the domain objects' implementations. However, you still need to be cognizant of whether your customers use other software to access the data before making data model changes.

APPLICABILITY

Use the Active Domain Object pattern when:

- You want to hide the physical data model and data access complexity from application logic. Doing so keeps application logic cleaner and more focused on the business objects and processes that it models.

- You want to encapsulate all data model and data access details relating to a single domain concept within a single component. Grouping all accesses to a table or set of related tables makes it easier to predict the effect of and manage data model and data access changes.

- You want to mask data model inconsistencies or obscurities from application code. Some legacy data models impose less-than-intuitive semantics that you are not at liberty to change. Encapsulating these details within a single component prevents them from polluting application code.

STRUCTURE

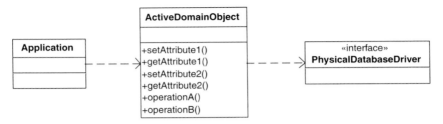

FIGURE 2.3: The static structure of the Active Domain Object pattern.

Figure 2.3 illustrates the static structure of the Active Domain Object pattern. An ActiveDomainObject defines logical attributes and operations that represent domain concepts and are convenient for applications to use. It implements these operations by interacting with a physical database driver. It also converts data between its physical form and its logical domain object form.

Active domain objects encapsulate the data model, data access details, and the mapping between themselves and the physical data.

INTERACTIONS

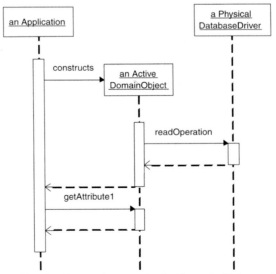

FIGURE 2.4: An application instantiates an ActiveDomainObject, which populates itself based on physical data. Once the ActiveDomainObject is initialized, the application can readily access its attributes.

Figure 2.4 portrays what happens when an application instantiates a single Active-DomainObject. The ActiveDomainObject issues an appropriate read or query operation to the database and populates its own contents based on this operation's results. Once it is initialized, the application can readily access its attributes and invoke subsequent operations.

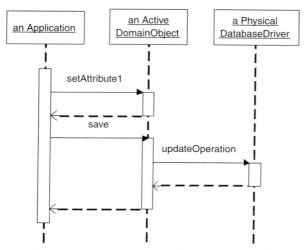

FIGURE 2.5: An application sets an attribute and saves an ActiveDomainObject, which updates the corresponding physical data.

Figure 2.5 illustrates what happens when an application sets one of an ActiveDomainObject's attributes. You can define set operations to update physical data immediately, but it is more common to update only an object's working copy in memory. This enables the application to set several attributes and save them at once, reducing the overall frequency of data access. In this scenario, the save operation writes any attribute changes by issuing a physical insert or update database operation.

CONSEQUENCES

The Active Domain Object pattern has the following consequences:

Benefits

- *Has clean application code*—Application code that works exclusively with domain objects is much cleaner and easier to develop and maintain than code that includes data model and data access details. When an application uses well-defined domain objects that expose only logical operations, its code can focus more on its own business logic.

- *Decouples application code from the data model*—When you relieve application code of the responsibility for understanding a data model, you are in a better position to alter the data model later.

- *Groups related data access code into a single component*—One or more related active domain objects implement the entire set of data access operations for a set of similarly related tables in the database. Grouping these operations together within a single component makes it easier to identify and repair defects in the data access implementation.

Drawbacks

- *Spreads data access across multiple domain objects*—Each active domain object is responsible for its own data access implementation. Spreading this responsibility across multiple objects means that employing overall data access strategies like statement caching requires you to update analogous code in every active domain object implementation.

- *Limits application control of data access*—Application code is limited to the logical attributes and operations that domain objects define. When domain objects are not well-designed or versatile enough for an application's data access requirements, the application code may need to resort to unnatural or awkward workarounds that ultimately lead to unexpected results.

STRATEGIES

As you define domain objects to use in applications, it is important to decide whether to model application concepts or data model concepts more closely. If you are creating an application and its data model from scratch, then you can align these concepts so they match. However, as applications mature, these two concept sets do not always change consistently. The whole motivation for defining domain objects is to make application code easier to write and maintain, so it makes sense to tailor domain objects toward application concepts. Here are some ideas to consider as you make this distinction:

- *Domain objects and tables*—You do not necessarily need to define domain objects that correspond directly to rows in a single table. For instance, you can define a domain object as a collection that represents query results. A domain object can correspond to a join rather than a table. You can define one domain object to correspond to only a subset of a table's columns and another domain object to correspond to the remaining columns. How you align domain objects with tables depends on the granularity that you expect applications to require.

- *Attributes and columns*—You do not necessarily need to define domain object attributes that correspond directly to table columns. If you do not expect applications to reference certain columns, then there is no reason to incorporate them in a domain object. Likewise, if applications only need to read specific data, then a domain object only needs to provide get operations for the corresponding attributes.

  Also consider whether the physical form of the data is convenient for the application. If it is not, then a domain object can convert transparently between its physical and logical forms. It may even make sense to form a single attribute from multiple columns or vice versa.

- *Separate collections from objects*—It is common to define domain objects that represent a single table row. Applications often need to manipulate several rows at a time to process query results or issue batch updates. It usually makes sense to consider collection domain objects differently from single-row domain objects.

  A collection domain object encapsulates query and batch update operations and usually hands back related single-row domain objects for the application to manipulate. You can package a collection domain object and single-row domain object together to form a single component that provides all domain operations for one or more related tables. These two classes can also share common aspects of their domain object mapping code.

- *Domain logic*—Domain objects are object-oriented and can define behavior. It follows that you can attach related behavior and processes as additional operations on a domain object. You may find that exposing common logical operations is less error-prone than exposing attributes and expecting application code to implement the same logic. You may also find that you do not need to expose some attributes at all if applications can sufficiently manipulate them through the domain object's operations.

- *No usage penalties*—It is essential that you define domain object attributes and operations to be both convenient and useful. Ensure that applications do not need to employ unnatural semantics or glue code to use your domain objects. If application developers employ odd sequences of code repeatedly, you may need to enhance or rethink your design. Effective use case analysis helps to avoid this problem.

- *No performance penalties*—Domain objects hide many details from callers and this fact makes application code easier to write and maintain. However, the trade-off is that callers have much less control over some aspects of data access such as resource management and physical database operations. Ensure that common usage patterns result in optimal data access operations.

Here are some other ideas to consider when implementing the Active Domain Object pattern:

- *Define a consistent connection management strategy*—Connection management addresses how active domain objects resolve and share the physical database connections they use for reading and writing the data they represent. You may find it helpful to use a consistent connection management strategy for all active domain objects in a system.

  One possibility is for active domain objects to manage their own connections. You might create and store a connection for each domain object, or share one among all domain objects of a particular type. This choice is clean and hides connections within domain object implementations, but it may not be the most efficient way to manage connections since the number of connections can be large and they tend to be left open long after the application code requires their services. These characteristics can have a significant effect on an application's scalability and performance.

  A second possibility is to have calling code pass a connection to active domain objects whenever data access is required. This takes the form of an extra parameter to relevant domain object operations and constructors and makes the class's public operation signatures more complex. In addition, it sometimes requires your code to pass connections several levels deep through a domain object's call stack. This strategy imposes the burden of connection management on the caller, but it does allow the caller to efficiently manage a small set of connections that all domain objects share.

A final approach is to define a *connection factory* object that is globally accessible and hands off a connection to any code that requests one. This enables active domain objects to request connections as needed, without requiring callers to pass them explicitly on operation or constructor calls. A connection factory encapsulates the connection management strategy within a single component and makes it easier to add new connection types or optimize and use a connection pool.

- *Maintain a saved state*—You may find it necessary to maintain a saved state for each active domain object. In most cases, this is simply a Boolean value that indicates whether a particular object's data matches the database. A domain object that an application creates to represent new data sets this flag to false. A domain object that loads its contents from the database sets this flag to true.

  An active domain object can use this state information when an application calls its save operation. If its saved state is true, it deduces that the data already exists in the database and it issues an update operation. If the saved state is false, the domain object knows that it is saving the data for the first time and it issues an insert operation.

  An active domain object can also use state information to keep track of whether its attributes have changed since it was last loaded or saved. In both of these cases, the saved state is only referenced within the active domain object's code, so you can define it to be a private attribute.

SAMPLE CODE

This example defines an active domain object that represents a customer's name and address. It corresponds to the example described in the "Context" section.

```
public class Customer {

    // SQL statements for data access.
    private static final String QUERY
        = "SELECT * FROM CUSTOMERS WHERE CUSTID = ?";

    private static final String INSERT
        = "INSERT INTO CUSTOMERS "
        + "(LAST, FIRST, ADDRESS, CITY, STATE, COUNTRY, "
```

```
            + "ZIP, CUSTID) VALUES(?, ?, ?, ?, ?, ?, ?, ?)";

    private static final String UPDATE
        = "UPDATE CUSTOMERS SET LAST = ?, FIRST = ?, "
        + "ADDRESS = ?, CITY = ?, STATE = ?, COUNTRY = ?, "
        + "ZIP = ? WHERE CUSTID = ?";

    // The customer's data attributes.
    private int id;
    private String name;
    private Address address;

    // Indicates whether the data in the active domain
    // object matches that in the database.
    private boolean saved = false;

    /**
    Constructs a Customer object.  This constructor is
    intended for application code that adds new customers
    to the database.  It leaves the saved flag false to
    indicate that the data is not stored in the database
    yet.
    */
    public Customer(int id, String name, Address address) {
        this.id = id;
        this.name = name;
        this.address = address;
    }

    /**
    Constructs a new Customer object.  This constructor
    is intended for application code to read information
    for a single customer.
    */
    public Customer(int id) throws DataException {
        this.id = id;

        try {
            Connection connection
                = ConnectionFactory.getConnection();
            PreparedStatement statement
                = connection.prepareStatement(QUERY);

            statement.setInt(1, id);
            ResultSet resultSet = statement.executeQuery();
            resultSet.next();

            String lastName = resultSet.getString("LAST");
            String firstName = resultSet.getString("FIRST");
```

```
            String address = resultSet.getString("ADDRESS");
            String city = resultSet.getString("CITY");
            String state = resultSet.getString("STATE");
            String country = resultSet.getString("COUNTRY");
            String zip = resultSet.getString("ZIP");

            resultSet.close();
            statement.close();
            connection.close();

            initialize(id, lastName, firstName, address,
                       city, state, country, zip);
        }
        catch(SQLException e) {
            throw new DataException("Unable to read customer "
                + id, e);
        }
    }

    /**
    Constructs a Customer object.  This constructor is
    called only by CustomerList as it populates its
    contents.
    */
    public Customer(int id,
                    String lastName,
                    String firstName,
                    String address,
                    String city,
                    String state,
                    String country,
                    String zip) {

        initialize(id, lastName, firstName, address,
            city, state, country, zip);
    }

    /**
    Initializes the contents of this object based on
    physical data.  This is the mapping of data from
    its relational form to its domain object form.
    */
    private void initialize(int id,
                            String lastName,
                            String firstName,
                            String address,
                            String city,
                            String state,
                            String country,
```

```
                              String zip) {

    // Combine the first and last names, since
    // that is how the application
    // needs them.
    StringBuffer buffer = new StringBuffer();
    buffer.append(lastName);
    buffer.append(", ");
    buffer.append(firstName);
    name = buffer.toString();

    // Combine the city and state, since
    // that is how the application
    // needs them.
    buffer = new StringBuffer();
    buffer.append(city);
    buffer.append(", ");
    buffer.append(state);
    String cityState = buffer.toString();

    // Initialize the address.
    this.address = new Address();
    this.address.setAddress1(address);
    this.address.setCityState(cityState);
    this.address.setCountry(country);
    this.address.setPostalCode(zip);

    // Set this to true, since this information
    // was read from the database.
    saved = true;
}

public String getName() {
    return name;
}

public void setName(String name) {
    this.name = name;
}

public Address getAddress() {
    return address;
}

public void setAddress(Address address) {
    this.address = address;
}
```

```
/**
Saves the customer information to the database.
This is the mapping of data from its domain object
form to its relational form.  It uses the saved flag
to determine whether to insert new data or update
existing data.
*/
public void save() throws DataException
{
    // Split the name into first and last, since
    // the CUSTOMERS table stores these items in separate
    // columns.
    String first;
    String last;
    int comma = name.indexOf(',');
    if (comma >= 0) {
        first = name.substring(comma + 1).trim();
        last = name.substring(0, comma).trim();
    }
    else {
        first = "";
        last = name;
    }

    // Split the city and state, since the CUSTOMERS table
    // stores these items in separate columns.
    String cityState = address.getCityState();
    String city = "";
    String state = "";
    if (cityState != null) {
        comma = cityState.indexOf(',');
        if (comma >= 0) {
            city = cityState.substring(0, comma).trim();
            state = cityState.substring(comma).trim();
        }
        else {
            city = cityState;
        }
    }

    try {
        Connection connection
            = ConnectionFactory.getConnection();

        // If the customer information came from
        // the database, then issue an update.
        if (saved) {
            PreparedStatement statement
                = connection.prepareStatement(UPDATE);
```

```
            statement.setString(1, last);
            statement.setString(2, first);
            statement.setString(3, address.getAddress1());
            statement.setString(4, city);
            statement.setString(5, state);
            statement.setString(6, address.getCountry());
            statement.setString(7,
                address.getPostalCode());
            statement.setInt(8, id);
            statement.executeUpdate();
            statement.close();
        }

        // If the customer information did not
        // come from the database, then issue an insert.
        else {
            PreparedStatement statement
                = connection.prepareStatement(INSERT);
            statement.setString(1, last);
            statement.setString(2, first);
            statement.setString(3, address.getAddress1());
            statement.setString(4, city);
            statement.setString(5, state);
            statement.setString(6, address.getCountry());
            statement.setString(7,
                address.getPostalCode());
            statement.setInt(8, id);
            statement.executeUpdate();
            statement.close();

            // Indicate that the information now exists
            // in the database.
            saved = true;
        }

        connection.close();
    }
    catch(SQLException e) {
        throw new DataException("Unable to save customer "
            + id, e);
    }
  }
}
```

Customer stores the customer's address in an Address object. Address is a domain object, but it is not active *per se*. Customer address information is stored within the same table as related customer information, so Customer takes care of the Address domain object's mapping. This fact enables the Address object to be reusable for other types of addresses, such as employee addresses that are stored in a different format. You can implement the Employee active domain object similarly to Customer and reuse the same Address object:

```
public class Address
{
    private String address1 = null;
    private String address2 = null;
    private String address3 = null;
    private String cityState = null;
    private String country = null;
    private String postalCode = null;

    public String getAddress1() {
        return address1;
    }

    public void setAddress1(String address1) {
        this.address1 = address1;
    }

    // Repeat for the rest of the attributes
    // that this class defines.
    // ...
}
```

ConnectionFactory encapsulates the connection management strategy for Customer and other active domain objects. This example creates a new connection for each request. In a real, scalable application, you should employ a connection sharing mechanism like a connection pool. See Resource Pool (117) for more information about connection pooling.

```
public class ConnectionFactory {

    public static Connection getConnection()
        throws SQLException {
        return DriverManager.getConnection("url",
            "user", "password");
    }
}
```

DataException represents any exception that is thrown within the context of an active domain object implementation. This exception class wraps concrete database exceptions like java.sql.SQLExceptions. Wrapping specific exceptions further decouples consuming applications from underlying JDBC implementations.

```
public class DataException
extends Exception {

    DataException(String message, Throwable cause) {
        super(message, cause);
    }
}
```

This block illustrates how simple it is for an application to access and change information for a single customer. Notice that there are no data model or access details at all. The application operates exclusively on active domain objects.

```
Customer customer = new Customer(id);
Address oldAddress = customer.getAddress();
customer.setAddress(newAddress);
customer.save();
```

CustomerList is an active domain object that represents a collection of customers. As a simple example, it represents an entire list of customers. You can also provide other constructors that initialize CustomerList objects to represent specialized queries, such as all customers that reside in a certain geographical region.

```
public class CustomerList
{
    private static final String QUERY
        = "SELECT * FROM CUSTOMERS";

    private List contents = new LinkedList();

    /**
    Constructs a CustomerList object that represents
    every customer in the database.
    */
    public CustomerList() throws DataException {

        try {
            Connection connection
                = ConnectionFactory.getConnection();
            PreparedStatement statement
                = connection.prepareStatement(QUERY);
            ResultSet resultSet = statement.executeQuery();
            while(resultSet.next()) {

                int id = resultSet.getInt("CUSTID");
                String lastName = resultSet.getString("LAST");
                String firstName
                    = resultSet.getString("FIRST");
```

```
                    String address
                        = resultSet.getString("ADDRESS");
                    String city = resultSet.getString("CITY");
                    String state = resultSet.getString("STATE");
                    String country
                        = resultSet.getString("COUNTRY");
                    String zip = resultSet.getString("ZIP");

                    Customer customer = new Customer(id, lastName,
                        firstName, address, city, state, country,
                      zip);
                    contents.add(customer);
                }
                resultSet.close();
                statement.close();
                connection.close();
            }
            catch(SQLException e) {
                throw new DataException(
                    "Unable to read customer list", e);
            }
        }


        /**
        Returns an iterator that lists every customer in the list.
        */
        public Iterator iterator() {
            return contents.iterator();
        }
    }
```

This block illustrates application code that issues catalogs to every customer in the database. Notice again that this code was written exclusively in terms of active domain objects.

```
CustomerList customerList = new CustomerList();
for(Iterator i = customerList.iterator(); i.hasNext(); ) {
    Customer customer = (Customer)i.next();
    String name = customer.getName();
    Address address = customer.getAddress();
    issueCatalog(name, address);
}
```

RELATED PATTERNS AND TECHNOLOGY

- Active Domain Object is also known as Active Record [Fowler 2002].

- An Enterprise JavaBean (EJB) that uses bean-managed persistence (BMP) is an example of an active domain object. BMP means that an EJB takes responsibility for its own domain object mapping and physical data access.

- Consider using the Data Accessor pattern (9) to abstract the data access portion of active domain objects. This further encapsulates data access details into a separate component.

- Object/Relational Map (53) describes an alternate strategy for domain object mapping. This pattern implements mapping in a separate component that is decoupled from domain objects.

- You can define active domain objects within one or more layers, as described in the Layers patterns (75).

- You can use Selection Factory (191), Domain Object Factory (203), and Update Factory (215) to define consistent, but hardwired domain object mapping strategies. You can manage these factories with Domain Object Assembler (227), a pattern that describes a strategy for implementing a generic domain object mapping infrastructure.

- Paging Iterator (253) works well for managing collections of domain objects that correspond to database query results.

Object/Relational Map

DESCRIPTION

Encapsulates the mapping between domain objects and relational data in a single component. An object/relational map decouples both application code and domain objects from the underlying data model and data access details.

CONTEXT

Programmers use object-oriented concepts to model real-world entities in a natural, familiar way. An object's behavior enables it to interact with other objects using application domain semantics. Domain objects related by aggregation and inheritance collaborate to implement elegant application-level solutions.

When it comes time to read or write the relational data that domain objects represent, an application's elegance often suffers. This happens because it is usu-

53

ally not possible to directly model the real world with relational data. Instead, you must morph real-world entities into a row and column format. This format sharply contrasts with the versatility that object-oriented models provide.

For example, consider some of the objects involved in an order processing application. An order is made up of a unique order identifier, the identifier of the customer who placed the order, the date that the customer placed the order, and a collection of zero or more line items that make up the order. Similarly, a line item consists of a line item identifier, a product identifier, the quantity that the customer ordered, and the product's unit price. Figure 3.1 illustrates the Order and LineItem classes that define domain objects for this application:

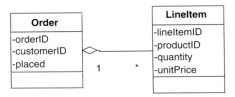

FIGURE 3.1:   Order and LineItem define the domain objects for the order processing application example.

The data model includes ORDERS and LINE_ITEMS tables that define similar concepts, although the relationship between these tables is not so straightforward. Figure 3.2 illustrates these tables. Since a single order contains zero or more line items, there is a one-to-many relationship between rows in the ORDERS table and those in the LINE_ITEMS table. To associate rows across these tables, LINE_ITEMS defines the ORDER_ID column as a foreign key (FK) that you can use to join with the ORDERS table.

ORDERS				LINE_ITEMS	
PK	ORDER_ID			PK	LINE_ITEM_ID
	CUSTOMER_ID PLACED			FK1	ORDER_ID PRODUCT_ID QUANTITY UNIT_PRICE

FIGURE 3.2:   The ORDERS and LINE_ITEMS tables store order processing application data as part of a relational data model. (Note: PK stands for primary key.)

Consider a simple business process that the application must perform. It carries out the following tasks to generate order invoices:

1. *Determine the appropriate queries*—The application queries the ORDERS and LINE_ITEMS tables to gather all the information it needs to generate order invoices. This may entail a single join operation across both tables, or it may require multiple queries involving the individual tables.

2. *Issue the queries*—The application initializes a database connection if one is not already available and interacts directly with the database driver to issue the queries.

3. *Parse the query results*—The application reads the data from the query results and organizes it by creating Order and LineItem object representations. This may also require converting data from its database format to a format more amenable to the application's semantics.

4. *Print the invoices*—The application uses the Order and LineItem objects to iterate through all the orders, calculate total prices, and print the invoices.

The first step requires tight coupling between the application and the data model, since the application forms the queries. Similarly, the second and third steps couple the application with data access code, in this case, the database driver and its resources.

The Object/Relational Map pattern decouples both the data model and data access details from an application and its domain objects. The mapping between object-oriented concepts and relational data becomes the responsibility of a separate component, allowing it to be changed independently of the application and domain objects. An object/relational map is commonly defined using an abstraction that hides all of its mapping details from applications. Figure 3.3 illustrates how the object/relational map abstraction and implementation achieve this decoupling:

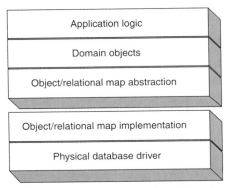

FIGURE 3.3: The Object/Relational Map pattern decouples the application logic and domain objects from the physical data model and data access details.

The object/relational map implementation is responsible for the mapping between domain objects and relational data and usually interacts directly with a physical database driver. One option is to define a custom implementation that hardwires all the mapping details for a single domain object, application, or system. Hardwiring these details in code makes it less amenable to changes, but it provides a cleaner decoupling than burying the same mapping within application code or domain objects. It may also be an effective prototyping strategy that allows you to develop applications before you build a more versatile solution.

Sophisticated object/relational map systems define mapping details using metadata. Metadata makes an implementation quite versatile, since you can change the mapping details without updating or recompiling application or domain object code. It is common to store mapping metadata in configuration files or a database. It is also common to define administration tools that allow users to view and update mapping details without having to understand the persistent metadata format.

The most fundamental issues that an object/relational map system deals with are how to map object-oriented concepts to relational database concepts. Table 3.1 describes a common analogy. These are general guidelines and are not required. You can define a class for each table that your application uses. The application or object/relational map instantiates object instances for each row as it referencse the rows. Each domain object exposes analogous column values as attributes.

In practice, these are not always direct correspondences. For example, an object/relational map often hides relational data that an application does not need, such as keys used purely for defining table relationships or identity attributes. In addition, the object/relational map can convert data in both direc-

TABLE 3.1: A Common Analogy for Mapping Between Object-Oriented and Relational Database

Object-Oriented Concept	Relational Database Concept
Class	Table
Object	Row
Attribute	Column

tions and calculate attributes on behalf of the application, encapsulating even more details of the data model. If you need to define domain objects that stray further from this analogy, you must ensure that the object/relational map system that you choose supports the mapping capabilities you require.

With an object/relational map in place, the steps for generating invoices within the order processing application become much easier to describe:

1. *Request the orders*—The application requests relevant orders and the object/relational map returns them as a collection of Order objects.

2. *Get each order's line items*—These are available directly from the Order object. Remember that in object-oriented terms, an Order contains a collection of LineItems and the Order class exposes the collection as one of its attributes.

3. *Calculate and report*—Calculate totals and print the invoice as before.

Notice that the application operates exclusively using domain objects and makes no explicit reference to the relational data model or data access. The same physical data access operations happen as did with the coupled approach described earlier, but this time, the object/relational map issues them transparently.

Implementing an object/relational map that handles simple cases like the order processing application requires is a reasonable undertaking. However, if you plan to make extensive use of object/relational mapping within your applications, you probably do not want to tackle creating a generic implementation from scratch. Writing an efficient, versatile, and metadata-driven object/relational map is a difficult task. Fortunately, there are many commercial products and standards available that you can employ directly within your application. Most of these products allow you to define map metadata using tools or configuration files and plug in a variety of database drivers for physical data access.

APPLICABILITY

Use the Object/Relational Map pattern when:

- You want to hide the physical data model and data access complexity from application logic and domain objects. Doing so keeps these components cleaner and more focused on the business objects and processes that they model.

- You want to encapsulate domain object mapping within a single component so that you can adapt to data model changes without changing application code or domain object definitions.

- You want the versatility to map domain objects to multiple data models without changing application code or domain object definitions. This versatility lets you integrate your application with multiple data models, regardless of how they are defined.

STRUCTURE

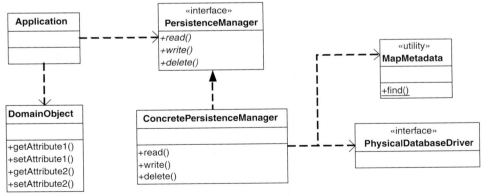

FIGURE 3.4: The static structure of the Object/Relational Map pattern.

Figure 3.4 illustrates the static structure of one variety of an Object/Relational Map implementation. The PersistenceManager interface defines database operations in terms of generic domain objects. It normally defines operations for reading, writing, and deleting domain objects. This interface does not expose any database details. As an alternative, you can spread the set of persistence operations across multiple interfaces that together form a conceptual PersistenceManager abstraction.

ConcretePersistenceManager provides the implementation of these operations in terms of physical database operations. It references some form of MapMetadata, which describes the domain object mapping. It also uses a PhysicalDatabaseDriver to interact with the relational database.

ConcretePersistenceManager encapsulates the data model, data access, and domain object mapping for an application.

Several variations on this structure exist in object/relational mapping standards and commerical object/relational mapping systems. One common variation decouples application code from the PersistenceManager by way of implicit framework or environment calls. Others generate mapping code that is invoked on an application's behalf.

INTERACTIONS

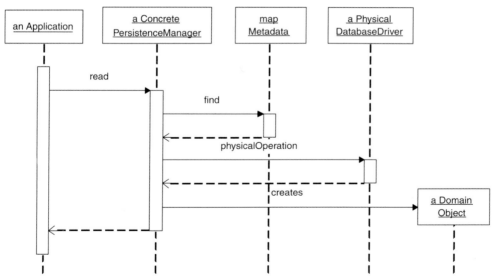

FIGURE 3.5: An application invokes the read operation on a ConcretePersistenceManager.

Figure 3.5 portrays what happens when an application invokes the read operation on a ConcretePersistenceManager. The ConcretePersistenceManager finds the relevant metadata that describes the mapping details and uses this information to issue operations to the physical database driver. Finally, it creates a new domain object using the relational data and metadata, and returns this object to the caller. Other PersistenceManager operations work similarly.

CONSEQUENCES

The Object/Relational Map pattern has the following consequences:

Tradeoff

- *Depends on additional commercial product*—Most applications already depend on a commercial database, one or more database drivers, and an application server. If you use object/relational mapping extensively, you are likely to benefit from integrating a commercial object/relational mapping product as well. Buying a commercial product saves you a significant amount of development expense. However, redistributing third-party software does require you to address additional legal, packaging, and installation issues.

Benefits

- *Has clean application code*—Application code that works exclusively with domain objects is much cleaner and easier to develop and maintain than code that includes data model and data access details. When an application uses well-defined domain objects that expose only logical attributes, its code can focus more on its own domain logic. In addition, you are in a better position to alter the data model or data access details later.

- *Maps to alternate data models*—The most versatile object/relational mapping mechanisms isolate configurable map metadata that you can change without affecting application code. Many object/relational map products store and interpret map metadata at runtime so that changes do not require any code to be recompiled.

  The concept of mapping to alternate data models has powerful consequences. It is common for data models to be bound by their applications. This characteristic severely restricts data model changes because they require extensive software upgrades. Encapsulating data model details within metadata enables you to make changes such as rearranging tables, moving to different platforms, or even moving to a different type of data store such as an XML-based or object-oriented database.

Metadata is also beneficial because it enables you to quickly adapt your applications to alternate data models. This is especially significant from a marketing and demonstration perspective since you can quickly configure your application to work with a prospective customer's legacy data. Prospects are more likely to be interested in your demonstration when they see it in the context of their own data.

Drawback

- *Limits application control of data access*—Application code is limited to the operations that the PersistenceManager interface defines. Since the Concrete-PersistenceManager encapsulates data access details, it is harder to tune its physical database operations and resource management to optimize data access performance for a particular application. This especially holds true if you employ a commercial object/relational mapping product.

STRATEGIES

If you use an object/relational map mechanism to manage domain objects, it makes sense to use the same strategy throughout your applications. Consistent data access is beneficial when it comes to understanding and analyzing applications' database interactions as a whole. This section describes various issues that arise as you implement the Object/Relational Map pattern.

Unmapped Attributes

In general, domain objects that participate in an Object/Relational Map instance correspond to a row in a physical database table or join. However, not all of a domain object's attributes are necessarily stored in the database. In some cases, they are computed or converted based on other sources. These attributes are called *unmapped attributes* because they do not map directly to a single piece of relational data. Unmapped attributes and associated behavior do not typically present any additional mapping issues and can automate processes and calculations involving a domain object's mapped attributes. For example, a LineItem object might publish a totalPrice unmapped attribute that it computes based on its mapped unitPrice and quantity attributes.

Object Identity

For a persistence manager to map domain objects to their corresponding rows in a table, you must define the notion of identity on both sides of the relationship. If a table defines a primary key, then it already defines unique identity for its rows. Similarly, if a domain object defines one or more attributes that map to the table's primary key, then they meet the criteria for domain object identity.

Some persistence managers require all mapped objects to define their identities. Consider the LINE_ITEMS table from the order processing application example described in the "Context" section. From a relational data model perspective, there is no technical reason for the LINE_ITEMS table to include a LINE_ITEM_ID column. After all, multiple rows in this table are associated with those in the ORDERS table based purely on their ORDER_ID column values. However, to account for the case where an application updates a single LineItem object, you need to introduce the LINE_ITEM_ID column as a primary key as well as the corresponding lineItemID attribute in the LineItem class. This enables the Concrete-PersistenceManager to update the correct row.

Some persistence managers use identity attributes for another reason. They transparently cache domain objects that applications frequently access. This enables faster access to these objects by optimizing physical database access. This variety of caching mechanism often uses a set of identity attributes as the cache key, since they uniquely identify any domain object in the system.

Aggregation Relationships

Another important concept in object/relational mapping is implementing aggregation relationships. From the perspective of a data model, aggregation involves matching foreign key data in one table with primary key data in another. The corresponding domain objects usually model similar relationships, but they translate to object aggregation, in which one domain object directly references others.

Consider two related tables, TABLE_A and TABLE_B, and their corresponding domain object classes, ObjectA and ObjectB. It is common to describe their relationship as one of the following types:

- *One-to-one*—Every row in TABLE_A corresponds to exactly one row in TABLE_B. Similarly, every ObjectA instance refers to a single ObjectB instance.

- *One-to-many*—Every row in TABLE_A corresponds to zero or more related rows in TABLE_B. Likewise, every ObjectA instance refers to a collection of ObjectB instances.

- *Many-to-many*—Any number of grouped rows in TABLE_A corresponds to a similar grouping of related rows in TABLE_B. Each ObjectA and ObjectB instance refers to a collection of the other type.

  An alternate strategy for a many-to-many relationship is to define TABLE_A and TABLE_B independently and define another table that lists related keys from each. ObjectA and ObjectB relate as before depending on the logical relationship of the tables.

Regardless of the relationship characteristics, it is the persistence manager's responsibility for resolving and managing ObjectB instances when an application refers to them through ObjectA's accessor methods. In the order processing application example, there is a one-to-many relationship between ORDERS and LINE_ITEMS. The Order class exposes this relationship through an accessor method called getLineItems, which returns the collection of related LineItems. The persistence manager can choose to implement the corresponding physical data access operations using one or more of the following strategies:

- *Issue a single join operation*—For read operations, the persistence manager issues a single join operation across the related tables that returns all the data required to populate a set of Orders and their related LineItems. There is no corresponding strategy for update and delete operations.

- *Issue multiple query operations*—The persistence manager can issue two physical query operations, one for each table. This works the same for read, update, and delete operations.

- *Use lazy initialization*—For read operations, the previous two strategies populate all the related domain objects regardless of whether the application even needs to access them. Lazy initialization is an alternative where the persistence manager does not populate aggregate domain objects until applications reference them. For example, when an application reads an Order object, the persistence manager only queries the ORDERS table. It waits until the application references an Order's LineItems to query the LINE_ITEMS table, and then it only requests the LineItems relating to that particular Order.

The benefit of lazy initialization is that it avoids reading superfluous data that applications do not need. In some cases, this can lead to noticeable reductions of network and memory utilization. However, it does require additional query operations, since it issues multiple small queries on the aggregate table. Sometimes, these additional queries have a more significant performance impact than reading the extra data.

Inheritance Relationships

It is also common for domain objects to relate by inheritance, but relational databases do not normally support an analogous concept. Consider a domain object class, Employee, and its subclass, Manager. Manager extends Employee, adding attributes that apply only to managers. It is common for a persistence manager to map these domain objects using one of these strategies:

- *Concrete table inheritance*—Map each type of concrete domain object to its own table. In this example, there is an EMPLOYEES table that contains data for all employees that are not managers and a MANAGERS table that contains data for all managers.

- *Class table inheritance*—Map each class in the inheritance hierarchy to its own table. In this example, there is an EMPLOYEES table that contains all common employee data for both non-managers and managers alike. There is also a MANAGERS table, but it only contains information specific for managers and is treated as supplemental to the data in the EMPLOYEES table.

- *Single table inheritance*—Map all domain objects within the inheritance hierarchy to the same table. In this example, there is a single EMPLOYEES table that contains columns that map to both Employee and Manager attributes. It also includes a column that indicates the exact concrete type for each row. Manager attributes are set to null for rows that correspond to employees who are not managers.

Single table inheritance makes query, batch update, and batch delete operations simpler and more efficient to implement since they only involve one table. The same operations using concrete or class table inheritance require joins or multiple database operations. However, single table inheritance does not make the most efficient use of database storage, since it requires the table to define the union of all attributes within an inheritance hierarchy.

SAMPLE CODE

This example uses a Java Data Objects (JDO) provider to define and implement an object/relational map. JDO is not an object/relational map standard. Rather, it is an object persistence standard. JDO providers vary in their support for object/relational mapping. The standard defines programming interfaces for persistence operations like storing and retrieving object data, but it does not dictate how to set up an object/relational map if one is required. This example uses a specific JDO provider that is part of the Object/Relational Bridge (OJB) product from the Apache Software Foundation's Jakarta Project.

This sample code illustrates the order processing application described in the "Context" section. LineItem defines domain objects that represent single line items in an order. The persistence manager is responsible for mapping the contents of this object to the LINE_ITEMS table in the database. At runtime, the persistence manager instantiates a LineItem object for every row in the LINE_ITEMS table that the application requests or references. Each of a LineItem object's attributes corresponds to a single piece of column data within its row.

```java
public class LineItem {

    private long orderID;
    private long lineItemID;
    private String productID;
    private int quantity;
    private BigDecimal unitPrice;

    public LineItem() { }

    public LineItem(long orderID,
                    long lineItemID,
                    String productID,
                    int quantity,
                    BigDecimal unitPrice) {

        this.orderID = orderID;
        this.lineItemID = lineItemID;
        this.productID = productID;
```

```
            this.quantity = quantity;
            this.unitPrice = unitPrice;
        }

    public long getOrderID() {
        return orderID;
    }

    public void setOrderID(long orderID) {
        this.orderID = orderID;
    }

    public long getLineItemID() {
        return lineItemID;
    }

    public void setLineItemID(long lineItemID) {
        this.lineItemID = lineItemID;
    }

    public String getProductID() {
        return productID;
    }

    public void setProductID(String productID) {
        this.productID = productID;
    }

    public int getQuantity() {
        return quantity;
    }

    public void setQuantity(int quantity) {
        this.quantity = quantity;
    }

    public BigDecimal getUnitPrice() {
        return unitPrice;
    }

    public void setUnitPrice(BigDecimal unitPrice) {
        this.unitPrice = unitPrice;
    }
    }
}
```

Notice how the code for LineItem makes no mention of the corresponding LINE_ITEMS table or its columns. Instead, it is defined using pure object-oriented domain concepts.

Order serves a similar purpose to LineItem in that it represents the domain concept of an order using object-oriented semantics. Again, the persistence manager is responsible for mapping the contents of Order objects to the ORDERS table in the database.

```java
public class Order {

    private long orderID;
    private long customerID;
    private Timestamp placed;
    private Collection lineItems;

    public Order() { }

    public Order(long orderID,
                 long customerID,
                 Collection lineItems) {

        this.orderID = orderID;
        this.customerID = customerID;
        this.placed
            = new Timestamp(System.currentTimeMillis());
        this.lineItems = lineItems;
    }

    public long getOrderID() {
        return orderID;
    }

    public void setOrderID(long orderID) {
        this.orderID = orderID;
    }

    public long getCustomerID() {
        return customerID;
    }

    public void setCustomerID(long customerID) {
        this.customerID = customerID;
    }

    public Timestamp getPlaced() {
        return placed;
    }

    public void setPlaced(Timestamp placed) {
        this.placed = placed;
```

```
    }

    public Collection getLineItems() {
        return lineItems;
    }

    public void setLineItems(Collection lineItems) {
        this.lineItems = lineItems;
    }
}
```

Notice the relationship between the Order and LineItem classes. Every Order object references a collection of LineItem objects. This models the one-to-many aggregation relationship between rows in the ORDERS and LINE_ITEMS tables. The persistence manager is also responsible for maintaining this relationship.

One of the benefits of an object/relational map is that application domain objects do not need to implement any mapping details. Most commercial object/relational map products require you to define these details using metadata. Some products store metadata in configuration files and others store it in the database itself. Some products provide graphical mapping tools for manipulating metadata while others require you to code it using XML or another defined format. The OJB JDO provider requires you to define mapping details using its own XML format. This is the XML definition that maps the LineItem class to the LINE_ITEMS table:

```
<class-descriptor class="LineItem" table="LINE_ITEMS">

    <field-descriptor id="1"
        name="orderID"
        column="ORDER_ID"
        jdbc-type="BIGINT"
    />

    <field-descriptor id="2"
        name="lineItemID"
        column="LINE_ITEM_ID"
        jdbc-type="BIGINT"
        primarykey="true"
    />

    <field-descriptor id="3"
        name="productID"
        column="PRODUCT_ID"
        jdbc-type="VARCHAR"
    />
```

```
    <field-descriptor id="4"
        name="quantity"
        column="QUANTITY"
        jdbc-type="INTEGER"
    />

    <field-descriptor id="5"
        name="unitPrice"
        column="UNIT_PRICE"
        jdbc-type="DECIMAL"
    />

</class-descriptor>
```

Next is a similar metadata definition for mapping from the Order class to the ORDERS table. Notice the <collection-descriptor> tag near the bottom. It defines the one-to-many relationship between rows in the ORDERS and LINE_ITEMS tables. It states that every Order object is related to zero or more LineItem objects whose orderID attribute values match.

```
<class-descriptor class="Order" table="ORDERS">

    <field-descriptor id="1"
        name="orderID"
        column="ORDER_ID"
        jdbc-type="BIGINT"
        primarykey="true"
    />

    <field-descriptor id="2"
        name="customerID"
        column="CUSTOMER_ID"
        jdbc-type="BIGINT"
    />

    <field-descriptor id="3"
        name="placed"
        column="PLACED"
        jdbc-type="TIMESTAMP"
    />

    <collection-descriptor
        name="lineItems"
        element-class-ref="LineItem"
        auto-retrieve="true"
        auto-update="true"
```

```
        auto-delete="true">
        <inverse-foreignkey field-id-ref="1"/>
    </collection-descriptor>

</class-descriptor>
```

The last XML declaration that OJB requires is a repository definition. This describes global information such as the underlying JDBC driver and transaction isolation level to use. You can customize these aspects for each table, but this example defines them in one location that applies to all tables. This repository definition also includes the mapping files that are described above.

```
<?xml version="1.0" encoding="UTF-8"?>

<!DOCTYPE descriptor-repository SYSTEM "repository.dtd" [
<!ENTITY lineItem SYSTEM "LineItem.xml">
<!ENTITY order SYSTEM "Order.xml">
]>

<descriptor-repository
    version="0.9.5"
    isolation-level="read-uncommitted">

    <jdbc-connection-descriptor
        jdbc-level="2.0"
    driver="org.apache.ojb.jdo.PersistenceManagerFactoryImpl"
        protocol="jdbc"
        subprotocol="mysql"
        dbalias="///test"
        username=""
        password=""
    />

    &lineItem;
    &order;

</descriptor-repository>
```

The next block shows the application code that initializes a JDO Persistence-Manager. Every JDO provider provides a PersistenceManagerFactory implementation that resolves new PersistenceManager objects when an application requests them.

```
// Initialize the PersistenceManagerFactory.
PersistenceManagerFactory pmFactory
    = (PersistenceManagerFactory)Class.forName(
```

```
            "org.apache.ojb.jdo.PersistenceManagerFactoryImpl"
            ).newInstance();

    // Resolve the PersistenceManager.
    PersistenceManager pm = pmFactory.getPersistenceManager();
```

This block shows how application code can create a new order and store it in the database. Notice that there is no reference to the data model or data access code at all.

```
    Collection newLineItems = new LinkedList();
    newLineItems.add(new LineItem(currentOrderID, 1, "698487", 2,
                            new BigDecimal("164.00")));
    newLineItems.add(new LineItem(currentOrderID, 2, "458305", 1,
                            new BigDecimal("78.89")));
    newLineItems.add(new LineItem(currentOrderID, 3, "988664", 10,
                            new BigDecimal("12.99")));

    Order currentOrder = new Order(currentOrderID,
                                currentCustomerID,
                                newLineItems);

    // Store the data in the database.  The PersistenceManager
    // takes care of the details.
    pm.makePersistent(currentOrder);
```

The last application code block for this example prints invoices for all orders in the database. Again, there is no database access code at all.

```
    Query orderQuery = pm.newQuery(Order.class);
    Collection orderCollection = (Collection)orderQuery.execute();
    for(Iterator i = orderCollection.iterator(); i.hasNext(); ) {

        Order order = (Order)i.next();

        // Print the order details.
        invoiceOut.println("Invoice for order: "
                            + order.getOrderID());
        invoiceOut.println("Customer ID:       "
                            + order.getCustomerID());
        invoiceOut.println("Order placed on:    "
                            order.getPlaced());
        invoiceOut.println();

        // Iterate through the order's line items and
        // print their details.
        BigDecimal orderTotal = new BigDecimal("0");
```

```
    Collection lineItems = order.getLineItems();
    for(Iterator j = lineItems.iterator(); j.hasNext(); )
    {
        LineItem lineItem = (LineItem)j.next();
        int quantity = lineItem.getQuantity();
        BigDecimal unitPrice = lineItem.getUnitPrice();
        BigDecimal lineItemTotal = unitPrice.multiply(
            new BigDecimal(Integer.toString(quantity)));

        invoiceOut.println(lineItem.getProductID() + "..."
            + quantity + " x "
            + unitPrice + " = "
            + lineItemTotal);

        orderTotal = orderTotal.add(lineItemTotal);
    }

    // Print the order total.
    invoiceOut.println();
    invoiceOut.println("Order total:       " + orderTotal);
    invoiceOut.println();
}

// Free resources associated with the query results.
orderQuery.close(orderCollection);
```

This example illustrates how you can define object/relational mapping details exclusively using metadata. You can adapt to data model changes simply by updating the map metadata and leaving the application code untouched.

RELATED PATTERNS AND TECHNOLOGY

There are many commercial products and standards available that enable you to quickly incorporate object/relational mapping capabilities into your applications. These are a few alternatives for Java applications:

- *Java Data Objects (JDO)*—JDO is a standard interface set that defines semantics for storing persistent objects. You write your application in terms of these interfaces, but at runtime, you plug in a specialized JDO provider, which implements the JDO interfaces.

  JDO is not strictly an object/relational map interface. Instead, it is designed for any persistent object technology, including object-oriented database management systems (OODBMS), XML-based databases, and proprietary storage systems. However, many JDO providers implement object/relational maps. Each JDO provider defines its own mechanism and tools for customizing map metadata. See the "Sample Code" section for an example of an application that uses JDO for object/relational mapping.

- *Container-managed persistence*—An EJB that uses container-managed persistence (CMP) is a type of domain object that is managed by an Object/Relational Map. CMP means that the EJB container takes responsibility for domain object mapping and physical data access.

- *Other third-party products*—Numerous third-party products are available to implement object/relational maps for a variety of platforms and databases. They vary in their degree of mapping versatility and integration with popular development environments.

The following patterns are related to the Object/Relational Map pattern:

- Active Domain Object (33) describes an alternate strategy for domain object mapping that implements mapping within each domain object rather than in a single, separate component.

- You can use the Object/Relational Map pattern within one or more layers, as described in Layers (75).

- You can use Selection Factory (191), Domain Object Factory (203), and Update Factory (215) to define consistent, but hardwired domain object mapping strategies. You can manage these factories with Domain Object Assembler (227), a pattern that describes a strategy for implementing a generic domain object mapping infrastructure.

- Paging Iterator (253) works well for managing collections of domain objects that correspond to database query results.

- [Fowler 2002] devotes a whole section to object/relational mapping patterns. Many of the patterns address concepts that this chapter introduces in greater detail. These patterns are of particular relevance if you implement your own general-purpose object/relational map or if you want to understand how commercial mapping products work so you can optimize the way your application uses them.

Layers

DESCRIPTION

Stack orthogonal application features that address data access issues with increasing levels of abstraction.

CONTEXT

The previous patterns in this section, Data Accessor (9), Active Domain Object (33), and Object/Relational Map (53), described strategies for decoupling the notions of the data model, domain object mapping, and data access details from application code. These notions are *orthogonal* because you can vary them independently of each other. For example, the Data Accessor pattern enables you to make data model changes without updating data access code. Likewise, if you employ an Object/Relational Map, you can change the domain object mapping implementation without altering application code.

Generally stated, software components are orthogonal if they address completely disjointed issues and can be assembled in any combination to build an overall solution. An application's data model is often orthogonal to its data access mechanism. The data model is the static structure of the data and data access addresses how to move the data between the physical database and the application code. Altering the data model, even drastically, does not usually require a change to the data access mechanism, and the converse is mostly true as well. Identifying orthogonal components in a system enables you to modularize it more effectively. Decoupling orthogonal components is nearly always a good idea because doing so grants you freedom to alter them independently.

Finer grained components can be orthogonal as well. Consider a data accessor instance that encapsulates all data access implementation code for a suite of applications. The code within this component addresses two distinct issues. The first is connection management, which involves initializing and resolving database connections. The other issue is generating SQL statements for database operations. There is very little overlap between the solutions for these issues so it makes sense to decouple them into separate modules.

As you think about orthogonal components, it is important to understand that orthogonality does not preclude dependence. In other words, just because two components solve completely different problems, it does not mean that you cannot build one of them using the other. For example, one way to decompose the data model and data access aspects of an application is to employ active domain objects that encapsulate their own mapping to the underlying data model. Rather than spreading data access code throughout active domain object implementations, you can utilize a common data accessor implementation within each. Active domain objects and data accessor implementation address orthogonal issues, and you can decouple them by defining a proper data accessor abstraction, but there remains a strong, dependent relationship of the active domain objects on this abstraction. Figure 4.1 illustrates this relationship as well as the decomposition of the connection management functionality from the rest of the data accessor implementation:

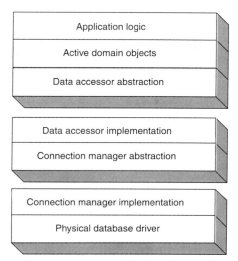

FIGURE 4.1: One way to decompose an application into orthogonal layers. Active domain objects encapsulate the data model and domain object mapping. The data accessor implementation is responsible for physical data access, and the connection manager implementation handles database connections and statement handles.

The Layers pattern describes how to stack multiple dependent, orthogonal components to form a robust and maintainable application. A *layer* is a set of components that implements a software abstraction in terms of less abstract entities. You can stack abstract layers that incrementally decompose a solution down to its ultimate physical implementation. Layers effectively manage the mapping from abstract concepts to a concrete implementation in steps, solving the problem one piece at a time. Figure 4.2 illustrates a stack of layers between application logic and physical database access in general terms:

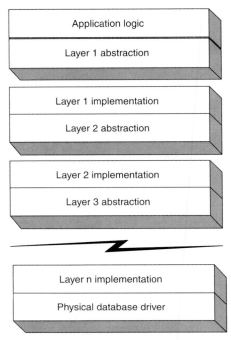

FIGURE 4.2: Layers decouple abstract entities to incrementally map an application domain abstraction to its physical implementation.

As with any orthogonal components, it is a good practice to decouple layers so that they are only dependent on lower level abstractions rather than implementations. You can achieve this by defining abstractions for each layer. When you follow this strategy, you can view a single-layer implementation as an adapter from one abstraction to another. For example, the data accessor implementation in Figure 4.1 is an adapter that implements the data accessor abstraction in terms of the connection manager abstraction. Of course, it is not a pure adapter. Rather, it is likely to include a substantial amount of functionality as well. However, this single focus makes layered components easier to build and maintain.

Data access code is amenable to building with layers because there are so many orthogonal facets to it. Here are some examples of data access details that are candidates for implementation within their own layer:

- *Domain object mapping*—You can map between domain objects and relational concepts within a single layer. Active Domain Object (33), Object/Relational

Map (53), and Domain Object Assembler (227) are domain object mapping patterns that you can confine to a single software layer.

- *Data conversion*—It is common for both databases and drivers to convert data between its physical and software formats slightly differently. This is especially true for timestamp data, BLOBs, complex objects, and character data stored using specific code pages. If you support multiple database platforms, you may find it useful to define a software layer that is devoted to normalizing tricky data conversion details.

- *Data operation mapping*—If you define logical database operations for your application to use like Data Accessor (9) suggests, then you can define the components that implement them in terms of physical operations within their own layer. The example given in this chapter takes this approach.

- *Resource management*—Database resource management is a good candidate for isolation within a single software layer because resource optimizations can have a significant effect on system performance and utilization. This includes strategies like connection pooling, statement caching, and resource timeouts. If you do not confine these operations within their own software layer, they may impose complex semantics on other components in your system. Defining one or more layers for resource management also makes it easier for you to start with a simple implementation and incorporate optimizations later.

- *Distribution*—If you plan to access data from multiple sources, it is beneficial to define a configurable directory rather than hardwiring data sources into your code. This allows you to readily adapt to new data source topologies. However, implementing a directory also adds complexity to an application's data access code, since every data access operation must target the appropriate data source. You can mitigate this complexity by defining a software layer whose inputs make no mention of physical data sources and outputs attach a data source to each operation.

- *Caching*—Caching data that your application accesses frequently can significantly improve its performance. Like other optimizations, caching introduces complexity, so it is yet another candidate for its own software layer. Caching layers typically define the same input and output operations, but intercept some input operations when cached data is available.

- *Authorization*—You can implement application-level authorization within a software layer by comparing operations to a set of authorization rules defined by an administrator. This usually involves checking rules for every data access operation, so it makes sense to confine authorization within its own software layer.

- *Logging*—Complete and consistent logging is extremely important when you debug defects that customers report. If you depend on application code to implement logging effectively, you run the risk of having to deal with missing or inaccurate diagnostic messages. You can implement logging within its own software layer, which intercepts and logs every data access operation consistently. You may even find it useful to define multiple logging layers that track operations as they pass through different abstraction levels.

APPLICABILITY

Use the Layers pattern when:

- You want to decouple the data model, data access details, domain object mapping, or any other orthogonal features that you plan to alter independently.

- You want to define multiple, incremental levels of software abstraction to simplify development and maintenance. You may also find that different abstraction levels are more amenable to supporting different types of client code. For example, you might write main application code in terms of the highest level of abstraction and graphical administration utilities using a lower level of abstraction.

- You want to prototype or build a system gradually using stubbed or simplified layer implementations and then fill in more scalable or optimized implementations later in the development process.

STRUCTURE

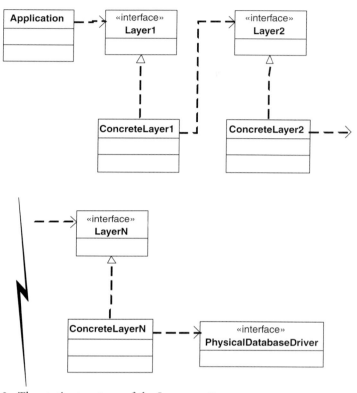

FIGURE 4.3: The static structure of the Layers pattern.

Figure 4.3 illustrates the static structure of the Layers pattern. Layers are numbered beginning with one. N represents the total number of layers. Application code works in terms of Layer1, the most abstract data access layer. Each ConcreteLayer$M$ implements its respective Layer$M$ interface in terms of the next, less abstract Layer$M+1$ interface. ConcreteLayer$N$, the least abstract layer, interacts directly with the physical database driver.

As you define your own layering structures, remember that layers do not have to strictly conform to the structure that Figure 4.3 shows. Here are some variations you may employ in your own layered designs:

- *Describe a layer with multiple interfaces*—It does not always make sense in object-oriented terms to define a layer with only one interface. One example is a data accessor layer that exposes logical database operations as well as operations for fetching query results. You can represent this type of layer abstraction more appropriately using two interfaces: one for database operations and one for result set operations.

- *Define an abstraction using classes*—In general, defining abstractions using interfaces is beneficial because it prevents higher level layers from depending on implementation details. This in turn prevents you from changing implementation details as easily. However, it is not imperative that you define each layer exclusively using interfaces. You may find it more convenient to define a particular abstraction using classes, especially for those objects that represent simple data structures like a single row of physical data or an exception.

- *Use non-strict layering*—Layers do not necessarily need to form a strict linear structure. Some layers may depend on multiple instances of the same layer type or multiple types of layers, especially if their implementation changes significantly depending on the runtime course of events. You may also find it convenient to skip layers on certain occasions, like for an optimized operation or a drastic behavior change. Non-strict layering adds significant complexity to the overall application structure, so document these cases well.

INTERACTIONS

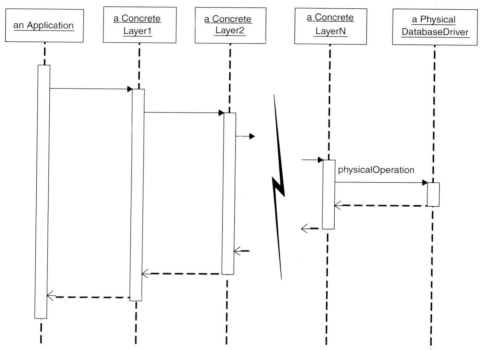

FIGURE 4.4: An application invokes an operation on a ConcreteLayer1 instance, which implements the system's highest level abstraction.

Figure 4.4 portrays what happens when an application invokes an operation on a ConcreteLayer1 instance, which implements the system's highest level abstraction. ConcreteLayer1 implements the operation with custom functionality that makes zero or more calls to operations in a ConcreteLayer2 instance. Likewise, ConcreteLayer2 invokes operations on the next layer, and so on, until the lowest level layer, a ConcreteLayerN instance, calls the physical database driver directly.

In reality, most layered data access implementations are not quite this simple. For example, it is quite common for a single call to a ConcreteLayerM instance to map to multiple ConcreteLayerM+1 calls.

CONSEQUENCES

The Layers pattern has the following consequences:

Benefits

- *Software design decomposition*—Layers are a convenient strategy for decomposing a large software design into smaller, more manageable components. This enables you to address large-scale issues earlier in your development process and fine-tune the details later.

- *Data access feature modularization*—Defining layers for orthogonal data access features enables you to build and maintain them concurrently and independently. Concurrent development and testing often lead to faster product development cycles. In addition, effective feature modularization can make software easier to debug, since you can isolate defective code more quickly based on the exact feature characteristic that is failing.

- *Data access detail encapsulation*—Each layer encapsulates the implementation of one or more data access details. This relieves the layers above it from any dependence on its details, making their coupling looser and implementations more focused.

- *Multiple layer implementation pluggability*—Defining clean layer abstractions enables you to plug in one or more implementations of a particular layer during runtime initialization. This can be a powerful strategy that you can employ to support multiple, diverse data access semantics and topologies with a single set of interfaces.

Drawback

- *Layer interaction and initialization complexity*—Layers interact with each other by way of clear abstractions. As you build more layers into your software structure, you must maintain their interactions to ensure that the overall solution is viable. Understanding how these interactions affect the entire structure gets significantly more complex with more layers, especially when the structure is not entirely linear. This complexity comes to light in initialization code, where layer implementations are coupled with each other.

STRATEGIES

Consider these strategies when implementing the Layers pattern:

- *Stub layer implementations for prototyping*—Splitting application functionality into layers enables you to define stubs for layers that enable you to develop components concurrently or build unoptimized versions for early demonstrations or prototypes. Stub layers are also helpful for building the entire layered structure early in your development process. This is important since it helps to ensure that the layers will interact as you predict. Sometimes unexpected layer interdependencies crop up, requiring you to redefine one or more layers in your system. It is much easier to fix this type of problem before you build a significant quantity of code that depends on the problematic structure.

- *Design from the top down or bottom up*—As you design an application's layered structure, your design goals affect which end of the stack to begin with. Starting at the top enables you to focus on application requirements and use cases first. Conversely, working from the bottom forces you to address core implementation details first.

- *Isolate layer initialization*—Figure 4.3 shows a recommended layering structure. Each layer depends on the next layer's abstraction, but you must plug in concrete implementations at runtime. Coupling layer implementations usually happens by passing a ConcreteLayer$M$+1 instance to a ConcreteLayer$M$ instance as a constructor parameter or by setting an attribute. At that point, the ConcreteLayer$M$ instance saves a reference to the ConcreteLayer$M$+1 instance so that it can invoke its operations.

  As the number of layers increases, it gets difficult to keep tabs on the combination and ordering of layers. It helps to isolate all layer initialization code within a single module, which also serves to precisely describe the application's overall layering structure application in one place. If you find that you need to rearrange layers, you can do so within the initialization module.

SAMPLE CODE

The following sections show sample code that defines and implements much of the layered structure defined in the example in the Context section. There are three layers: the connection management layer, the data accessor layer, and the active domain objects layer.

Connection Management Layer

The connection management layer is the bottom-most layer in this example. It is responsible for managing database connections and statement handles. The ConnectionManager interface defines this layer's abstraction. It exposes operations for executing SQL queries and updates to any data source defined in the system.

```
public interface ConnectionManager {

    /**
    Executes an SQL query statement.

    @param dataSource The data source.
    @param sql The SQL statement.
    @return The ResultSet.  It is the caller's
            responsibility to close this ResultSet
            when it finishes using it.
    */
    ResultSet executeQuery(String dataSource,
                           String sql)
                           throws SQLException;

    /**
    Executes an SQL update statement.

    @param dataSource The data source.
    @param sql The SQL statement.
    @return The number of affected rows.
    */
    int executeUpdate(String dataSource,
                      String sql)
                      throws SQLException;
}
```

The ConcreteConnectionManager is a simple implementation that plugs the data source name directly into a JDBC URL to establish new connections. It creates at most one connection for each data source and reuses that connection for subsequent operations.

```java
public class ConcreteConnectionManager
implements ConnectionManager {

    // Maps data sources to connections.
    private Map connections = new HashMap();

    public ResultSet executeQuery(String dataSource,
                                  String sql)
                    throws SQLException {
      Connection connection = resolveConnection(dataSource);
      Statement statement = connection.createStatement();
      return statement.executeQuery(sql);
    }

    public int executeUpdate(String dataSource,
                             String sql)
                    throws SQLException {
      Connection connection = resolveConnection(dataSource);
      Statement statement = connection.createStatement();
      int rowsUpdated = statement.executeUpdate(sql);
      statement.close();
      return rowsUpdated;
    }

    private Connection resolveConnection(String dataSource)
        throws SQLException {

        // If the map already contains a connection for
        // this data source, then use it.  Otherwise,
        // initialize a new one.
        synchronized(connections) {
            Connection connection
                = (Connection)connections.get(dataSource);

            if (connection == null) {
                connection = DriverManager.getConnection(
                    "jdbc:subprotocol://" + dataSource,
                    myUser, myPassword);
                connections.put(dataSource, connection);
            }
            return connection;
        }
    }
}
```

ConcreteConnectionManager's implementation has a few problems. First of all, any two clients that invoke operations using the same data source name utilize the same database connection. This works fine most of the time. However, like most call-level interfaces, JDBC maintains at most one active transaction per database connection. As a result, ConcreteConnectionManager forces multiple operations to run within the same transaction. Applications may not always expect this behavior. You can fix this problem by building a connection pool that this layer encapsulates. Each operation uses its own connection from the pool and returns it when it is done.

Another problem with ConcreteConnectionManager is that it contains a statement handle leak. The executeQuery operation creates a new statement handle, but neglects to close it. In JDBC, closing a statement handle forces the physical database driver to implicitly close the result set as well, thus rendering the query results unavailable to client code. You cannot expect the client to close the statement handle, because the client does not have a reference to it. You can solve this problem by wrapping the result set object in a Resource Decorator (103) that maintains a reference to the statement handle. The decorator can take care of closing the statement handle when the client code closes the result set.

A final problem with ConcreteConnectionManager is that the executeQuery operation returns an open result set. It clearly documents that the client is responsible for closing this result set when it is done. However, if the client's developer does not heed this documentation or writes defective code, his/her code may leave the result set and its associated database resources open indefinitely. You can account for this possibility by incorporating a Resource Timer (137) that automatically closes the result set after a configured amount of time.

It is safe to say this implementation has significant scalability problems. However, it works fine on a small scale and certainly suffices for initial prototyping and development testing. It is an example stub implementation that demonstrates how you can solve problems after you build the remaining layers in the system. Later, you can enhance it to incorporate additional functionality, such as a more sophisticated data distribution mechanism or user and password management.

Data Accessor Layer

The data accessor layer is responsible for implementing physical data access operations on behalf of its client. The DataAccessor interface defines this layer's abstraction using logical database operations and does not expose any SQL or call-level interface semantics at all. This is the same interface that the sample code for Data Accessor (9) previously defined.

```
public interface DataAccessor {

    List read(String table,
              String[] columns,
              Row selectionRow,
              String[] sortColumns) throws DataException;

    void insert(String table, List rows) throws DataException;

    void update(String table,
                Row selectionRow,
                Row updateRow) throws DataException;

    void delete(String table, Row selectionRow)
        throws DataException;
}
```

The ConcreteDataAccessor implementation is similar to that shown in the "Sample Code" section for the Data Accessor pattern. The difference is that it is implemented here in terms of the ConnectionManager interface rather than the physical database driver. This illustrates how the data accessor layer now sits on top of the connection management layer. ConcreteDataAccessor effectively acts as an adapter from the DataAccessor interface to the ConnectionManager interface.

```
public class ConcreteDataAccessor
implements DataAccessor {

    private ConnectionManager connectionManager;

    /**
    Constructs a ConcreteDataAccessor object.

    @param connectionManager The connection manager.
    */
    public ConcreteDataAccessor(
        ConnectionManager connectionManager) {

        this.connectionManager = connectionManager;
    }

    public List read(String table,
                     String[] columns,
                     Row selectionRow,
                     String[] sortColumns)
                        throws DataException {
        try {
            // Generate the SQL SELECT statement based on
```

```java
// the client input.
StringBuffer buffer = new StringBuffer();
buffer.append("SELECT ");

// List the columns if the caller specified any.
if (columns != null) {
    for(int i = 0; i < columns.length; ++i) {
        if (i > 0)
            buffer.append(", ");
        buffer.append(columns[i]);
    }
}
else
    buffer.append(" * ");

// Include the resolved qualified table name.
buffer.append(" FROM ");
buffer.append(resolveQualifiedTable(table));

// Generate the WHERE clause if the caller
// specified a selection row.
if (selectionRow != null) {
    buffer.append(
        generateWhereClause(selectionRow));
}

// Generate the ORDER BY clause if the caller
// specified sort columns.
if (sortColumns != null) {
    buffer.append(" ORDER BY ");
    for(int i = 0; i < sortColumns.length; ++i) {
        if (i > 0)
            buffer.append(", ");
        buffer.append(sortColumns[i]);
        buffer.append(" ASC");
    }
}

// Use the ConnectionManager to execute the query.
String dataSource = resolveDataSource(table);
ResultSet resultSet
    = connectionManager.executeQuery(dataSource,
        buffer.toString());
ResultSetMetaData rsmd = resultSet.getMetaData();
int columnCount = rsmd.getColumnCount();

// Create a list of result rows based on the
// contents of the result set.
List resultRows = new LinkedList();
```

```
        while(resultSet.next()) {
            Row resultRow = new Row();
            for(int i = 1; i <= columnCount; ++i) {
                resultRow.addColumn(
                    rsmd.getColumnName(i),
                    resultSet.getObject(i));
            }
            resultRows.add(resultRow);
        }

        // Release database resources and return.
        resultSet.close();
        return resultRows;
    }
    catch(SQLException e) {
        throw new DataException("Unable to read table "
            + table, e);
    }
}

// See the full listing in the "Sample Code" section for
// Data Accessor (9).  You can reimplement the other
// public operations analogously.

}
```

Notice that ConcreteDataAccessor defines a ConnectionManager parameter in its constructor. This does not necessarily dictate any overall layer initialization strategy, but it does ensure that the client will assign a ConnectionManager implementation before ConcreteDataAccessor needs to invoke any database operations.

Active Domain Object Layer

The next layer is a set of active domain objects that is responsible for mapping itself to the physical data model. CustomerList maps itself to the contents of the CUSTOMERS table. Its constructor reads the contents of this table and populates a list of Customer objects. This code is similar to that previously shown in the "Sample Code" section for Active Domain Object (33), except it uses the data accessor layer rather than interacting with a physical database driver directly.

```
public class CustomerList
{
    private List contents = new LinkedList();

    /**
    Constructs a CustomerList object that represents
```

```
every customer in the database.
*/
public CustomerList() throws DataException {
    DataAccessor dataAccessor
        = DataAccessorFactory.getDataAccessor();

    List resultData = dataAccessor.read("CUSTOMERS",
                                    null, null, null);

    for(Iterator i = resultData.iterator();i.hasNext();) {
        Row row = (Row)i.next();
        int id
            = ((Integer)row.getColumnValue("CUSTID"))
            .intValue();
        String lastName
            = (String)row.getColumnValue("LAST");
        String firstName
            = (String)row.getColumnValue("FIRST");
        String address
            = (String)row.getColumnValue("ADDRESS");
        String city
            = (String)row.getColumnValue("CITY");
        String state
            = (String)row.getColumnValue("STATE");
        String country
            = (String)row.getColumnValue("COUNTRY");
        String zip
        = (String)row.getColumnValue("ZIP");

        Customer customer = new Customer(id, lastName,
            firstName, address, city, state, country,
            zip);
        contents.add(customer);
    }
}

/**
Returns a customer list iterator.
*/
public Iterator iterator() {
    return contents.iterator();
}
}
```

Recall that the active domain objects in the "Sample Code" section for Active Domain Object (33) used a ConnectionFactory in order to resolve physical database connections. This example takes the same approach except that it defines a DataAccessorFactory for resolving DataAccessor implementations:

```
public class DataAccessorFactory {

    private static final ConnectionManager connectionManager
        = new ConcreteConnectionManager();

    public static DataAccessor getDataAccessor() {
        return new ConcreteDataAccessor(connectionManager);
    }
}
```

RELATED PATTERNS AND TECHNOLOGY

- [Buschmann 1996] describes Layers from a more general architectural perspective.

- Some concrete layer implementations are instances of Adapter [Gamma 1995] since they adapt their own layer's abstraction to the abstraction for the subsequent layer.

- You can define more than one layer using the same abstraction. This comes in handy if the layers implement different features for the same logical database operations. Stacking multiple layers that implement the same abstraction forms an instance of a Chain of Responsibility [Gamma 1995]. Since the layers implement the same abstraction, you can combine them in different orders.

- Instances of Data Accessor (9), Active Domain Object (33), Object/Relational Map (53), and Domain Object Assembler (227) can make layers within a single system. It is also convenient to encapsulate resource and cache patterns within one or more layers.

Part 2

Resource Patterns

All input and output in software involves resource management. A *resource* is an entity that represents storage or devices reserved for use by a specific application instance. A file handle is a simple example. A file handle represents an open file and a channel that enable input and output to that file. The file handle also acts as a software interface to the contents of the file, hiding the hardware-level details. In general, resources are abstractions that simplify the low-level complexity of dealing with input and output.

In addition to encapsulating input and output details, resources also serve semantic purposes. Resources store contextual information and enable controlled, concurrent access to the underlying storage or devices. This part of the book describes the semantic characteristics of resources, gives an overview of common resources that are involved in data access, and introduces patterns that are useful for managing resources.

RESOURCES AND CONTEXT

Resources store context. Consider how an application writes to a file:

```
FileWriter out
    = new FileWriter("/home/user1/output.txt", false);
out.write("This is a test.");
out.write("This is another test.");
out.write("This is yet another test.");
```

The FileWriter object is the file handle. It stores contextual information about how the file was opened. This context includes the file's name and whether it was opened for reading, writing, or appending. In addition, the file handle also stores state information, specifically a pointer to the location of the last operation. Saving this state ensures that subsequent writes do not overwrite data.

All file input and output operations require this contextual information. Without the notion of open files and file handles, the same code might look like this:

```
File.write("/home/user1/output.txt", 0,
           "This is a test.");
File.write("/home/user1/output.txt", 15,
           "This is another test.");
File.write("/home/user1/output.txt", 36,
           "This is yet another test.");
```

Without the benefit of a file handle's contextual information, the code has to pass the file name on every operation and maintain its own file pointer. Listing the filename repeatedly clutters the code and file pointer calculations are extremely error-prone. In general, resources that store contextual information save programmers from copying and pasting a lot of redundant code and managing state information from one operation to the next.

In addition, a resource's context helps to eliminate redundant initialization operations. A file handle might reference hardware-level details about the physical location of a file's data or a record from a volume's file access table. A file handle resolves this information when an application initializes it, and then references it on every operation. If there is no file handle in which to store these low-level details, the file system needs to resolve them for every operation. Resource initialization tends to be expensive, and storing the details for repeated use significantly reduces performance overhead.

RESOURCES AND CONCURRENCY

Resources often represent data or objects that are available to multiple applications distributed across a network. For example, a shared file system's contents are accessible to multiple users and serve as a cornerstone for team development and project management. Similarly, a single table's contents are available to a variety of applications, as well as reporting, data entry, and management tools. When multiple users access the same files or tables in incompatible ways, unpredictable results occur.

Consider a set of servers that logs requests and responses to a single file. This log is useful for gathering operational statistics and debugging. If two server instances write entries to the file at the same time, there is a good chance that the messages will blend together into an unreadable mess. Clearly, this file requires concurrent writes to be synchronized.

Resources play an important role in robust concurrency solutions. Resources often manage some level of synchronization that restricts concurrent access. For example, a file handle associates multiple writes with a single server instance so that the file system can ensure that no other instances write to the same file until the current write operation is complete. It can further restrict access so that only one server instance can open a given file at a time, if required. In this case, it blocks or rejects any other instance's requests for similar file handles.

DATA ACCESS RESOURCES

The following general-purpose, low-level resources provide unstructured data access and are useful in a wide range of applications:

- A *buffer* is an unstructured block of memory allocated from the heap for a specific purpose. The system's heap manager prevents other applications from allocating the buffer's memory until the original requester explicitly frees it.

- A *file handle* controls access to a physical file. File systems implement concurrency to prevent multiple users from making inconsistent updates to the file.

- A *socket* is a network connection handle to another application or server.

A substantial amount of relational database access code today employs a standard call-level interface like ODBC, OLE DB, or JDBC. Interface standards have matured in recent years, but most retain the same well-known resource concepts.

The following list describes the most common resources that applications use when calling data access interfaces. While these are not universal, most call-level interfaces define analogous entities.

- A *connection* is a handle to a database manager or server that exposes fundamental database operations. Connections often enforce user authentication and authorization and encapsulate one or more sockets. Because of its considerable initialization overhead, creating a new database connection tends to be among the slowest database operations in an application.

- A *statement handle* stores contextual and state information for one thread or module's database operations. A *prepared statement* is an optimized form of statement handle that stores compiled database instructions and parameter values so that an application can quickly execute them multiple times.

- A *result set* provides access to query results stored within a database. Result sets usually allow applications to fetch results as either single rows or blocks to avoid requiring massive amounts of bandwidth and client memory. A result set maintains a pointer to the current position using an open *cursor*. In some cases, particularly when updating result data, open cursors lock individual rows or complete tables to prevent other processes from updating them at the same time.

  Some databases allow you to read and manipulate disconnected result sets. A *disconnected result set* contains an entire set of query results in memory and does not require an active connection. Later on, when your application re-establishes a connection, it can synchronize changes made to the result set data. Disconnected result sets impose fewer concurrency constraints than connected result sets, but require additional attention when synchronizing potentially inconsistent changes.

- A *transaction* groups a set of database operations together so that either all or none of the operations get committed to the database. Database drivers often implement transactions using extensive row and table locking.

This list is not comprehensive. You will run across other resources, but the management techniques and patterns that this section describes often still apply.

RESOURCE MANAGEMENT

Resources play an important role in simplifying input and output code, improving the performance of database operations, and enforcing consistent, concurrent data access. On the other hand, resources also impose some important responsibilities on applications.

Resources usually consume significant amounts of storage as long as they remain open. For example, a database connection requires client memory to store its contextual information and it allocates server memory to maintain server-side context. In addition, it usually keeps a socket open on both sides to enable fast communication between the two sockets.

Resources often implement synchronization by restricting concurrent access to one or more objects. A file handle opened for writing often instructs the file system to lock out any other requests for the same file. The file system blocks other applications or users from accessing the file until the writing application closes its handle. This characteristic usually manifests to end users as a slow or unresponsive system since processes spend a significant amount of time waiting for locked resources.

Since open resources consume storage and reduce concurrency, it is important to understand how applications use and manage resources. There are no easy solutions for all cases, but this list describes a few ideas that apply to most:

*   *Always release resources*—Anytime your code opens or allocates a resource, it is also responsible for closing or freeing it. While you might not intentionally neglect to close a resource, it is common to mistakenly inject a condition where the resource close operation gets skipped. This condition is commonly known as a *resource leak.* As your program gradually consumes more resources, the supply available for other applications similarly depletes. Resource leaks are exceptionally difficult to debug because the ultimate symptom is either an error indicating that no more resources are available or a slow system whose performance continually degrades. In either case, the error provides absolutely no indication of the resource leak's source.

    Environments that provide automatic garbage collection theoretically solve this problem. Once your program finishes using a resource, the garbage collector closes it for you. This strategy works effectively for resources like buffers that are managed within the garbage-collected environment, but it does not work well for database resources. There is an unpredictable window between the time your program finishes using a resource and the time the environment collects it. As this interval increases, concurrency issues become more pronounced. Even worse, many database drivers keep internal references to resources for their own management. Since the garbage collector does not differentiate between your applications' and the driver's references, it assumes that all referenced resources are still in use and does not close them.

A better strategy for avoiding resource leaks is to open and close resources with rigid, symmetric structure. This means that any isolated component that opens a resource is responsible for closing it as well. It also helps to confine resource management within a single component so that it is easier to write and maintain, and requires fewer accommodations for special cases.

- *Minimize the interval that a resource is left open*—Since it is common for resources to lock objects for the purpose of synchronization, it is best to minimize the interval between the time when an application opens and closes each resource.

  Consider an application that performs extensive calculations while writing a report to a file. It is a good idea to calculate the report data before opening the file. That way, the file handle is open just long enough to write the report. The file system locks the file for a smaller interval, making its previous contents available to other applications until just before it writes the new report data.

- *Pool resources to conserve initialization expense*—Some resources, like database connections and sockets, are quite expensive to initialize. These resources consume client and server storage, but they do not necessarily restrict concurrency. In these cases, consider pooling resources. Pooling resources means keeping a set of resources open at all times so that your application can use them quickly without incurring initialization overhead on each operation.

RESOURCE PATTERNS

Resource patterns define common design strategies for managing resources at the application or middleware level. This part of the book contains chapters for each of the following patterns:

- **Resource Decorator** (103)—Dynamically attaches additional behavior to an existing resource with minimal disruption to application code. A resource decorator enables the extension of a resource's functionality without subclassing or changing its implementation.

- **Resource Pool** (117)—Recycles resources to minimize resource initialization overhead. A resource pool manages resources efficiently while allowing application code to freely allocate them.

- **Resource Timer** (137)—Automatically releases inactive resources. A resource timer alleviates the effect of applications or users that allocate resources indefinitely.

- **Resource Descriptor** (159)—Isolates platform- and data source-dependent behavior within a single component. A resource descriptor exposes specific platform idiosyncrasies that relate to particular database resources as generic, logical operations and enables the majority of data access code to remain independent of its physical environment.

- **Retryer** (171)—Automatically retries operations whose failure is expected under certain defined conditions. This pattern enables fault tolerance for data access operations.

If you employ a strategy that isolates data access code within a single component like the decoupling patterns in Part 1 of this book describe, then you are in a better position to confine the use of resource patterns within that component as well. This enables you to add new database features like customized logging, connection pooling, statement caching, automated resource cleanup, and retry functionality without negatively affecting application code.

Resource Decorator

DESCRIPTION

Dynamically attaches additional behavior to an existing resource with minimal disruption to application code. A resource decorator enables the extension of a resource's functionality without subclassing or changing its implementation.

CONTEXT

A *database driver* is a middleware entity that mediates interactions between an application and its physical data. Database drivers that implement a standard interface like ODBC or JDBC make it possible for an application to avoid hardwiring references to a specific database platform. Applications invoke generic operations defined by the interface, and database drivers implement that interface in conjunction with a specific database product. Standard driver interfaces enable simple applications to support a wide range of database products that can be effectively plugged in at runtime. Figure 5.1 illustrates how this relationship decouples a Java application from its supporting JDBC drivers:

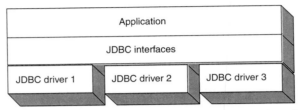

FIGURE 5.1: Applications interact with JDBC drivers via JDBC interfaces. This enables you to plug in any new JDBC driver at runtime without updating or recompiling application code.

Suppose that you want to extend the behavior of an existing database driver. For example, most driver implementations provide a logging facility, but the messages they issue are geared toward debugging internal driver problems and are usually not helpful to application developers. Rather than poring over the underlying byte data flowing between the client and server, application developers are usually interested in things like the SQL statements being executed and their corresponding parameter values. You can enable your own logging dynamically by attaching customized behavior to existing database drivers. This is a convenient way to debug your application's SQL statements, even within a customer's environment.

The database drivers that your application uses are normally commercial products that are tuned for communication with particular database platforms. With a few exceptions, you do not have source code for database drivers, so adding your own logging implementation directly to them is rarely a feasible solution.

A database driver is usually made up of several related classes. You can extend its behavior by creating subclasses for each class. The problem with this idea is that to build a comprehensive solution, you need to provide a similar set of subclasses for every database driver you support.

The Resource Decorator pattern is an elegant solution that avoids creating subclasses for each supported database driver. It is an instance of the Decorator pattern [Gamma 1995] and applies directly to database resources. Resource Decorator allows you to attach additional behavior to any existing driver implementation with a single set of classes and minimal disruption to application code.

Consider the problem of identifying resource leaks. In JDBC terms, common resources are represented by the Connection, Statement, and ResultSet interfaces.

If an application neglects to close any of these resources when it is finished using them, they continue to consume both client and server storage. ResultSets left open sometimes leave database locks in place, which prevents other applications from accessing the same data. To make matters worse, JDBC drivers tend to maintain internal references to these resources, preventing the Java Virtual Machine (JVM) from garbage collecting them effectively.

You can use Resource Decorator to implement a solution that tracks certain operations and ensures that applications close all resources in a timely manner. You can define a "leak detection" decorator that attaches to any JDBC driver and continuously reports facts about how applications are utilizing resources. A key concept of this solution is that neither the JDBC driver nor the main application code need to change to make use of the leak detection decorator. This works because the decorator implements the same JDBC interfaces as the driver. The application invokes the decorator's operations as if it was any other JDBC driver and the decorator dispatches those operations to the physical JDBC driver in turn. Figure 5.2 shows how resource decorators fit between a Java application and its supported JDBC drivers:

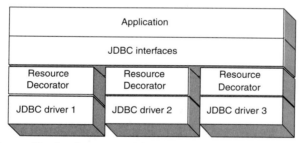

FIGURE 5.2: An application interacts with a Resource Decorator like any another JDBC driver. You can plug it in at runtime without updating or recompiling application or JDBC driver code.

Resource decorators are useful primarily as debugging and logging aids, but they can also provide other functions such as tweaking SQL statements, enforcing application-level security, preventing write operations, caching result set data, and adding result set scrolling support when it is not available from a driver.

APPLICABILITY

Use the Resource Decorator pattern when:

- You need to attach additional behavior to a resource, but changing its source code is not feasible. Most database resources are provided by commercial vendors. In the rare case that source code is available, changing, compiling, and supporting new versions is expensive and creates maintenance issues.

- You need to attach identical behavior to multiple resource implementations. Many applications support multiple database platforms, yet require the same extra functionality for each platform.

- You need to associate an additional behavior with many resource operations without spreading that behavior across your application code.

- You need the ability to dynamically enable an additional behavior without changing application or resource code.

STRUCTURE

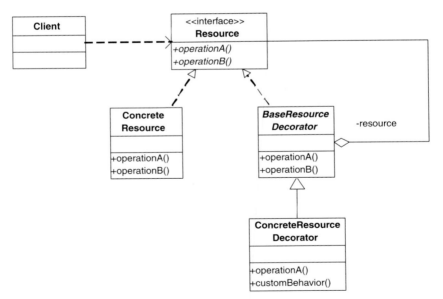

FIGURE 5.3: The static structure of the Resource Decorator pattern.

Figure 5.3 illustrates the static structure of the Resource Decorator pattern. The Resource interface represents any database resource, such as a connection, statement handle, or result set. A ConcreteResource class implements this interface in conjunction with a database platform or middleware product. You normally write client code in terms of the Resource interface, but interact directly with a ConcreteResource at runtime. This enables your code to work readily with any compliant Resource implementation.

BaseResourceDecorator is an abstract class that maintains a reference to any other Resource implementation. It itself is a full Resource implementation that delegates every operation to its referenced Resource.

On its own, BaseResourceDecorator does not provide much value. Its benefits come when you extend it and add specific, additional behavior. ConcreteResourceDecorator inherits BaseResourceDecorator's automatic operation delegation and adds its own custom behavior. The end result is a full Resource implementation that you can attach to any other Resource implementation. The ConcreteResourceDecorator class only contains code related to its additional behavior, while all delegation logic happens in BaseResourceDecorator.

The client code continues to refer only to the Resource interface, but you can plug in one or more ConcreteResourceDecorators that are wrapped around the ConcreteResource of your choice.

INTERACTIONS

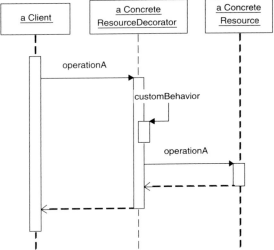

FIGURE 5.4: A client invokes operationA on a ConcreteResourceDecorator.

Figure 5.4 portrays what happens when a client invokes operationA on a Concrete-ResourceDecorator. In this sequence, ConcreteResourceDecorator invokes its custom behavior before delegating the operation to its assigned ConcreteResource. In practice, it can implement its custom behavior before, after, or even instead of delegating operations.

CONSEQUENCES

The Resource Decorator pattern has the following consequences:

Benefits

- *Attaches additional behavior to any resource*—When you think of extending an object's behavior, subclassing and inheritance often come to mind. However, a subclass must relate to a specific superclass and your application cannot dynamically alter this static relationship at runtime. When applications support multiple database drivers, it is not practical to define identical subclasses for each driver. In addition, the object factories common in standard resource interfaces make it difficult to plug in subclasses for resource objects that are constructed within a driver's factory.

  As an alternative, the Resource Decorator pattern defines the relationship between a Decorator object that defines an additional behavior and any driver resource using a dynamic reference that it connects at runtime.

- *Requires minimal changes to application code*—Assuming that application code is written in terms of generic resource interfaces, replacing resources with decorators that implement the same interfaces only requires changes to application initialization routines. You can hardwire this initialization, but make sure to isolate it in a single component so that it is easy to update. If you plan to let users or administrators alter this behavior, consider allowing them to designate a specific resource implementation in a registry entry, configuration file, or administration console.

- *Has combinatorial characteristics*—A resource decorator ultimately delegates operations to a driver resource. However, it references any resource implementation. Since decorators themselves meet this criterion, you can set up decorators to attach behavior to other decorators. This enables you to attach multiple, otherwise decoupled behaviors to a single driver resource in any combination.

Drawback

- *Requires complete implementations*—For a decorator to implement a resource interface completely, it must implement all of the interface's operations. Even though its delegation implementation is trivial, the number of operations that some resource intefaces define is often in the hundreds. It helps to write this code with an editor's cut and paste feature, but it is easy to inject mistakes in the delegation logic. Compilers will find some, but not all, of these errors.

STRATEGIES

Consider these strategies when implementing the Resource Decorator pattern:

- *Define client code in terms of generic Resource interfaces*—Client code ultimately interacts with ConcreteResource objects. However, you should write client code exclusively in terms of generic Resource interfaces. Doing so will keep it decoupled from specific ConcreteResources and ConcreteResourceDecorators. This is beneficial because it enables you to plug in other ConcreteResources or Concrete-ResourceDecorators dynamically.

- *Assign BaseResourceDecorator's reference Resource at construction time*— Dynamic assignment assures that the reference Resource is assigned prior to any subsequent operation invocations. This requires you to define Resource parameters in both the BaseResourceDecorator and ConcreteResourceDecorator constructors. ConcreteResourceDecorator simply passes the Resource on to BaseResourceDecorator during construction and BaseResourceDecorator maintains the reference.

- *Implement BaseResourceDecorator completely*—This ensures that its delegation behavior is consistent for all operations. The compiler will enforce this in cases where the Resource interface is defined with no default or optional behavior.

- *Implement ConcreteResourceDecorators sparingly*—BaseResourceDecorator handles delegating operations to its reference Resource implementation. ConcreteResourceDecorator inherits this functionality, so it does not necessarily need to implement every operation. Instead, it should implement only those operations whose behavior it modifies. In these operations, the ConcreteResourceDecorator code implements its additional behavior before, after, or instead of delegating the operation to BaseResourceDecorator, which in turn delegates it to its reference Resource implementation.

- *Define related ConcreteResourceDecorators for related Resource interfaces*—Many Resource interfaces include factory operations. A factory operation's job is to instantiate another type of related Resource implementation. An example of this is JDBC's createStatement operation. This operation is part of the Connection interface, but it creates new Statement objects.

  Factory operations are common because they allow a ConcreteResource to construct its own related implementations for other types of associated resources. They ensure that applications work with a consistent set of related Resource implementations. Likewise, you may need to implement BaseResourceDecorators and ConcreteResourceDecorators for multiple, related Resource interfaces.

  Suppose that ResourceA and ResourceB are related interfaces, and ResourceA defines a factory operation called newResourceB. ConcreteResourceADecorator implements this method by delegating the operation to its reference ResourceA implementation. It wraps the resulting ResourceB object in a ConcreteResourceBDecorator and returns it to the caller. Figure 5.5 illustrates this sequence:

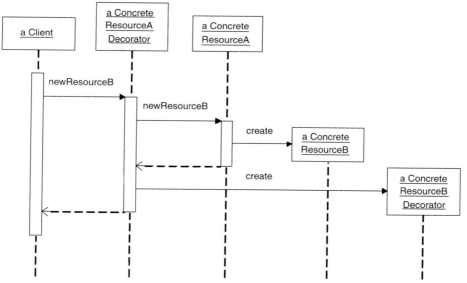

FIGURE 5.5: The operational sequence for ConcreteResourceADecorator's newResourceB implementation.

SAMPLE CODE

The first part of this example illustrates BaseConnectionDecorator and BaseStatementDecorator classes. These classes define base delegation semantics for the JDBC Connection and Statement interfaces, respectively. They implement JDBC's java.sql.Connection and java.sql.Statement interfaces by dispatching all operations to a reference instance that is assigned in their constructors.

```
public class BaseConnectionDecorator
implements Connection {

    private Connection reference;

    public BaseConnectionDecorator(Connection reference) {
        this.reference = reference;
    }

    public void close() throws SQLException {
        reference.close();
    }

    public Statement createStatement() throws SQLException {
```

```
            return reference.createStatement();
    }

    // Repeat for the rest of the operations
    // that the Connection interface defines.
    // ...
}

public class BaseStatementDecorator
implements Statement {

    private Statement reference;

    public BaseStatementDecorator(Statement reference) {
        this.reference = reference;
    }

    public void close() throws SQLException {
        reference.close();
    }

    public ResultSet executeQuery(String sql)
    throws SQLException {
        return reference.executeQuery(sql);
    }

    // Repeat for the rest of the operations
    // that the Statement interface defines.
    // ...
}
```

The next set of classes defines concrete decorator implementations called Leak-DetectionConnectionDecorator and LeakDetectionStatementDecorator. These classes print messages whenever the caller creates and closes connections and statements. In addition, they log the number of connections and statements open at a given time. The messages are intended to be a debugging aid. If either number continually increases, it is a good indication that there is a resource leak in the client code.

Notice how LeakDetectionConnectionDecorator implements createStatement by wrapping the concrete Statement object with a LeakDetectionStatementDecorator. This is an example of a factory operation. A full implementation of this solution would do the same for PreparedStatement, CallableStatement, and ResultSet objects.

```
public class LeakDetectionConnectionDecorator
extends BaseConnectionDecorator {

    private static int openConnections = 0;
    private static int nextId = 0;
    private int id;
    private PrintStream out;

    /**
    Constructs a LeakDetectionConnectionDecorator object.

    @param reference The reference Connection implementation.
    @param out The print stream to which this object writes
              debug messages.
    */
    public LeakDetectionConnectionDecorator(
        Connection reference, PrintStream out) {

        // Initialize the reference and print stream.
        super(reference);
        this.out = out;

        // Assign this connection a unique identifier.
        id = nextId++;

        // Report that a connection has been created and
        // dump the current stack trace.
        out.println("Connection " + id + " was created. "
            + "Open connections = " + (++openConnections)
            + ".");
        (new Throwable()).printStackTrace(out);
    }

    public void close() throws SQLException {

        // Delegate the close operation.
        super.close();

        // Report that a connection has been closed.
        out.println("Connection " + id + " was closed. "
            + "Open connections = " + (--openConnections)
            + ".");
    }

    public Statement createStatement() throws SQLException {

        // Wrap the concrete Statement in a
        // LeakDetectionStatementDecorator object.
        Statement statement = super.createStatement();
```

```
        return new LeakDetectionStatementDecorator(
            statement, out);
    }

    // There is no need to override methods to which we are
    // not attaching additional behavior.  To complete this
    // example, we need to override the other methods that
    // create Statements to decorate all such objects
    // appropriately.
}


public class LeakDetectionStatementDecorator
extends BaseStatementDecorator {

    private static int openStatements = 0;
    private static int nextId = 0;
    private int id;
    private PrintStream out;

    /**
    Constructs a LeakDetectionStatementDecorator object.

    @param reference The reference Statement implementation.
    @param out The print stream to which this object writes
            debug messages.
    */
    public LeakDetectionStatementDecorator(
        Statement reference, PrintStream out) {

        // Initialize the reference and print stream.
        super(reference);
        this.out = out;

        // Assign this statement a unique identifier.
        id = nextId++;

        // Report that a statement has been created and
        // dump the current stack trace.
        out.println("Statement " + id + " was created. "
            + "Open statements = " + (++openStatements)
            + ".");
        (new Throwable()).printStackTrace(out);
    }

    public void close() throws SQLException {

        // Delegate the close operation.
        super.close();
```

```
            // Report that a statement has been closed.
            out.println("Statement " + id + " was closed. "
                + "Open statements = " + (--openStatements)
                + ".");
        }

        public ResultSet executeQuery(String sql)
        throws SQLException {

            // Wrap the concrete ResultSet in a
            // LeakDetectionResultSetDecorator object.
            // (This class is not included in this example,
            // but is similar to this one.)
            ResultSet resultSet = super.executeQuery(sql);
            return new LeakDetectionResultSetDecorator(
                resultSet, out);
        }

        // There is no need to override methods to which we are
        // not attaching additional behavior.  To complete this
        // example, we need to override the other methods that
        // create ResultSets to decorate all such objects
        // appropriately.
    }
```

This sample application code shows the only additional line needed to attach leak detection functionality to a JDBC Connection object. The fact that the application incorporates the additional functionality with a single line of code makes it easy to use it during development and then remove it for production.

```
// Get the appropriate physical connection.
Connection connection = DriverManager.getConnection(...);

// Attach leak detection to the connection.
connection = new LeakDetectionConnectionDecorator(connection,
System.out);

// The rest of the application works the same with
// or without the additional functionality.
// ...
```

You can easily augment this code to attach the additional behavior based on a configuration file or flag. A more extensive approach is to package the LeakDetectionConnectionDecorator and related classes as a discrete JDBC driver complete with its own URL and connection property definitions. This enables you to plug it in to nearly any application that allows you to configure a JDBC driver.

RELATED PATTERNS AND TECHNOLOGY

- The Resource Decorator pattern is an instance of Decorator [Gamma 1995], which describes its foundation in generic terms.

- If you attach multiple decorators to the same resource, you form an instance of a Chain of Responsibility [Gamma 1995].

- Resources are not only defined by commercial database platforms and middleware products. Data Accessor (9) forms a logical resource that your application or system manages. It follows that you can use a Resource Decorator to attach additional behavior to a Data Accessor.

- Resource Pool (117) incorporates a Resource Decorator to redefine what happens when an application closes a pooled resource.

- Resource Timer (137) uses a Resource Decorator to monitor a resource's activity.

Resource Pool

DESCRIPTION

Recycles resources to minimize resource initialization overhead. A resource pool manages resources efficiently while allowing application code to freely allocate them.

CONTEXT

Connection initialization is notorious for being one of the slowest data access operations. Since connecting to a database is a prerequisite for any data access, it offers an opportunity to introduce significant bottlenecks to even the most straightforward applications. Simple standalone applications tend to initialize database connections when they begin and leave the connections open as long as they continue running.

Server and middle-tier programs like Java servlets and enterprise applications can also take this approach. However, applications in these environments usually need to service multiple concurrent users and sharing the same database connections is usually not feasible. One reason is that many threads contend for the same connection. This condition manifests as either non-threadsafe behavior that is difficult to debug or extensive blocking that noticeably reduces response time. You can alleviate this condition by creating a database connection for each active session. This strategy often results in many more active connections than an application actually needs at any given point in time because most of these connections sit idle while end-users peruse data that the application presents to them.

A prevalent and much more effective solution to this problem is a *resource pool*. A resource pool manages a set of active resources that is recycled for repeated use. A single application or server session no longer needs to monopolize a particular database connection to avoid connection initialization overhead. Instead, it checks out a connection from a global pool whenever it needs to access the database. As long as the application or session code is using the connection, no other application or session is able to access it. When it is done with its database work, the application or session code checks the connection back into the pool for others to use.

If a client requests a resource from the pool and none are available, it is the resource pool's responsibility to create a new resource. This enables the application to easily and efficiently gain access to a new resource without any concern for whether the resource is recycled or brand new.

APPLICABILITY

Use the Resource Pool pattern when:

- Your application needs to repeatedly open and close database resources that are slow to initialize.

- Keeping resources open for extended intervals does not negatively impact concurrency. A resource pool leaves resources open so they can be recycled.

STRUCTURE

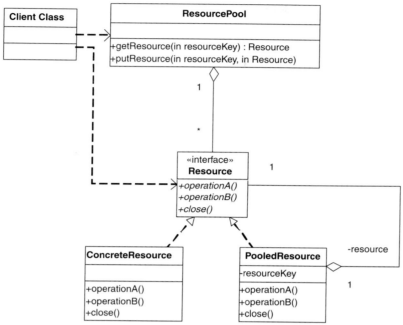

FIGURE 6.1: The static structure of the Resource Pool pattern.

Figure 6.1 illustrates the static structure of the Resource Pool pattern. The Resource interface represents any database resource, such as a connection or statement handle. A ConcreteResource class implements this interface in conjunction with a specific database platform or middleware product. You normally write client code in terms of the Resource interface, but interact directly with a Concrete-Resource at runtime. This enables your code to work readily with any compliant Resource implementation.

The ResourcePool class manages a pool of one or more recycled resources. Clients call the getResource operation whenever they need to use a Resource. ResourcePool wraps each of the ConcreteResources that it manages in a PooledResource. PooledResource specializes the notion of Resource Decorator (103), which attaches customized close behavior to any Resource implementation and delegates all remaining operations. Closing a PooledResource has the effect of returning the ConcreteResource to the ResourcePool for recycling without physically closing it.

If all Resources are identical, then the ResourcePool can hand back any available Resource in conjunction with any request. Most of the time, however, this is not the case. For example, a single ResourcePool instance can manage connections for multiple users or data sources. In cases like this, its getResource operation defines one or more parameters that make up a resource key. Resource key values place additional constraints on the exact Resource that a ResourcePool can return. Similarly, a PooledResource retains a reference to its resource key that it uses when it puts itself back into the ResourcePool.

INTERACTIONS

ResourcePool and PooledResource cooperate to manage and recycle ConcreteResources on behalf of client code. Figure 6.2 shows what happens when a client requests a Resource from an empty ResourcePool. The ResourcePool discovers that it has no existing Resources available so it creates a new ConcreteResource and decorates it with a PooledResource. ResourcePool returns the PooledResource to the client.

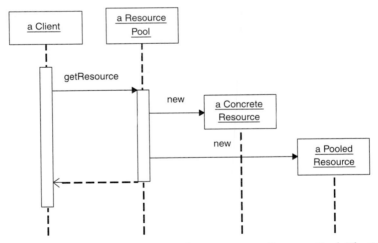

FIGURE 6.2: A client requests a Resource from an empty ResourcePool. The ResourcePool creates a new ConcreteResource and decorates it with a PooledResource.

The PooledResource delegates all operations to its referenced ConcreteResource. The only exception is for the close operation. When the client calls close, the PooledResource intercepts each call and puts the ConcreteResource into the ResourcePool for recycling. Figure 6.3 shows this interaction:

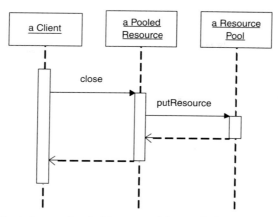

FIGURE 6.3: A client closes a PooledResource. The PooledResource checks itself back into the ResourcePool.

Figure 6.4 portrays a subsequent getResource operation. Now that the Concrete-Resource is checked back into the ResourcePool, the ResourcePool can recycle it. The next time the client calls getResource, the ResourcePool removes this Concret-eResource from the pool and decorates it with a PooledResource.

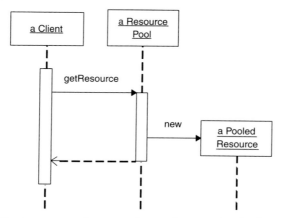

FIGURE 6.4: A client requests a Resource from a ResourcePool. This time, there is a recy-cled Resource available.

A side-effect of leaving ConcreteResources open is that clients can potentially use them even after returning them to the ResourcePool. When this happens, mul-tiple processes share the same ConcreteResources. This condition can in turn lead to inconsistent results and concurrency problems that are difficult to diagnose. ResourcePool creates a new PooledResource decorator for every request as a precaution to prevent this possibility. PooledResource maintains its own closed state. Once it has returned its ConcreteResource to the pool, it rejects any subsequent operations.

CONSEQUENCES

The Resource Pool pattern has the following benefits:

Benefits

- *Reduced resource initialization overhead*—Initializing new database resources is one of the slowest of all database operations. A resource pool recycles resources with the goal of minimizing the overall quantity that an application initializes. Resource pools significantly improve response time for server applications since each individual session or request no longer requires a brand new resource.

- *Minimal client code change*—If you define a resource pool to model the same semantics that the physical resource manager or programming interface dictates, then client code will require only simple changes to take advantage of the pool.

- *Resource semantics that match application logic*—Repeatedly requesting a resource from a pool does not cause noticeable performance problems. With a resource pool, clients are free to request and discard resources as dictated by application logic, and can avoid extensive passing or sharing of resources. Less sharing leads to cleaner application code and fewer concurrent access problems.

- *Centralized resource management*—A resource pool centralizes the management of all resources that a single application or suite of applications uses. This makes it inherently easier to optimize, incorporates new administrative and monitoring features, and controls resource utilization.

STRATEGIES

This section describes some issues to consider when you implement the Resource Pool pattern.

Resource Keys

A resource key identifies resource characteristics. Clients specify resource keys to indicate certain criteria when they request resources from a pool. A resource pool uses keys to discern whether any of its pooled resources match requests.

In a typical implementation, every pooled resource is identified by a resource key. The type and structure of the resource key does not matter as long as it follows these semantics:

- Two resources that can be used in the same context must have equivalent resource keys. The more your resource key semantics follow this rule, the greater degree of resource recycling you will achieve.

- Two resources that cannot be used in the same context must have distinct resource keys. Without this rule, applications may use resources initialized for other users or data sources. This condition can cause security problems or other undefined results.

Normally, a resource key encapsulates all the initialization parameters passed to the physical resource manager or programming interface. In the case of a database connection, these usually include the data source location, user, password, and connection properties.

Resource Pool Properties

You can define configuration properties that affect how a resource pool initializes new resources and to enforce thresholds. Here are some examples of resource pool properties:

- *Initial size*—The initial number of resources in the pool. Priming the resource pool reduces the delay caused when an application responds to its first end-user requests. For example, a servlet can prime its connection pool during its initialization so that there is no delay when the first client request arrives.

- *Growth increment*—The number of resources to initialize when the pool is depleted. You can choose to allocate multiple additional resources when the pool runs out rather than allocating one resource at a time. Increasing this number results in longer delays when the pool is empty, but these delays happen less frequently. Different applications prefer different behavior.

- *Maximum resources*—The maximum number of resources a pool can manage. Placing a threshold on the number of resources in a pool minimizes the effect of resource leaks or too many concurrent users. Resource leaks occur when clients neglect to return resources to the pool when they finish using them. Controlling this threshold at the resource pool level results in better diagnostics when this condition occurs. These conditions may cause memory leaks or system crashes if the pool does not enforce this threshold.

  If no resources are available and this threshold has been reached, the resource pool can let clients wait until resources are available or reject requests for new resources outright until old resources are returned to the pool.

A resource pool implementation can encapsulate each of these properties completely. You can also provide an associated administrative facility such as a configuration file or graphical console to allow administrators to tailor these settings based on what works best in their particular environments.

Closing Resources

Be aware of resources whose close operations affect other dependent resources. For example, the JDBC specification states that closing a connection implicitly closes any related statement handle as well. Likewise, closing a statement handle implicitly closes its open result set, if any.

When you override resource close operations that carry stipulations like these, you can consider whether to break the contract that the specification dictates. If you choose to implement the specification precisely, ensure that your close operations release dependent resources as clients expect. If you choose to ignore this aspect of the specification, then pooled resources might leave dependent resources open and simply return themselves to the pool when they are closed. Applications that depend on the specification behavior may potentially leak dependent resources if they do not get closed implicitly. This sounds like a significant side-effect, but it does simplify a pooled resource's implementation. You can also argue that clients should explicitly close all resources despite what the specification allows.

Resource Pool Cleaning

You can incorporate an automated cleaning mechanism that reduces the number of resources a pool manages when its utilization decreases. For example, a resource pool is likely to create a significant number of new resources to account for the additional load that the high number of users during the workday causes. However, during the night, the load drastically decreases and most of the pool's resources sit idle but still consume client and server storage.

One strategy to alleviate this condition is to incorporate an automated cleaning routine that runs periodically, perhaps in a low-priority background thread, and closes a fraction of a pool's inactive resources. Resource Timer (137) describes a mechanism for monitoring and reacting to resource inactivity that you can employ to solve this problem.

Another cleaning issue is dealing with client code that neglects to return resources to the pool. This usually happens due to a defect in the client's own code that causes essential cleaning operations to be skipped. You can use the Resource Timer pattern to alleviate this problem as well, this time to automatically close resources after a period of inactivity.

SAMPLE CODE

Two common Resource Pool instances are connection pools and statement caches. A connection pool recycles database connections with the primary goal of avoiding repeated connection initialization overhead. A statement cache works similarly, but on a more granular scale. It recycles prepared statements within a single connection, helping to minimize the overhead that comes with repeatedly compiling the same SQL statements. This section shows sample code for both of these instances.

Connection Pool

The ConnectionPool class implements a generic connection pool for standard JDBC connections. It stores connections in its contents object, which maps connection keys to lists of available connections. Each connection key is a combination of a database URL, user, and password.

```
public class ConnectionPool {

    // The contents of the connection pool.
    // This maps connection keys to lists of
    // available connections.
    private Map contents = new HashMap();

    /**
    Gets a connection from the connection pool.
    This creates a new connection if none are
```

```
    available in the pool.
    */
    public Connection getConnection(String url,
                                    String user,
                                    String password)
        throws SQLException {

        // Form the connection key.  For simplicity, this
        // example stores it as a string that incorporates
        // each of the connection parameters.
        StringBuffer buffer = new StringBuffer();
        buffer.append(url);
        buffer.append(":");
        buffer.append(user);
        buffer.append(":");
        buffer.append(password);
        Object connectionKey = buffer.toString();

        // Check to see if there is a matching
        // connection list in the pool.  If there is
        // not, create a new one.
        List connectionList;
        synchronized(contents) {
            connectionList
                = (List)contents.get(connectionKey);
            if (connectionList == null) {
                connectionList = new LinkedList();
                contents.put(connectionKey, connectionList);
            }
        }

        // Check to see if there is a connection in
        // the connection list.  If there is at least
        // one connection, remove it from the list.
        // Otherwise, create a new one.
        Connection connection;
        synchronized(connectionList) {
            if (connectionList.size() > 0) {
                connection
                    = (Connection)connectionList.remove(0);
            }
            else {
                connection
                    = DriverManager.getConnection(url,
                    user, password);
            }
        }

        // Decorate the connection with a PooledConnection.
```

```
        // This will cause it to be returned to the pool
        // when the client closes it.
        connection = new PooledConnection(this,
            connectionKey, connection);

        return connection;
    }

    // PooledConnection.close calls this.
    void putConnection(Object connectionKey,
                    Connection connection) {

        // Resolve the connection list for the specified
        // connection key.
        List connectionList;
        synchronized(contents) {
            connectionList
                = (List)contents.get(connectionKey);
        }

        // Add the connection to the list.
        synchronized(connectionList) {
            connectionList.add(connection);
        }
    }
}
```

The PooledConnection class decorates any JDBC connection with modified behavior for its close operation. Rather than delegating close operations to the physical connection, PooledConnection returns the connection to the ConnectionPool instead. PooledConnection also ensures that clients are not able to invoke any of a connection's operations after returning them to the ConnectionPool.

This class extends BaseConnectionDecorator, which is a general-purpose decorator for java.sql.Connection objects. See the "Sample Code" section for Resource Decorator (103) for details regarding BaseConnectionDecorator.

```
class PooledConnection
extends BaseConnectionDecorator
implements Connection {

    private ConnectionPool connectionPool;
    private Object connectionKey;
    private Connection reference;
    private boolean closed = false;

    public PooledConnection(ConnectionPool connectionPool,
```

```
                              Object connectionKey,
                              Connection reference)   {
        super(reference);
        this.connectionPool = connectionPool;
        this.connectionKey = connectionKey;
        this.reference = reference;
    }


    /**
    Do not really close the reference connection.   Instead,
    just return it to the pool.
    **/
    public void close() throws SQLException {
        if (!closed) {
            closed = true;
            connectionPool.putConnection(
                connectionKey, reference);
        }
    }

    public Statement createStatement() throws SQLException {
        if (closed)
            throw new SQLException("Connection is closed.");
        return super.createStatement();
    }

    // Repeat for the rest of the operations
    // that the Connection interface defines.
    // ...

}
```

Without the connection pool, client code initializes new connections using the standard java.sql.DriverManager:

```
Connection connection
    = DriverManager.getConnection(url, user, password);
```

ConnectionPool intentionally mirrors DriverManager's semantics so that the only change to the client code is the target object of the getConnection method invocation:

```
Connection connection
    = connectionPool.getConnection(url, user, password);
```

Statement Cache

Most relational databases expose the notion of statement handles. Applications use statement handles as contexts for executing database operations. You can also use statement handles to run multiple operations in succession. However, if you execute the same operation repeatedly, you can benefit from preparing or compiling a statement and storing it using an intermediate representation. From the database's perspective, preparing a statement entails parsing the request and creating an *access plan* for the operation. The access plan is a structure that describes the most efficient strategy for executing a particular database operation. Clients do not interact directly with access plans, but understanding how they work helps when you fine-tune your data model and data access operations for optimal performance. Preparing a statement can be expensive depending on the operation's complexity. You should strive to minimize the number of times your application prepares statements as a means to improve performance.

When you use a prepared statement to execute the same operation multiple times, the database reuses its intermediate representation to execute the operation more quickly. Applications that issue database operations using SQL have the choice of preparing statements that include literal values or parameter markers. SQL statements with literals look like this:

```
SELECT * FROM ACCOUNTS WHERE ACCOUNT_ID = 1234

UPDATE ORDERS SET SHIP_STATUS = 'Shipped' WHERE ORDER_ID = 8888
```

Prepared statement handles for operations like these have very little chance of being recycled because they include specific literal values. For example, an application can only use the UPDATE statement when marking order 8888's status as shipped, something that probably happens only once.

By contrast, SQL statements with parameter markers designate placeholders rather than exact literal values. You can plug in different parameter values each time you execute them:

```
SELECT * FROM ACCOUNTS WHERE ACCOUNT_ID = ?

UPDATE ORDERS SET SHIP_STATUS = ? WHERE ORDER_ID = ?
```

Applications can reuse these statements to query information for any account or change the ship status for any order. Statements with parameter markers are inherently recyclable, so statement caching is much more effective when an application uses them extensively.

Caching statement handles allows your application to reuse prepared statements and saves the expense of repeatedly re-preparing them. A statement cache manages a set of prepared statements that are recycled for repeated use.

In this example, StatementCachingConnection is an instance of Resource Decorator (103), which attaches a statement cache to any concrete java.sql.Connection implementation. It extends BaseConnectionDecorator, which is a general-purpose decorator for java.sql.Connection objects. See the "Sample Code" section for the Resource Decorator pattern for the details regarding BaseConnectionDecorator.

StatementCachingConnection keeps the statement cache contents in a map that associates statement keys with lists of matching prepared statement handles. A statement key is a combination of SQL statement text and the requested result set scrollability and concurrency attributes.

```java
public class StatementCachingConnection
extends BaseConnectionDecorator
implements Connection {

    // The contents of the statement cache.
    // This maps statement keys to lists of
    // available statements.
    private Map statementCache = new HashMap();

    public StatementCachingConnection(Connection delegate) {
        super(delegate);
    }

    /**
    Get an appropriate statement from the cache, if
    available.
    **/
    public PreparedStatement prepareStatement(String sql,
        int resultSetType,
        int resultSetConcurrency)
        throws SQLException {

        // Form the statement key.  For simplicity, this
        // example stores it as a string that incorporates
        // each of the prepareStatement parameters.
        StringBuffer buffer = new StringBuffer();
        buffer.append(sql);
        buffer.append(":");
        buffer.append(resultSetType);
```

```
        buffer.append(":");
        buffer.append(resultSetConcurrency);
        Object statementKey = buffer.toString();

        // Check to see if there is a matching
        // statement list in the cache.  If there is
        // not, create a new one.
        List statementList;
        synchronized(statementCache) {
            statementList
                = (List)statementCache.get(statementKey);
            if (statementList == null) {
                statementList = new LinkedList();
                statementCache.put(statementKey,
                                    statementList);
            }
        }

        // Check to see if there is a statement in
        // the statement list.  If there is at least
        // one, remove it from the list.
        // Otherwise, prepare a new one.
        PreparedStatement statement;
        synchronized(statementList) {
            if (statementList.size() > 0) {
                statement = (PreparedStatement)
                    statementList.remove(0);
            }
            else {
                // Delegate the prepareStatement call.
                statement = super.prepareStatement(sql,
                    resultSetType, resultSetConcurrency);
            }
        }

        // Decorate the statement to be a CachedStatement.
        // This will cause it to be returned to the cache
        // when the client closes it.
        statement = new CachedStatement(this,
            statementKey, statement);

        return statement;
    }

    // ... similar for other overloaded prepareStatement
    //     and prepareCall methods.


    // CachedStatment.close calls this.
```

```
       void putStatement(Object statementKey,
                    PreparedStatement statement) {

           // Resolve the statement list for the specified
           // statement key.
           List statementList;
           synchronized(statementCache) {
               statementList
                   = (List)statementCache.get(statementKey);
           }

           // Add the statement to the list.
           synchronized(statementList) {
               statementList.add(statement);
           }
       }
   }
```

StatementCachingConnection overrides the prepareStatement operations to reference its internal statement cache. Each prepareStatement operation forms a statement key and uses this key to find any matching statement handles that are already prepared.

If it does not find any matching statement handles, StatementCachingConnection prepares a new one. This detail makes it easy for clients to efficiently prepare new statement handles without requiring additional behavior to interact with the cache. Clients simply call prepareStatement without any regard for whether the returned statement handle is brand new or recycled.

Whenever StatementCachingConnection prepares a new statement, it wraps it in a CachedStatement object. CachedStatement decorates any java.sql.Prepared-Statement object with modified behavior for its close operation. Rather than delegating close operations to the physical statement handle, CachedStatement returns the statement handle to the cache. CachedStatement also ensures that a client is not able to invoke any of its operations after it returns its statement handle to the cache.

This class extends BasePreparedStatementDecorator, which is a general-purpose decorator for java.sql.PreparedStatement objects. BasePreparedStatement-Decorator is analogous to the BaseStatementDecorator class that the "Sample Code" section for the Resource Decorator pattern (103) defined.

```
   class CachedStatement
   extends BasePreparedStatementDecorator
   implements PreparedStatement {

       private StatementCachingConnection connection;
```

```
private Object statementKey;
private Statement reference;
private boolean closed = false;

public CachedStatement(
    StatementCachingConnection connection,
    Object statementKey,
    PreparedStatement reference) {

    super(reference);
    this.connection = connection;
    this.statementKey = statementKey;
    this.reference = reference;
}

/**
Do not really close the reference statement.  Instead,
just return it to the cache.
**/
public void close() throws SQLException {
    if (!closed) {
        closed = true;
        connection.putStatement(
            statementKey, reference);
    }
}


public ResultSet executeQuery()
throws SQLException {
    if (closed)
        throw new SQLException("Statement is closed.");
    return super.executeQuery();
}

// Repeat for the rest of the operations
// that the statement interface defines.
// ...
```

```
}
```

To enable statement caching with a new java.sql.Connection object, client code decorates it with a StatementCachingConnection:

```
Connection connection
    = DriverManager.getConnection(url, user, password);
```

```
connection
    = new StatementCachingConnection(connection);
```

Most database environments confine statement handles to a single connection, so it makes sense to manage a statement cache within each connection. When you build a connection pool and statement cache that cooperate, the statement cache is only effective when applications happen to utilize the same connection each time they prepare a particular operation. Over time, you end up with several connections with the same set of prepared statements. Figure 6.5 illustrates this condition:

FIGURE 6.5: Over time, the same statements get prepared for multiple connections, even when statement caching is involved.

You can improve this situation by integrating the connection pool and statement cache facilities. If clients can describe the database operations they plan to prepare when they request connections from the pool, then the connection pool can look for existing connections that already have those statements prepared. Figure 6.6 portrays a connection pool with more efficient integrated statement caching:

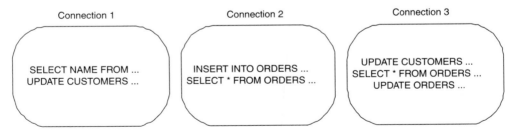

FIGURE 6.6: Integrating statement caching with a connection pool can result in fewer prepared statements.

Another optimization technique that can improve a statement cache's effectiveness is *statement morphing*. Statement morphing is the process of replacing literal values in database operations with parameter markers. This improves their chances for reusability. You can incorporate transparent statement morphing directly into the StatementCachingConnection implementation.

It may not make sense to cache every statement that an application prepares. Some types of statements may never be prepared by any application again, so caching them would actually hinder resource utilization. One way to address this issue is to define categories of statement handles to cache. Some candidates for caching might be queries, updates, statements with parameter markers, and statements that open updatable cursors. The statement cache implementation can usually determine a statement's category with some fundamental analysis of the statement parameters. You can experiment with statement categories by watching which statement types get recycled in a real environment.

RELATED PATTERNS AND TECHNOLOGY

- Pool Allocation [Noble 2001] describes similar concepts in terms of memory allocation.

- Connection pools and statement caches are pervasive data access optimizations. Many database drivers and most application servers provide some form of connection pool support. The JDBC 2.0 standard provides many support classes similar to those that this pattern describes.

- You can pool logical resources, such as those that specialize Data Accessor (9). This can improve resource utilization and also helps to manage multiple resources within a central component.

- PooledResource specializes Resource Decorator (103), since it decorates any resource with customized close behavior.

- Resource Timer (137) describes a strategy for cleaning up inactive resources. In one capacity, you can use it to counter defective clients that neglect to return inactive resources to the pool. In another, you can automatically trim the size of the pool when a large number of its resources go unused.

- A common problem in connection pools is that some databases implicitly close connections after given inactivity conditions are met. When a connection pool attempts to recycle a closed connection, unpredictable results often occur.

Retryer (171) describes a strategy that can be used to transparently detect and discard stale connections and then replace them with fresh connections.

- Cache Statistics (361) describes a consistent mechanism for publishing resource pool statistics such as pool size and number of hits and misses. A hit happens when the resource pool recycles an existing pooled resource. A miss indicates that the pool cannot find a resource to match a request and needs to create a brand new resource.

Resource Timer

DESCRIPTION

Automatically releases inactive resources. A resource timer alleviates the effect of applications or users that allocate resources indefinitely.

CONTEXT

A *resource leak* occurs when an application does not close all the resources it opens. As an offending application gradually consumes more resources, the supply available for other applications similarly depletes. This is called a leak because system storage slowly diminishes and performance gradually degrades much like a tire losing air.

Resource leaks are a common software defect and are often difficult to debug. Developer tests do not necessarily identify leaks, since automated unit test suites do not usually run long enough for leaks to noticeably affect the system. In addition, isolated test environments often involve only a small number of users or sessions. This is not enough for subtle leaks to impact performance or utilization.

Integration testers or end-users tend to be the first to notice a resource leak's symptoms. They may notice performance or scalability problems or errors indicating that no more resources are available. Unfortunately, these symptoms do not offer any suggestions about the source of the leak. To make matters worse, it is often extremely difficult for programmers to recreate resource leaks in their debugging environment, so they are usually left to pore over the application's resource management code, looking for clues.

The best solution to this problem is to avoid leaks in the first place by employing disciplined resource management strategies. Any module that allocates a resource is ultimately responsible for cleaning it up. Isolating the code that uses a resource within a single component makes it easier to handle all possible conditions.

Unfortunately, despite your best intentions, resource leaks will still occur. Suppose you are responsible for designing a data access library that other developers will use to build applications. Resource utilization depends heavily on the quality of the application code.

At an even higher level, end-users can cause similar symptoms. For example, a graphical application that incorporates the contents of a large set of query results into its user interface needs to keep the corresponding physical result set open so that it can fetch additional data as the user scrolls down. Depending on the exact database implementation, leaving a result set open may prevent other users from updating one or more of its rows. It is common for users to vacate their desks without closing all open application forms, essentially rendering some data inaccessible to others.

Garbage collection offers a promise for a solution. Programming platforms like Java and C# automatically free memory that your code allocated but no longer references. This works quite well for fine-grained objects like buffers and internal data structures. However, it is not usually effective for database resources because most resource managers and database drivers retain references to each resource they create. These references prevent garbage collectors from identifying them as objects that are no longer needed.

The Resource Timer pattern offers a more refined solution. A timer keeps track of a resource's inactivity. A resource is *inactive* when an application has not invoked any of its operations. A resource timer expires when it reaches its *inactivity threshold*.

This is the interval that the timer waits before automatically cleaning up an inactive resource. A resource timer does this work independently of application code so that leaks caused by application defects or user behavior get resolved over time.

You can build resource timers to work with a variety of resource types. However, it is up to each type of resource to precisely define what activity it entails and what cleaning operations occur automatically when the resource is inactive.

Some examples of where you can readily apply the Resource Timer pattern include:

- An open result set often locks rows or tables, preventing other applications from reading or updating them. You can use a resource timer to automatically close a result set if its application does not fetch any of its data or explicitly close it within a designated period of time.

- An active transaction nearly always locks database objects that are involved in it, and this prevents other applications from accessing them. You can use a resource timer to automatically roll back a transaction if its application neglects to execute subsequent operations within its context or explicitly commit it or roll it back within a designated period of time.

- A pooled resource that is not returned to its pool prevents it from being recycled for use by other components. This ultimately causes the resource pool to initialize more resources than it otherwise requires. You can use a resource timer to automatically return inactive resources to the pool after a designated period of time.

APPLICABILITY

Use the Resource Timer pattern when:

- Application defects can cause resources to be left open for an indefinite period of time. This happens when errors result in an application's cleaning routines being skipped.

- End-user behavior can cause resources to be left open for an indefinite period of time. This happens when applications leave resources open while awaiting user input or confirmation.

- Open resources restrict concurrent access to shared system entities. This is symptomatic of resources that lock database objects or files.

- Open resources consume a significant amount of storage overhead.

STRUCTURE

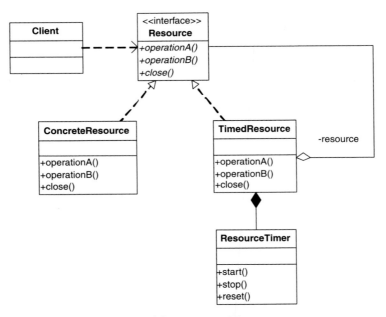

FIGURE 7.1: The static structure of the Resource Timer pattern.

Figure 7.1 illustrates the static structure of the Resource Timer pattern. The Resource interface represents any database resource, such as a connection, result set, or transaction. A ConcreteResource class implements this interface in conjunction with a database platform or middleware product. You normally write client code in terms of the Resource interface, but interact directly with a ConcreteResource at runtime. This enables your code to work readily with any compliant Resource implementation.

TimedResource is another Resource implementation that is a specialized Resource Decorator (103). TimedResource attaches a ResourceTimer to any Resource implementation. It is the TimedResource's responsibility to designate what activity it entails. It does this by resetting its ResourceTimer for each operation that corresponds to resource activity. In many cases, it does this for every operation.

The additional TimedResource functionality is mostly transparent to clients. Once a client decorates a ConcreteResource object with a TimedResource object, it interacts with it as if it was any other Resource implementation.

INTERACTIONS

TimedResource uses its ResourceTimer to monitor resource inactivity. It starts the timer when the client first opens it. Figure 7.2 portrays TimedResource initialization:

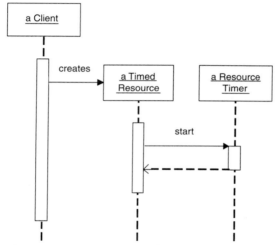

FIGURE 7.2: TimedResource starts ResourceTimer when the client first opens it.

TimedResource delegates all operations to its reference ConcreteResource object. For operations that indicate resource activity, it also resets the Resource-Timer. Figure 7.3 illustrates this interaction. You can choose to reset the Resource-Timer before or after delegating operations. It is best to reset the timer before delegating to prevent it from expiring during long-running operations.

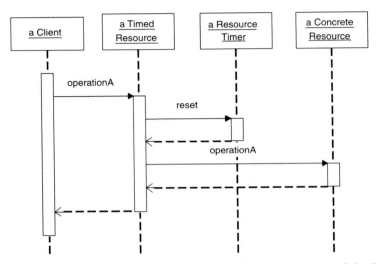

FIGURE 7.3: The client invokes an operation that indicates resource activity. Timed-Resource resets the ResourceTimer and delegates the operation to its referenced Concrete-Resource object.

When the client explicitly closes a TimedResource, the TimedResource stops its ResourceTimer and delegates the close operation to its referenced ConcreteResource object. Figure 7.4 shows this sequence:

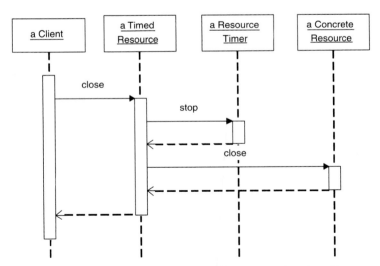

FIGURE 7.4: The client explicitly closes a TimedResource. The TimedResource stops its ResourceTimer and delegates the close operation to its referenced ConcreteResource object.

Figure 7.5 shows what happens when the ResourceTimer expires. It notifies the TimedResource, usually by sending an event. The TimedResource reacts by implicitly closing its referenced ConcreteResource object.

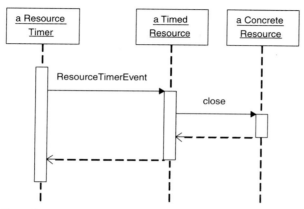

FIGURE 7.5: When the ResourceTimer expires, it sends an event to the TimedResource. The TimedResource implicitly closes its referenced ConcreteResource object.

CONSEQUENCES

The Resource Timer pattern has the following consequences:

Benefits

- *Automatically cleans up inactive resources*—Resource Timer defines a strategy for mitigating the negative effects on system utilization and performance incurred by defective applications and neglectful users that leave resources open indefinitely.

- *Requires minimal changes to application code*—Assuming that application code is written in terms of generic resource interfaces, replacing concrete implementations with timers only requires changes to resource initialization routines.

Drawbacks

- *Unintentional timeouts*—There are cases when an application or user really intends to keep a resource open and inactive beyond its configured inactivity threshold. These cases are difficult to identify and accommodate. If you anticipate this requirement, it is best to ensure that your application's configuration allows this functionality to be disabled in special cases.

- *Increased thread complexity and overhead*—Many timer implementations involve some semblance of a timing thread. It is common to create a thread for every timed resource in the system. Threads add complexity and overhead of their own and can contribute to system scalability issues if you do not manage them diligently.

STRATEGIES

Consider these strategies when implementing the Resource Timer pattern:

- *Make inactivity thresholds configurable*—Your customers will use the software you build in ways that you may not anticipate. Their regular use cases may require certain resources to be left open and inactive beyond the default threshold that you choose. For this reason, it is a good idea to make inactivity thresholds configurable. Command-line arguments, configuration files, and graphical administration consoles are common mechanisms for exposing configurable options to users and administrators.

   You may also consider defining multiple thresholds for different resource types, since use cases are bound to affect them differently. For example, you might find that it is common and desirable for user and application behavior to leave read-only result sets open indefinitely, while implementing a reasonable inactivity threshold for updatable result sets and transactions.

- *Log timer expirations*—Timer expirations indicate that user behavior or application logic has caused inactive resources to remain open. You cannot do much to change user behavior, but you can usually fix application logic. However, users and administrators are much less likely to notice and report resource leaks when resource timers are in place. For this reason, it is beneficial to log timer expirations in an error or debug log so that developers can identify potential resource management problems before their effects become noticeable to users.

- *Ensure that expiration errors are informative*—If a user leaves a resource inactive for too long, the resource timer will clean it up effectively. When the user returns to the application, it should present him or her with an appropriate error message. Keep in mind that most users do not understand what resources and timers are, but learning that their search results expired should give them enough information to issue the same search again.

- *Account for closing a resource multiple times*—One benefit of using Resource Decorator (103) within this pattern is that it completely hides the timing behavior from client code. Since the timing logic is transparent, well-behaved client code is likely to explicitly close its resources, even after timers have already closed one or more of the resources implicitly.

  If you impose the burden of checking to see if resources are already closed to client code, then you compromise the Resource Timer solution's transparency. It is cleaner to build this logic into your TimedResource objects. If a client closes a resource that a timer already closed implicitly, TimedResource simply ignores the operation. You can accomplish this easily by defining a private boolean flag within TimedResource.

- *Use thread logistics*—Many timer solutions use daemon threads. A *daemon thread* is an independent task that runs concurrently with other program logic and handles periodic housekeeping or services requests in the background. A Resource-Timer can create a daemon thread that sleeps most of the time, but wakes up under two conditions. First, when a TimedResource resets its ResourceTimer in reaction to resource activity, it wakes the daemon thread to reset its state. The second condition happens when the daemon thread reaches the inactivity threshold. It wakes itself and notifies its TimedResource accordingly.

- *Employ event mechanism*—A ResourceTimer notifies the corresponding Timed-Resource when it expires. In implementation terms, this means that the ResourceTimer needs to invoke one of TimedResource's operations. However, hardwiring it to call the close operation on a specific Resource interface couples your ResourceTimer implementation directly with that resource type. As a result, you need to build different ResourceTimer implementations for connections, result sets, and transactions, despite the fact that the implementation is otherwise identical for each.

  Generic event notification mechanisms allow you to let TimedResources register themselves as ResourceTimer observers. When a ResourceTimer expires, it notifies its observers without coupling to a specific resource type. Many programming languages and environments define a standard paradigm for event notification or callbacks.

SAMPLE CODE

This example defines TimedConnection, which implements the Resource Timer pattern in conjunction with any JDBC connection. Figure 7.6 shows the entities that collaborate in this implementation. Numerous classes and interfaces are involved, but most are small and have isolated responsibilities.

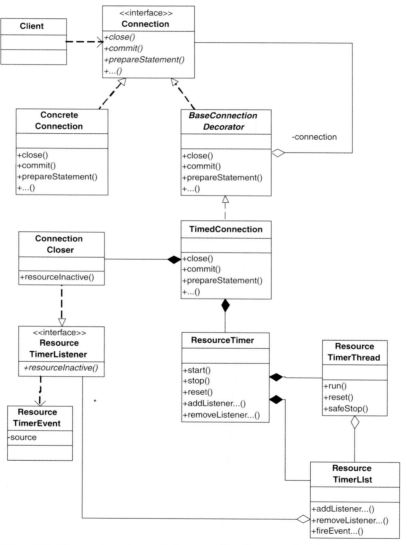

FIGURE 7.6: The entities that collaborate to implement TimedConnection.

ResourceTimerListener and ResourceTimerEvent define the event mechanism that enables ResourceTimer to notify TimedConnection when it expires. These entities work with any type of resource. ResourceTimerListener defines a listener interface that relates directly to the ResourceTimerEvent class. Any object that needs to be notified when a ResourceTimer expires implements this interface. ResouceTimerEvent defines·the representation of the actual timer expiration event. These entities follow the common convention for strongly typed events in Java.

```
public interface ResourceTimerListener
extends EventListener {

    /**
    This method is called when a resource
    remains inactive beyond the configured
    inactivity threshold.
    */
    void resourceInactive(ResourceTimerEvent event);
}

public class ResourceTimerEvent
extends EventObject {

    ResourceTimerEvent(ResourceTimer eventSource) {
        super(eventSource);
    }

}
```

ResourceTimer maintains a list of registered ResourceTimerListeners so that it can notify each of them when it expires. In this example, TimedConnection only registers one ResourceTimerListener for each ResourceTimer, but the common convention for events in Java provides for multiple registered listeners. This also makes the ResourceTimer class a bit more versatile and may enable it to better adapt to future changes. ResourceTimerListenerList manages the list of listeners on behalf of a ResourceTimer.

```
class ResourceTimerListenerList
{
    private List contents = new LinkedList();
    private ResourceTimer eventSource;

    /**
    Constructs a ResourceTimerListenerList object.
    */
    ResourceTimerListenerList(ResourceTimer eventSource) {
        this.eventSource = eventSource;
    }

    /**
    Registers a ResourceTimerListener to be notified
    when a resource remains inactive beyond the
    configured inactivity threshold.
    */
    void addResourceTimerListener(
        ResourceTimerListener listener) {

        synchronized(contents) {
            contents.add(listener);
        }
    }

    /**
    Deregisters a ResourceTimerListener so that it is no
    longer notified when a resource remains inactive
    beyond the configured inactivity threshold.
    */
    void removeResourceTimerListener(
        ResourceTimerListener listener) {

        synchronized(contents) {
            contents.remove(listener);
        }
    }

    /**
    Notifies all registered ResourceTimerListeners
    when a resource remains inactive beyond the
    configured inactivity threshold.
    */
    void fireResourceInactiveEvent() {

        // Make a copy of the listener list so that
        // we do not send notifications within a
        // synchronized block.  If we do not do this,
        // any listeners that attempt to deregister
```

```
        // themselves cause deadlock.
        List contentsClone;
        synchronized(contents) {
            contentsClone = new LinkedList(contents);
        }

        // Send the event to each registered listener.
        ResourceTimerEvent event
            = new ResourceTimerEvent(eventSource);
        for(Iterator i = contentsClone.iterator();
            i.hasNext(); ) {
            ResourceTimerListener listener
                = (ResourceTimerListener)i.next();
            listener.resourceInactive(event);
        }
    }
}
```

ResourceTimerThread is another utility class that defines a daemon thread task to monitor resource inactivity. Most of the time, this task sleeps. It wakes up under two conditions. The first is when ResourceTimer calls its reset or safeStop operations. If it is reset, then it begins sleeping again. The other condition happens when it wakes up because the inactivity threshold passes. In this case, it notifies all registered listeners that it is expired.

```
class ResourceTimerThread
extends Thread
{
    private long inactivityThreshold;
    private ResourceTimerListenerList listenerList;

    private boolean reset = false;
    private boolean stop = false;
    private Object signal = new Object();

    /**
    Constructs a ResourceTimerThread object.
    */
    ResourceTimerThread(long inactivityThreshold,
        ResourceTimerListenerList listenerList) {

        this.inactivityThreshold = inactivityThreshold;
        this.listenerList = listenerList;

        // Make this a daemon thread.  This indicates that
        // the JVM may safely end even when
        // this thread is still running.
```

```
        setDaemon(true);
}

/**
The main thread task.
*/
public void run() {

    // Continue to loop as long as the thread
    // has not been stopped.
    while(!stop) {
        try {
            synchronized(signal) {

                // Wait for the allowed period of
                // inactivity.
                signal.wait(inactivityThreshold);

                // If the timer was reset, just loop
                // again.
                if (reset) {
                    reset = false;
                }

                // If the timer was not reset or stopped,
                // then the resource has
                // been inactive longer then the specified
                // threshold.  Send an event to indicate
                // this condition and stop this thread.
                else if (!stop) {
                    listenerList
                      .fireResourceInactiveEvent();
                    stop = true;
                }
            }
        }
        catch(InterruptedException ignore) {
            // If the wait is interrupted, simply loop
            // again.
        }
    }
}

/**
Resets the timer thread to start measuring inactivity
again.
*/
void reset() {
    synchronized(signal) {
```

```
                reset = true;
                signal.notify();
            }
        }

        /**
        Stops the timer thread.
        */
        void safeStop() {
            synchronized(signal) {
                stop = true;
                signal.notify();
            }
        }
    }
}
```

ResourceTimer collaborates with ResourceTimerListenerList and ResourceTimerThread to implement the ResourceTimer functionality that this pattern describes:

```
public class ResourceTimer {

    private ResourceTimerListenerList listenerList;
    private ResourceTimerThread thread = null;
    private boolean started = false;

    /**
    Constructs a ResourceTimer object.
    */
    ResourceTimer(long inactivityThreshold) {
        listenerList = new ResourceTimerListenerList(this);
        thread = new ResourceTimerThread(inactivityThreshold,
            listenerList);
    }

    /**
    Registers a ResourceTimerListener to be notified
    when a resource remains inactive beyond the
    configured inactivity threshold.
    */
    void addResourceTimerListener(
        ResourceTimerListener listener) {
        listenerList.addResourceTimerListener(listener);
    }

    /**
    Deregisters a ResourceTimerListener to be notified
    when a resource remains inactive beyond the
```

```
configured inactivity threshold.
*/
void removeResourceTimerListener(
    ResourceTimerListener listener) {
    listenerList.removeResourceTimerListener(listener);
}

/**
Starts the resource timer.
*/
synchronized void start() {
    if (!started) {
        started = true;
        thread.start();
    }
}

/**
Stops the resource timer.
*/
synchronized void stop() {
    if (started) {
        started = false;
        thread.safeStop();
    }
}

/**
Resets the resource timer.
*/
synchronized void reset() {
    thread.reset();
}
}
```

The TimedConnection class attaches a ResourceTimer to any JDBC connection. TimedConnection starts its ResourceTimer when the client initializes it and resets the ResourceTimer on each of its operations. Figure 7.7 shows the interactions that happen when a client invokes any of TimedConnection's operations:

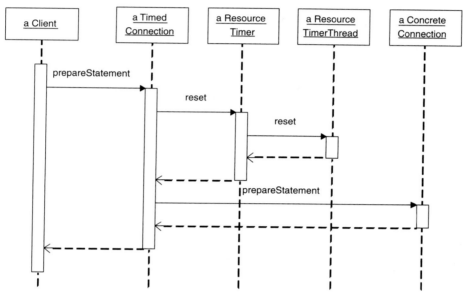

FIGURE 7.7: A client invokes any of TimedConnection's operations. TimedConnection resets its ResourceTimer in turn.

TimedConnection defines its own custom ResourceTimerListener implementation, ConnectionCloser, in an inner class. ConnectionCloser closes the referenced Connection object when ResourceTimer indicates that the inactivity threshold has passed. Figure 7.8 illustrates what happens when the ResourceTimerThread expires. ResourceTimerThread uses the ResourceTimerListenerList to notify ConnectionCloser that the inactivity threshold has passed.

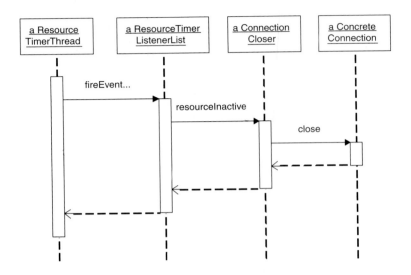

FIGURE 7.8: ResourceTimerThread uses ResourceTimerListenerList to notify Connection-Closer that the inactivity threshold has passed.

TimedConnection extends BaseConnectionDecorator, which is a general-purpose decorator for java.sql.Connection objects. See the "Sample Code" section for the Resource Decorator pattern (103) for details regarding BaseConnectionDecorator. This is the complete source code for TimedConnection:

```
public class TimedConnection
extends BaseConnectionDecorator
implements Connection {

    private ResourceTimer timer;
    private boolean closed = false;

    /**
    Constructs a TimedConnection object.
    */
    public TimedConnection(Connection reference) {
        super(reference);

        // Initialize the resource timer that monitors
        // periods of inactivity longer than 10 minutes
        // (600000 milliseconds).
        timer = new ResourceTimer(600000);
```

```java
    // Register a ConnectionCloser (see the inner class
    // below) as a listener to be notified when this
    // connection remains inactive longer than this
    // period.
    timer.addResourceTimerListener(
        new ConnectionCloser());

    // Start the timer.
    timer.start();
}

/**
ConnectionCloser is a custom ResourceTimerListener
implementation that closes this connection when it
remains inactive beyond the configured inactivity
threshold.
*/
private class ConnectionCloser
implements ResourceTimerListener {

    public void resourceInactive(
        ResourceTimerEvent event) {
        try {
            close();
        }
        catch(SQLException ignore) {
        }
    }
}

/**
Closes the connection.
*/
public void close()
throws SQLException
{
    // There is a chance that the resource timer
    // already closed the connection, so take the extra
    // precaution to delegate the close operation only
    // once.
    if (!closed) {
        closed = true;

        // Stop the resource timer, since it is no
        // longer needed.
        timer.stop();

        super.close();
```

```
        }
    }

    // Override the rest of the Connection operations to
    // indicate activity by resetting the timer.

    public void commit() throws SQLException {
        timer.reset();
        super.commit();
    }

    public PreparedStatement prepareStatement(
        String sqlStatement) throws SQLException {
        timer.reset();
        return super.prepareStatement(sqlStatement);
    }

    // Repeat for the rest of the operations
    // that the Connection interface defines.
    // ...
}
```

To utilize this class in conjunction with a new java.sql.Connection object, client code simply decorates it with a TimedConnection:

```
Connection connection = DriverManager.getConnection(url,
    user, password);

connection = new TimedConnection(connection);
```

RELATED PATTERNS AND TECHNOLOGY

- The TimedResource class specializes Resource Decorator (103), since it decorates any resource with customized timing behavior.

- You can incorporate the Resource Timer pattern into a Resource Pool (117) implementation to counter the effect that defective clients that neglect to return inactive resources to the pool have on overall resource utilization. You can also use it to automatically trim the size of the pool when a large number of its resources go unused.

- You can incorporate the Resource Timer pattern into a Transaction (379) implementation to roll back inactive transactions that defective client code neglects to commit or rollback.

Resource Descriptor

DESCRIPTION

Isolates platform- and data source-dependent behavior within a single component. A resource descriptor exposes specific platform idiosyncrasies that relate to particular database resources as generic, logical operations and enables the majority of data access code to remain independent of its physical environment.

CONTEXT

Despite the proliferation of data access standards and programming interfaces, programmers must still address database-, driver-, and platform-dependent issues on a regular basis. Sometimes incompatibilities result from multiple interpretations of vague specifications, but these aspects are usually refined in subsequent specification versions. Here are some examples of other common environment differences:

- *Error analysis*—Database standards and driver specifications define operational semantics precisely but neglect to dictate uniform error reporting. Even when a specification does describe a consistent scheme for delivering errors to clients, many database driver implementations define their own native error codes and messages.

  Many applications simply present database errors directly to users. However, those that incorporate filtering or depend on certain error codes or messages to make decisions need to handle different sets of error codes for different database drivers.

- *SQL differences*—While SQL statements are mostly portable among database products, many products inject some subtle twists into the SQL syntax that they support. This is often a result of historical or support-level details. Database platforms also extend SQL syntax to provide additional features and optimizations that the specification does not directly support. As a result, applications that support multiple database platforms often need the ability to choose among different SQL statements that represent the same logical data access operation.

- *Specification support levels*—Driver specifications often define operations before database drivers support them. For example, JDBC 2.0 added operations for updatable result sets. When it was first released, many drivers provided empty implementations for the new operations. At the time, applications that supported multiple database platforms and could take advantage of updatable result sets were likely to require two implementations. The first, full-featured implementation utilized updatable result sets while the other defined a less complete solution. The application had to decide when it could use the preferred implementation based on the support provided by the database driver at runtime.

A possible solution is to pepper your data access code with statements that check the level or exact implementation of the underlying database driver. For example, this block of code checks to see if updatable result sets are available based on the database connection's class and the programmer's understanding of each driver's support level:

```
Grid grid;

if (connection instanceof
    com.ibm.as400.access.AS400JDBCConnection
    || connection instanceof com.mysql.jdbc.Connection)
    grid = new UpdatableGrid(connection);

else
    grid = new ReadOnlyGrid(connection);
```

Hardwiring checks for particular database drivers in application code is detrimental for several reasons. One reason is that it clutters application logic. More importantly, it sprinkles database support-level details throughout application code. This makes the application code inherently more difficult to maintain, especially when it comes time to integrate support for a new database product or a new version of a database product that supports new features.

Database driver specifications provide some assistance for problems like these. Most specifications expose the notion of *database metadata*. Database metadata is a collection of information that describes the support levels and contents of a database and its entities in generic terms. Examples of database metadata include a list of the indices that are defined on a given table, the SQL scalar functions that a driver supports, and a driver's official product name and version information. JDBC's DatabaseMetaData interface includes an operation called supportsResultSetConcurrency that reports whether or not a driver implements updatable result sets. You can modify the application code shown earlier to use this operation instead of issuing explicit driver checks:

```
Grid grid;

DatabaseMetaData databaseMetaData
    = connection.getMetaData();

if (databaseMetaData.supportsResultSetConcurrency(
    ResultSet.TYPE_SCROLL_SENSITIVE,
    ResultSet.CONCUR_UPDATABLE))
    grid = new UpdatableGrid(connection);

else
    grid = new ReadOnlyGrid(connection);
```

Database metadata appears to solve the problem in this example. However, as anyone who has attempted to use this strategy can attest, database driver developers tend to forget to update their driver's metadata as they incorporate new features. When this happens, applications that use metadata to determine implementation details do not immediately take advantage of new, advertised driver features. This does not mean that the new features are not available. Rather, it means that the driver's metadata is not accurate.

Resource Descriptor describes a way to customize environment-dependent features and operations within isolated components. An instance of Resource Descriptor specializes the notion of database metadata in terms of logical data access operations that you can tune specifically for your application. In addition, you can use it to override any inaccurate database metadata that a database driver provides.

APPLICABILITY

Use the Resource Descriptor pattern when:

- Your application needs to support multiple database products while keeping its code neutral to particular runtime environments or resource types.

- You need to implement data access operations differently depending on a particular runtime environment or resource type. Database products, drivers, and other middleware can affect your application's behavior differently.

- You want to avoid hardwiring logic that is specific to a given platform or database within your application code.

- Standard database metadata operations do not report accurate results for the environments that your application supports.

- You want to package all code that directly supports a given environment within a single component.

STRUCTURE

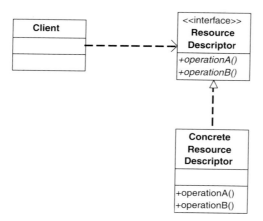

FIGURE 8.1: The static structure of the Resource Descriptor pattern.

Figure 8.1 illustrates the static structure of the Resource Descriptor pattern. The ResourceDescriptor interface defines operations for any aspects of application code that change depending on the runtime environment or resource type. These operations can retrieve attributes or implement functional behavior. ConcreteResourceDescriptor implements this interface in terms of a specific database product or driver. You write client code in terms of the ResourceDescriptor interface, but interact directly with the ConcreteResourceDescriptor at runtime. This enables your client code to remain neutral to its environment.

INTERACTIONS

Client code interacts with ConcreteResourceDescriptors as needed. You can choose to imbed operations that are specific to a given environment or resource type within ConcreteResourceDescriptor. Alternately, you can define multiple implementations within generic data access code and choose among them based on public ResourceDescriptor attributes.

CONSEQUENCES

The Resource Descriptor pattern has the following benefits:

Benefits

- *Isolates environment dependencies without hardwiring*—Resource descriptors encapsulate environment dependencies within their own modules, leaving application code and generic data access code free of hardwired conditional operations. This leads to maintainable code as well as the ability to add support for new database products without modifying application or data access code.

- *Provides tailored database metadata*—You can define any information that you want within your resource descriptors, making them more straightforward to use within application code.

STRATEGIES

Your data access code must interact with a particular ResourceDescriptor implementation at runtime. It is best to provide an environment-neutral mechanism that resolves appropriate ResourceDescriptor implementations based on an existing piece of contextual information, such as a database connection or data source representation. Here are some alternatives:

- *Static resolution module*—You can define a global, static resolution operation for resolving appropriate ResourceDescriptor instances. This is straightforward to implement and it groups all supported ResourceDescriptor implementations together. The downside to this choice is that you need to update the resolution module every time you incorporate support for a new environment. Here is an example of a static ResourceDescriptor resolution method:

```
public static ResourceDescriptor resolveDescriptor(
    Class resourceClass) {

    if (resourceClass
        == com.ibm.as400.access.AS400JDBCDriver.class)
        return new iSeriesResourceDescriptor();

    else if (resourceClass
        == com.mysql.jdbc.Connection.class)
        return new MySQLResourceDescriptor();

    else
        throw new IllegalArgumentException(
            "No descriptor is registered for "
```

```
        + resourceClass + ".");
    }
```

- *Operation parameters*—Just as you might pass a database connection around to operations that require it, you can pass a ResourceDescriptor implementation as an additional parameter to relevant operations. Here is an example of a domain method with an additional ResourceDescriptor parameter:

```
public void processAccount(int accountID,
    Connection connection,
    ResourceDescriptor resourceDescriptor) {

    // ...
}
```

This is a clean approach that avoids the requirement for any static or global resolution code, but it does contribute to parameter obfuscation, specifically for operations that already define numerous parameters.

- *Global registry*—You can define a static global registry that contains Resource-Descriptor instances for each supported environment. This registry defines methods for registering and resolving instances in a generic manner and enables each ResourceDescriptor implementation to effectively register itself. This is beneficial if you plan to add support for new environments in later application service releases, since simply loading a new ResourceDescriptor implementation integrates it into the overall system. The ResourceDescriptor-Registry class in the "Sample Code" section below illustrates this alternative.

If you use the Resource Descriptor pattern extensively, your ResourceDescriptor interface may include numerous, unrelated operations. When this happens, consider splitting it into multiple interfaces, each of which defines operations that relate to a specific resource type or operational category.

SAMPLE CODE

The ResourceDescriptor interface defines any attributes and operations that application or data access code requires and are dependent on a particular runtime environment. This example defines a few hypothetical, but common operations that tend to vary among JDBC drivers:

```
public interface ResourceDescriptor {

    /**
    Indicates if the resource supports updatable
    result sets.
    */
    boolean supportsUpdatableResultSets();

    /**
    Returns the qualified name in the format
    that the underlying database recognizes.
    */
    String getQualifiedName(String schema, String table);

    /**
    Determines whether an exception indicates
    a stale connection.
    */
    boolean isStaleConnection(SQLException e);

}
```

iSeriesResourceDescriptor implements ResourceDescriptor in terms of IBM's Toolbox for Java JDBC driver for iSeries (formerly AS/400) databases. This driver supports updatable result sets, uses a dot character to qualify table names, and throws SQLExceptions with a SQL state set to "08003" to indicate stale connections.

This class's static initializer registers itself with the ResourceDescriptorRegistry so that client code can resolve it quickly based on a specific java.sql.Connection implementation class:

```
public class iSeriesResourceDescriptor
implements ResourceDescriptor {

    static {
        // Register this descriptor for iSeries connections.
        ResourceDescriptorRegistry.registerDescriptor(
            com.ibm.as400.access.AS400JDBCConnection.class,
            new iSeriesResourceDescriptor());
    }

    public boolean supportsUpdatableResultSets() {
        return true;
    }

    public String getQualifiedName(String schema,
                                   String table) {
```

```
        StringBuffer buffer = new StringBuffer();
        buffer.append(schema);
        buffer.append(".");
        buffer.append(table);
        return buffer.toString();
    }

    public boolean isStaleConnection(SQLException e) {
        return e.getSQLState().equals("08003");
    }

}
```

ResourceDescriptorRegistry defines a static, global map for registering and resolving ResourceDescriptor implementations. ResourceDescriptor implementations are responsible for registering themselves, as the iSeriesResourceDescriptor did in the previous example. Client code passes any resource class object to the resolveDescriptor operation. If the class object has been registered, this operation returns the corresponding ResourceDescriptor implementation.

```
public class ResourceDescriptorRegistry
{
    private static Map contents = new HashMap();

    /**
    Adds a descriptor to the registry.
    */
    public static void registerDescriptor(
        Class resourceClass,
        ResourceDescriptor descriptor) {

        contents.put(resourceClass, descriptor);
    }

    /**
    Resolves a descriptor from the registry.
    */
    public static ResourceDescriptor resolveDescriptor(
        Class resourceClass) {

        ResourceDescriptor descriptor
            = (ResourceDescriptor)contents.get(resourceClass);

        if (descriptor != null)
            return descriptor;
        else
            throw new IllegalArgumentException(
```

```
                    "No descriptor is registered for "
            + resourceClass + ".");
    }
}
```

The following client code uses ResourceDescriptorRegistry to resolve a particular ResourceDescriptor implementation. It then enlists the assistance of the resulting ResourceDescriptor to determine whether an error indicates a stale connection. This code is a modified version of the attempt method from the QueryOperation class that the "Sample Code" section for Retryer (171) describes.

```
public boolean attempt() throws RetryFailedException {

    try {
        connection = connectionPool.getConnection(url,
            user, password);
        statement = connection.createStatement();
        resultSet = statement.executeQuery(sqlStatement);
        return true;
    }
    catch(SQLException e) {

        ResourceDescriptor descriptor
            = ResourceDescriptorRegistry.resolveDescriptor(
            connection.getClass());

        // If the connection is stale, then return false
        // to indicate that the operation failed but
        // can be tried again with a new connection.
        if (descriptor.isStaleConnection(e))
            return false;

        // Throw a RetryFailedException for any other
        // errors.  Retrying is not likely to remedy
        // them.
        else
            throw new RetryFailedException(
                "Query operation attempt error", e);

    }
}
```

RELATED PATTERNS AND TECHNOLOGY

- JDBC's DatabaseMetaData interface is a specialized Resource Descriptor that exposes a significant amount of information about a database's support and contents.

- In many cases, a ResourceDescriptor does not contain any state or class data. When this is true, consider defining ConcreteResourceDescriptors as Singleton classes [Gamma 1995] so that the system only instantiates and shares a single copy of each type.

- Resource Descriptor is a useful strategy for isolating environment dependencies that arise in implementations of the Data Accessor (9), Active Domain Object (33), and Object/Relational Map (53) patterns.

- Resource Descriptor is especially useful for analyzing errors in Retryer (171) implementations, since error details vary widely among database drivers.

Retryer

DESCRIPTION

Automatically retries operations whose failure is expected under certain defined conditions. This pattern enables fault-tolerance for data access operations.

CONTEXT

Enterprise applications typically utilize many independent, commercial system and middleware products, such as application servers, network managers, firewalls, and multiple database platforms. While the interactions between these products are usually precisely defined by standard interfaces, their implementations are not always straightforward. It is common for commercial products to impose semantics that conflict with your applications' expectations, including the following:

- *Non-standard configuration semantics*—Some database operations require pre-requisite initialization procedures before working correctly or efficiently. For example, the IBM iSeries integrated database dictates that applications cannot update a table within a transaction unless the table is configured for journalling. The only way to determine programmatically if a table is configured for journalling is to invoke a proprietary programming interface. This additional configuration step significantly degrades performance when you have to call it every time your application updates a table. Fortunately, it is only required the first time your application uses the table in the context of a transaction, so this condition rarely occurs.

  Rather than incurring the expense of checking a table's journalling configuration every time you want to involve it in a transaction, you can simply execute all operations under the assumption that the table is configured properly. In the rare case that it is not, your application will receive an error, analyze it, automate the journal configuration, and retry the operation.

- *Unexpected product interactions*—Database servers, firewalls, and network managers sometimes inadvertently close sockets that are reserved for use by pooled database connections. This condition results in a *stale connection* and can stem from configurable system administration policies, network problems, or hardware defects. When your application checks a connection out of the pool, there is no standard mechanism for your application code, the pool, or the connection to test whether its socket is usable. Often, the only way to detect a closed socket is for your application to try to use the connection and analyze the resulting error.

- *Commercial product defects*—A resource may become unresponsive or unusable as a result of a driver or database defect over which you have no control. Database resource implementations are somewhat state-dependent to ensure that applications invoke operations in the appropriate order. Like any other software, database resource implementations are not immune to defects of their own. State-dependent defects sometimes result in a given resource instance not being usable at all. If a defect is buried deep within database driver code, then you often have no recourse other than to reinitialize the resource and try again.

The common theme in these problems is that data access operations fail because of conditions outside of your applications' control. In addition, these errors should not cause any application to terminate, since it can reasonably recover from them. Your applications have no feasible mechanism to test for these conditions before they happen, so they must react to them afterward. Client code must analyze the severity of the errors, recover from them as much as possible, and potentially retry operations that failed as a result.

Error analysis, recovery, and retry logic is not complicated, but it does benefit from a structured approach. Otherwise, this logic clutters your application code and makes it more difficult to modify when you change your overall retry strategy. The Retryer pattern describes a generic structure and logic for automatically retrying data access operations that are expected to fail under certain conditions. This pattern defines a clear separation between retry logic and retryable database operations.

APPLICABILITY

Use the Retryer pattern when:

- Your applications need to react to certain, defined error conditions without terminating. There is often a set of recovery operations that an application can call to alleviate the original failure.

- Your applications are unable to detect certain recoverable error conditions ahead of time, so you must react to them after they occur.

- You want to decouple retry logic from data access code.

STRUCTURE

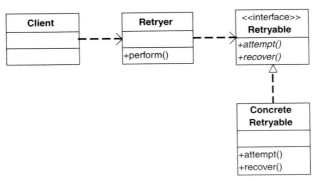

FIGURE 9.1: The static structure of the Retryer pattern.

Figure 9.1 illustrates the static structure of the Retryer pattern. The Retryable interface represents any data access operation that is potentially retryable. Concrete-Retryable implements this interface to define logic for a specific operation. The attempt operation contains the majority of its logic and returns true if the data access operation is successful or false if an expected error occurs. It throws an exception if an unexpected error occurs. Similarly, the recover operation contains any recovery logic and is called following a failed attempt.

Client code does not invoke a Retryable's attempt and recover operations directly. Instead, it uses a Retryer for this purpose, which acts as a harness that encapsulates all the generic retry logic.

INTERACTIONS

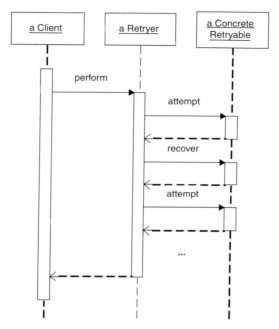

FIGURE 9.2: A client uses a Retryer to invoke a Retryable operation.

Figure 9.2 portrays what happens when a client uses a Retryer to invoke a Retryable operation. The Retryer invokes the ConcreteRetryable's attempt operation and checks its return value. If the attempt returns true, then the operation is successful and the Retryer returns control back to the client. If it returns false, then the Retryer calls recover, which the ConcreteRetryable implements to perform any logic required to recover from the failed attempt. It then waits for a period of time if configured to do so. This gives the external system time to recover from its own errors. After waiting, the Retryer invokes an attempt again. It repeats this cycle until either an attempt is successful or it reaches its permitted maximum number of attempts. In most cases, a small limit is desirable to prevent infinite loops.

The other condition that can occur is when either the attempt or recover operation throws an exception. Exceptions from these operations indicate that an error occurred other than those anticipated by ConcreteRetryable. When this happens, it normally does not make sense to call recover or attempt again. Instead, the Retryer simply dispatches the exception to the client.

CONSEQUENCES

The Retryer pattern has the following benefits:

Benefits

- The Retryer object encapsulates all retry logic, keeping it separate from application and data access code. If you redefine semantic details for retry logic, you only need to change the code within the Retryer class.

- Retryable implementations define a data access operation's characteristics clearly, including its logic, expected error conditions, and corresponding recovery logic.

STRATEGIES

Consider these strategies when implementing the Retryer pattern:

- *Command semantics*—Retryer is a specialization of the Command pattern [Gamma 1995]. As a result, you must define data access operations using command semantics. Rather than simply creating data access or resource objects and invoking their operations as method calls, you need to group a sequence of related physical or logical operations into a single Retryable implementation.

  The attempt operation does not normally define any parameters that relate to data access logic. All concrete Retryable class definitions must precisely implement the Retryable interface, so you can only define input parameters through constructor or custom mutator operations. Similarly, the class must save return values for subsequent calls to accessor operations.

  The Retryer class is responsible for invoking attempt and recover as needed, and client code is responsible for interacting with a Retryable's input and output parameters directly. This is a template implementation that illustrates these parameter logistics:

```
public class ConcreteRetryable implements Retryable {

    private Object inputParameter;
    private Object outputParameter;
```

```
    public ConcreteRetryable(Object inputParameter) {
        this.inputParameter = inputParameter;
    }

    public Object getOutputParameter() {
        return outputParameter;
    }

    public boolean attempt() throws RetryFailedException {
        try {
            outputParameter
                = dataAccessOperation(inputParameter);
            return true;
        }
        catch(ExpectedException e) {
            return false;
        }
        catch(Exception e) {
            throw new RetryFailedException(
                "Retryable operation attempt error", e);
        }
    }

    public void recover() throws RetryFailedException {
        try {
            anotherDataAccessOperation(inputParameter);
        }
        catch(Exception e) {
            throw new RetryFailedException(
                "Retryable operation recovery error", e);
        }
    }
}
```

- *Success and failure definition*—A Retryable implementation class strictly defines its own notion of success and failure. There may be occasions where operations fail for unexpected reasons that do not necessarily indicate that they should be retried. In most cases, retrying operations when an unexpected error occurs is futile. Retryable implementations indicate this fact by throwing an exception to be dispatched to the client.

- *Retryer configuration*—It is a good idea to provide a configuration mechanism for settings such as the maximum number of attempts or the interval to wait between attempts. This enables the install program or administrator to tailor an application so that it works best within a particular environment's constraints.

SAMPLE CODE

This is a sample definition of the Retryable interface:

```
public interface Retryable {

    /**
    Attempts a retryable operation one time.

    @returns true if the operation is successful or
            false if the operation fails and needs
            to be retried.

    @throws  RetryFailedException if an unexpected error
            occurs and retrying the operation will not
            fix it.
    */
    boolean attempt() throws RetryFailedException;

    /**
    Recovers from an operation failure.
    */
    void recover() throws RetryFailedException;
}
```

The Retryer class is the harness for repeatedly attempting a Retryable operation until it succeeds. It encapsulates all generic retry logic.

```
public class Retryer {

    private Retryable operation;

    public Retryer(Retryable operation) {
        this.operation = operation;
    }

    /**
    Retries the operation until it succeeds.

    @param maximumAttempts The maximum number of times
                          to attempt the operation or
                          -1 to retry the operation
                          indefinitely.

    @param attemptInterval The number of milliseconds to
                          wait in between attempts or
                          0 to indicate no waiting.
    */
```

```
public void perform(int maximumAttempts,
                    int attemptInterval)
                throws RetryFailedException {

    boolean succeeded = false;

    // Retry until you reach the maximum number
    // of attempts or the operation succeeds.
    // If maximumAttempts is less than zero, then
    // there is no limit on the number of attempts.
    for(int i = 1;
        (i <= maximumAttempts
            || maximumAttempts < 0)
           && !succeeded;
        ++i) {

        // Attempt the operation.  If it was successful,
        // then set the succeeded flag so that the loop
        // ends.
        if(operation.attempt()) {
            succeeded = true;
        }

        // Otherwise recover, sleep, and loop again.
        else {
            operation.recover();
            if (attemptInterval > 0) {
                try {
                    Thread.sleep(attemptInterval);
                }
                catch(InterruptedException ignore) {
                }
            }
        }
    }

    // If the operation never succeeds, then
    // indicate this by throwing an exception.
    if (!succeeded)
        throw new RetryFailedException(
            "Maximum failed attempts was reached.");
}
}
```

A RetryFailedException indicates that an operation failed because of an unexpected error and should not be attempted again. Retryer also throws this exception when an operation fails beyond its configured maximum number of attempts.

```
public class RetryFailedException extends Exception {

    public RetryFailedException(String message) {
        super(message);
    }

    public RetryFailedException(String message,
        Throwable cause) {
        super(message, cause);
    }
}
```

All of the sample code up to now defines generic retry logic and support. The next class defines a concrete Retryable implementation. QueryOperation gets a connection from the pool and uses it to issue a database query operation. It indicates failure if the connection is stale. Most likely, this stems from the underlying network support inadvertently closing the connection's socket, so retrying the operation with another connection is a viable and transparent solution. Any other exceptions indicate that there is an error that cannot be remedied by simply retrying the operation in this manner.

This class uses a ConnectionPool for resolving new database connections. See the "Sample Code" section for the Resource Pool pattern (117) for a definition of this class. QueryOperation explicitly neglects to return stale connections to the pool so that future operations do not attempt to use them.

QueryOperation maintains references to all objects involved in its input and the data access resources it uses to issue its query. This enables QueryOperation to strictly implement the Retryable interface while exposing necessary details to client code. In addition, clients must call close to explicitly release the database resources that this class uses.

```
public class QueryOperation implements Retryable {

    // Private variables that are input to the
    // query operation.
    private ConnectionPool connectionPool;
    private String url;
    private String user;
    private String password;
    private String sqlStatement;

    // Private variables that are resources
    // created for the query operation.
    private Connection connection;
```

```
    private Statement statement;
    private ResultSet resultSet;

    public QueryOperation(ConnectionPool connectionPool,
                          String url,
                          String user,
                          String password,
                          String sqlStatement) {

        this.connectionPool = connectionPool;
        this.url = url;
        this.user = user;
        this.password = password;
        this.sqlStatement = sqlStatement;
    }

    public boolean attempt() throws RetryFailedException {

        try {
            connection = connectionPool.getConnection(url,
                user, password);
            statement = connection.createStatement();
            resultSet = statement.executeQuery(sqlStatement);
            return true;
        }
        catch(SQLException e) {

            // If the connection is stale, then return false
            // to indicate that the operation failed but
            // can be tried again with a new connection.
            // This is likely to be a highly database driver-
            // dependent test, so if you support multiple
            // databases, consider building this check into
            // an instance of the Resource Descriptor pattern.
            if (e.getSQLState().equals("08003"))
                return false;

            // Throw a RetryFailedException for any other
            // errors.  Retrying is not likely to remedy
            // them.
            else
                throw new RetryFailedException(
                    "Query operation attempt error", e);
        }
    }

    /**
    Returns the result set after the operation runs
    successfully.
```

```
*/
public ResultSet getResultSet() {
    return resultSet;
}


/**
Closes the resources held by this operation, if any.
You need to leave resources open until you are done reading
the result set.
*/
public void close() throws SQLException {
    if (resultSet != null)
        resultSet.close();
    if (statement != null)
        statement.close();
    if (connection != null && !connection.isClosed())
        connection.close();
}

}
```

This block of client code instantiates a QueryOperation object and uses a Retryer to run it:

```
QueryOperation operation
    = new QueryOperation(connectionPool,
                         url,
                         user,
                         password,
                         "SELECT * FROM ACCOUNTS");

Retryer retryer = new Retryer(operation);

// Retry the operation indefinitely until
// it succeeds.  Wait 5 seconds between
// attempts to give the network a chance
// to recover from problems.
retryer.perform(-1, 5000);

// Process the reslt set.
ResultSet resultSet = operation.getResultSet();
while(resultSet.next()) {
    // ...
}

// Release the database resources that the operation
```

```
// left open.
operation.close();
```

RELATED PATTERNS AND TECHNOLOGY

- Retryer specializes Command [Gamma 1995], which defines objects that implement one or more logical or physical operations using precisely defined semantics. Command is useful for defining undo operations, keeping logs of user commands, and journalling operations for error recovery.

- Database drivers adhere to operational standards closely, but vary widely when it comes to identifying error conditions. Error analysis is fundamental within a concrete Retryable implementation since it needs to distinguish anticipated errors from more serious failures. To keep your error analysis code platform and database driver independent, consider using Resource Descriptor (159) to isolate specific error codes for each database or platform you support.

Part 3

Input and Output Patterns

Active Domain Object (33) and Object/Relational Map (53) describe architectural strategies for building application logic using domain objects. Domain objects directly model application or business concepts rather than relational database entities and enable you to decouple the physical data model and data access details from your application logic. You can alter the resulting application code independently from the data access code. In addition, application code that uses domain objects is generally easier to read and maintain.

When you design domain objects, you must define their domain object mapping as well. A domain object mapping describes the translation between domain objects and corresponding relational data. In the Active Domain Object pattern, each domain object is responsible for defining and encapsulating its own mapping, while in Object/Relational Map, the mapping happens in a generic, orthogonal component. Figure P3.1 illustrates a domain object mapping example that translates between Vehicle objects and rows in the VEHICLES table:

185

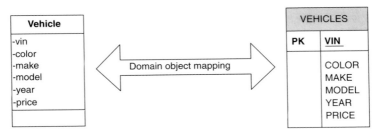

FIGURE P3.1: A domain object mapping example that translates between Vehicle domain objects and rows in the VEHICLES table.

Database input and output operations are a primary function of domain object mapping. As applications create new domain object instances and read their attributes, the mapping implementation issues analogous database read operations. Similarly, when applications alter domain object attributes, the mapping implementation updates the database copy.

A domain object mapping is also responsible for converting data between its physical database form and the form the application code expects. Numeric and text data usually present no conversion issues at all. However, data that designates non-numeric, semantic information usually requires some amount of conversion because its database representation is not in a form that is straightforward for applications to use. For example, the COLORS column in the VEHICLES table stores its value as a coded integer, while the Vehicle class defines it using a typesafe enum class [Bloch 2001].

This chapter introduces patterns for defining and implementing database input and output operations. The primary goal of these patterns is to use a uniform strategy for implementing these operations across multiple domain object types.

INPUT AND OUTPUT OPERATIONS

Within the context of a domain object mapping implementation, input and output operations translate between domain objects and relational data in both directions. Since mappings exist to enable application code to work exclusively with domain objects, you should define mapping interfaces in terms of domain object operations. Mappings implement the operations by accessing relational data. Here are some examples of input and output operations expressed in domain object terms:

- *Populate a domain object*—Populating a domain object entails finding relevant data and creating a corresponding domain object instance. In data access terms, you need to issue one or more database read operations and copy the results into the attributes of a new domain object instance.

- *Persist a domain object*—Persisting a domain object involves inserting or updating a row of data corresponding to the attributes of a domain object instance. To implement this, you need to issue the appropriate database insert or update operations that copy the attributes of the domain object instance to corresponding table columns.

- *Delete a domain object*—Deleting a domain object entails deleting the data that corresponds to a domain object instance. In data access terms, you need to issue analogous database delete operations.

A domain object mapping adapts the physical database driver's programming interface to a customized interface based on domain objects. Figure P3.2 shows how a domain object mapping relates to application logic, domain objects, and the underlying database driver:

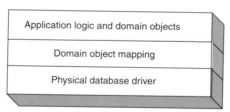

FIGURE P3.2: The domain object mapping adapts the physical database driver's programming interface to a customized interface based on domain objects.

IDENTITY OBJECTS

Besides translating data between domain objects and physical database forms, another important factor of domain object mapping is identifying objects. When an application invokes an input or output operation using domain objects, it must identify target data.

Consider a vehicle inventory table that contains all cars and trucks in stock at an automobile dealership. Any application code that queries this table must somehow indicate a relevant subset of this table's rows. For example, when a customer wants to learn more about a specific car on the lot, the salesperson looks up its details by entering the car's vehicle identification number (VIN) into the application. The application ultimately issues a SQL query like this:

```
SELECT * FROM VEHICLES WHERE VIN = '34FG4234NBJDDDD43'
```

In another scenario, a less decisive customer asks the salesperson to find all cars that are priced at $15,000 or less and whose model year is 1990 or later. The application also issues this query using SQL:

```
SELECT * FROM VEHICLES WHERE YEAR >= 1990 AND PRICE <= 15000
```

These expressions should never appear directly in application code that otherwise uses domain objects. One reason is that it makes explicit mention of data model entities, namely the VEHICLES table and its columns. Second, it includes specific SQL syntax, which may change if you decide to move your data to another database platform.

Identity objects alleviate this problem. An identity object uses domain concepts to identify the target relational data set. It is common for identity objects to correspond to a table's primary key. An identity object identifies a domain object, just as a set of primary key values uniquely identifies a row of table data.

In the VEHICLES table, the primary key is likely to be the VIN column, since VINs are guaranteed to be unique. The analogous identity object is simply a String representation of the VIN. The application code can find any car by its VIN like this:

```
Vehicle vehicle = vehicleInventory.find("NKWDE6764SD171396");
```

Identity objects do not always correspond directly to a table's primary key, especially in cases where applications search on columns other than those included in the primary key. An alternative identity object can define multiple attributes that correspond to search criteria. In this respect, a single identity object does not uniquely identify a single domain object, but rather a set of domain objects that matches its criteria. When you design an identity object's attributes and programming interface, consider the types of search operations that you expect applications to require. Identity objects may go so far as to allow applications to set value ranges or expressions that include pattern-matching characters.

For example, when a customer asks a salesperson to find all cars whose price is $15,000 or less and whose model year is 1990 or later, the application can designate this information using an identity object called VehicleCriteria:

```
VehicleCriteria criteria = new VehicleCriteria();
criteria.setMaximumPrice(15000);
criteria.setMinimumYear(1990);
List vehicles = vehicleInventory.find(criteria);
```

These examples illustrate find operations that use identity objects to query and read target data.

Identity objects are also important for output operations since they identify specific database rows to update, insert, and delete. For example, if the dealer chooses to mark down a car's price by 15 percent, the application can work as follows:

```
int price = vehicle.getPrice();
vehicle.setPrice(price * 0.85);
vehicleInventory.update(vehicle);
```

Notice that the application does not explicitly indicate an identity object when it calls this update operation. However, update's implementation implicitly extracts the Vehicle object's identity, the VIN in this case, to issue the appropriate SQL UPDATE statement.

INPUT AND OUTPUT PATTERNS

Input and output patterns describe design aspects for defining domain object mapping operation interfaces in terms of domain and identity objects and implementing them cleanly and with minimal code. The first set of input and output patterns are specializations of Abstract Factory [Gamma 1995]. The common theme among these factory patterns is isolating the mapping between domain and identity objects and their corresponding physical data. Encapsulating these mappings helps to minimize the effect of database format changes and also removes these details from application logic.

These patterns also define a consistent structure for mapping that works for a wide variety of domain object types and tables. You can define a single set of factory interfaces that works for all domain object types that your system uses. These factories enable you to build a generic infrastructure for caching, logging, and other orthogonal concepts using the interfaces while remaining independent from specific domain object type details. These patterns are:

- **Selection Factory** (191)—Generates query selections based on identity object attributes.

- **Domain Object Factory** (203)—Populates domain objects based on query result data.

- **Update Factory** (215)—Generates update operations based on modified domain object attributes.

The remaining input and output patterns take advantage of the generic nature of these factories to build all-purpose domain object mapping classes. In each of these, one or more front-end classes manage the factories on behalf of the client and invoke them as part of more abstract mapping operations.

- **Domain Object Assembler** (227)—Populates, persists, and deletes domain objects using a uniform factory framework.

- **Paging Iterator** (253)—Iterates efficiently through a collection of domain objects that represents query results.

You can combine these patterns to build a robust domain object mapping framework that strictly decouples generic mapping logic from the customized conversion details for specific types. This separation enables you to incorporate additional domain object types as your applications require them. In addition, it allows you to incorporate common optimizations and enhancements that apply immediately to operations for all domain object types.

Selection Factory

DESCRIPTION

Generates query selections based on identity object attributes.

CONTEXT

A primary task for any domain object mapping is to identify the set of target relational data on which to operate. Applications indicate this set using identity objects. An identity object can correspond directly to a table's primary key and refer to exactly one row of data or it can define criteria that match multiple rows across multiple tables.

If your goal is to enable applications to invoke operations using identity objects exclusively, then you must define a domain object mapping component that translates them to relational terms. The relational concept that is analogous to an identity object is called a *selection*. A selection is an entity or expression that you send to a database to indicate the data set on which to operate. Databases use selections for both read and write operations. In SQL, WHERE clauses are selections.

To illustrate a mapping from identity objects to selections, let's revisit the vehicle inventory table that maintains stock details for a car dealership. The VEHICLES table contains a row for every automobile that the dealer currently has for sale. The application uses two types of identity objects. The first is simply a VIN that is unique for every automobile on the lot. The second identity object is a VehicleCriteria object, which defines various, optional attributes that are useful for broader inventory searches. During application runtime, the domain object mapping translates either of these identity object types to a corresponding WHERE clause for use in SQL operations. Figure 10.1 illustrates this translation:

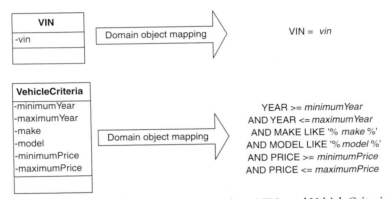

FIGURE 10.1: The domain object mapping translates VINs and VehicleCriteria objects to corresponding SQL WHERE clauses.

The Selection Factory pattern describes a strategy for encapsulating the details of translating from identity objects to selections using a single factory object. Since these details are likely to vary among different identity object types and target database entities, you can define factory objects for each translation variation. Application and middleware code can utilize these factory objects at any time. Figure 10.2 illustrates Selection Factory's role in domain object mapping:

FIGURE 10.2: A selection factory maps identity objects to selections.

APPLICABILITY

Use the Selection Factory pattern when:

- You need to define a common infrastructure for translating identity objects to selections as part of an overall domain object mapping strategy.

- You need to define customized mapping details for individual identity object types or database entities and hide these details from both applications and generic domain object mapping infrastructure code.

STRUCTURE

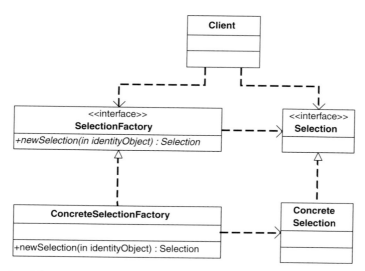

FIGURE 10.3: The static structure of the Selection Factory pattern.

Figure 10.3 illustrates the static structure of the Selection Factory pattern. The Selection interface defines the selection representation for your system and ConcreteSelection implements it. If your domain object mapping interacts directly with a physical database that supports SQL, you can simply use string values to represent SQL WHERE clauses. If you are using Layers (75) and your domain object mapping sits on top of a Data Accessor (9), you can define a Selection representation that is independent of any particular database technology.

The SelectionFactory interface defines a single operation for generating a new Selection object based on an identity object. ConcreteSelectionFactory implements this interface for a specific identity object type or target database entity. Your overall domain object mapping is likely to require multiple SelectionFactory implementations with customized mapping details encapsulated within each of them. Client code and generic domain object mapping infrastructure code refer only to the SelectionFactory and Selection interfaces, keeping them decoupled from any specific mapping details.

INTERACTIONS

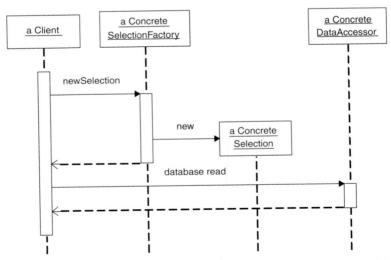

FIGURE 10.4: A client uses a ConcreteSelectionFactory to map an identity object to a ConcreteSelection.

Figure 10.4 portrays what happens when a client requires a new selection object. It creates an identity object, often based on user or batch input, and passes it to the

ConcreteSelectionFactory's newSelection operation. newSelection creates and returns a ConcreteSelection, which the client can use to issue a database read or update operation.

CONSEQUENCES

The Selection Factory pattern has the following consequences:

Benefits

- *Domain object mapping encapsulation*—A selection factory encapsulates the translation of identity objects that are defined using domain concepts to selections that identify data using data model details. This enables effective decoupling of application code from the data model and data access components.

- *Isolation of identity object and database entity details*—Translation details vary for different identity object types and database entities. You can define a different selection factory implementation for each type of translation, keeping them isolated from each other.

- *Consistent client interface*—Selection Factory defines a consistent client interface that applications and other middleware code can use generically without requiring references to specific implementations. This enables you to plug in alternate implementations in later releases without requiring changes to client code.

STRATEGIES

A SelectionFactory implementation determines database selection criteria based on an identity object's attributes. An implementation usually requires clients to pass specific types of identity objects because it depends on particular attribute values to generate the corresponding selection.

Depending on your application's requirements, you may also find it necessary to include ordering information within a Selection object. Ordering information defines how lists of domain objects are sorted and corresponds to an SQL ORDER BY clause.

A SelectionFactory implementation's constructor often defines parameters for any information it needs to create new selections, but is not defined as identity object attributes. For example, an implementation may need to access the JDBC

DatabaseMetaData information to determine how to qualify column names in the resulting SQL WHERE clause. It is the responsibility of the code that initializes the SelectionFactory implementation to pass this information.

If you find that there are many similarities among SelectionFactory implementations and few exceptions, consider defining a generic implementation that handles mappings declaratively. A generic implementation can infer domain object mapping details based on a consistent convention of attribute, table, and column names. Alternately, it can reference mapping metadata stored in a configuration file or system database. This approach is also useful when you want to define new domain objects without writing additional mapping code.

SAMPLE CODE

The first interface in this example is SelectionFactory. This interface defines the semantics for all concrete SelectionFactory implementations. This example uses SQL WHERE clauses to represent selections.

```
public interface SelectionFactory {

    /**
    Returns a SQL WHERE clause that corresponds
    to the identity object.
    */
    String newSelection(Object identityObject);

}
```

VehicleCriteria was introduced in the "Context" section of this chapter. This class defines identity objects that specify various criteria that collectively match zero or more rows in the VEHICLES table. Its make and model attributes correspond directly to columns of the same name, while minimumYear, maximumYear, minimumPrice, and maximumPrice define ranges for the YEAR and PRICE columns, respectively.

```
public class VehicleCriteria {

    private int minimumYear;
    private int maximumYear;
    private String make;
    private String model;
    private int minimumPrice;
```

```java
    private int maximumPrice;

    public int getMinimumYear() {
        return minimumYear;
    }

    public void setMinimumYear(int minimumYear) {
        this.minimumYear = minimumYear;
    }

    public int getMaximumYear() {
        return maximumYear;
    }

    public void setMaximumYear(int maximumYear) {
        this.maximumYear = maximumYear;
    }

    public String getMake() {
        return make;
    }

    public void setMake(String make) {
        this.make = make;
    }

    public String getModel() {
        return model;
    }

    public void setModel(String model) {
        this.model = model;
    }

    public int getMinimumPrice() {
        return minimumPrice;
    }

    public void setMinimumPrice(int minimumPrice) {
        this.minimumPrice = minimumPrice;
    }

    public int getMaximumPrice() {
        return maximumPrice;
    }

    public void setMaximumPrice(int maximumPrice) {
        this.maximumPrice = maximumPrice;
```

```
        }
    }
```

VINSelectionFactory is a SelectionFactory implementation that generates inventory table selections based on VINs:

```
public class VINSelectionFactory
implements SelectionFactory {

    public String newSelection(Object identityObject)
    {
        String vin = (String)identityObject;
        StringBuffer buffer = new StringBuffer();
        buffer.append("VIN = '");
        buffer.append(vin);
        buffer.append("'");
        return buffer.toString();
    }

}
```

Next is some client code that initializes a VINSelectionFactory and uses it to generate a WHERE clause that corresponds to a VIN. It then builds the rest of the SQL SELECT statement and issues it as a query operation. Notice that other than the VINSelectionFactory initialization, this code does not cater to any particular SelectionFactory implementation.

```
// Initialize the selection factory.
SelectionFactory selectionFactory
    = new VINSelectionFactory();

// Use the selection factory to find
// a specific VIN.
String vin = "NKWDE6764SD171396";
String selection
    = selectionFactory.newSelection(vin);

// Issue the query.
ResultSet resultSet
    = statement.executeQuery("SELECT * FROM VEHICLES WHERE "
                              + selection);
```

VehicleCriteriaSelectionFactory is another SelectionFactory implementation that generates inventory table selection VehicleCriteria objects. VehicleCriteriaSelectionFactory uses any VehicleCriteria non-null and non-zero attribute value to build a conjoined WHERE clause.

```
public class VehicleCriteriaSelectionFactory
implements SelectionFactory {

    public String newSelection(Object identityObject)
    {
        VehicleCriteria vehicleCriteria
            = (VehicleCriteria)identityObject;
        StringBuffer buffer = new StringBuffer();
        boolean firstExpression = true;

        int minimumYear
            = vehicleCriteria.getMinimumYear();
        if (minimumYear != 0) {
            buffer.append("YEAR >= ");
            buffer.append(minimumYear);
            firstExpression = false;
        }

        int maximumYear
            = vehicleCriteria.getMaximumYear();
        if (maximumYear != 0) {
            if (!firstExpression)
                buffer.append(" AND ");
            buffer.append("YEAR <= ");
            buffer.append(maximumYear);
            firstExpression = false;
        }

        String make = vehicleCriteria.getMake();
        if (make != null) {
            if (!firstExpression)
                buffer.append(" AND ");
            buffer.append("MAKE LIKE '%");
            buffer.append(make);
            buffer.append("%'");
            firstExpression = false;
        }

        String model = vehicleCriteria.getModel();
        if (model != null) {
            if (!firstExpression)
                buffer.append(" AND ");
            buffer.append("MODEL LIKE '%");
            buffer.append(model);
            buffer.append("%'");
```

```
            firstExpression = false;
        }

        int minimumPrice
            = vehicleCriteria.getMinimumPrice();
        if (minimumPrice != 0) {
            buffer.append("PRICE >= ");
            buffer.append(minimumPrice);
            firstExpression = false;
        }

        int maximumPrice
            = vehicleCriteria.getMaximumPrice();
        if (maximumPrice != 0) {
            if (!firstExpression)
                buffer.append(" AND ");
            buffer.append("PRICE <= ");
            buffer.append(maximumPrice);
            firstExpression = false;
        }

        return buffer.toString();
    }

}
```

Next is another client code example that passes a VehicleCriteria object to the VehicleCriteriaSelectionFactory. VehicleCriteria indicates that you want to get a list of all automobiles that were made in 1990 or later and whose price is $15,000 or less. The VehicleCriteriaSelectionFactory generates the corresponding WHERE clause and the client builds the rest of the SQL SELECT statement and issues it as a query operation. Notice again that the only code that refers to a particular SelectionFactory implementation is the initialization.

```
// Initialize the selection factory.
SelectionFactory selectionFactory
    = new VehicleCriteriaSelectionFactory();

VehicleCriteria vehicleCriteria = new VehicleCriteria();
vehicleCriteria.setMaximumPrice(15000);
vehicleCriteria.setMinimumYear(1990);

// Use the selection factory to generate
// the selection for these criteria.
String selection
    = selectionFactory.newSelection(vehicleCriteria);
```

```
// Issue the query.
ResultSet resultSet
    = statement.executeQuery("SELECT * FROM VEHICLES WHERE "
                              + selection);
```

RELATED PATTERNS AND TECHNOLOGY

- Selection Factory specializes Abstract Factory [Gamma 1995], which describes the generic application of factory interfaces.

- Selection Factory is similar to the Finder class that Row Data Gateway [Fowler 2002] defines. The difference is that the Finder class is responsible for issuing database query operations in addition to mapping identity objects to selections.

- As an alternative to depending on a particular database technology, you can design the Selection and ConcreteSelection interfaces to use logical database concepts that are defined as part of a Data Accessor (9) implementation.

- Selection Factory is useful for implementing the Active Domain Object (33) and Object/Relational Map (53) patterns.

- Consider isolating an entire set of Selection Factory implementations within a single middleware layer among other Layers (75).

- You can use Selection Factory in conjunction with Domain Object Factory (203) and Update Factory (215) to build a comprehensive domain object mapping solution.

- Selection Factory is a fundamental component of the framework that Domain Object Assembler (227) defines.

Domain Object Factory

DESCRIPTION

Populates domain objects based on query result data.

CONTEXT

Another primary function for any domain object mapping is populating domain objects based on physical query results. Each row of result data contains representations of the attributes needed to create a new domain object and initialize its attributes. In some cases, this is as simple as copying data directly from the result set to the new domain object. However, it is also common to include additional mapping and translation.

Consider a database table that contains customer names and addresses. Suppose that several product distribution applications use this table for many common operations. Sprinkling this table's physical details throughout these applications is detrimental to their maintainability and severely restricts future changes to the table and its supporting database. Defining a Customer domain object with which the applications can interact helps to encapsulate the physical table details in a single module.

The domain object mapping is responsible for translating physical result data into domain objects. Figure 11.1 illustrates the translation from query results that involve the CUSTOMERS table to a Customer object's attributes:

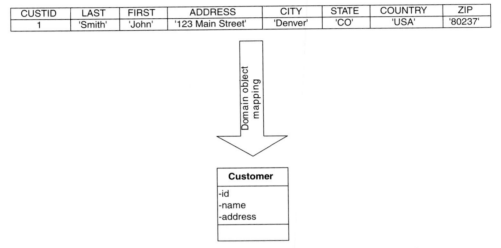

CUSTID	LAST	FIRST	ADDRESS	CITY	STATE	COUNTRY	ZIP
1	'Smith'	'John'	'123 Main Street'	'Denver'	'CO'	'USA'	'80237'

FIGURE 11.1: The domain object mapping translates a row of data from the CUSTOMERS table to a Customer object's attributes.

The Domain Object Factory pattern describes a strategy for encapsulating the details of this type of translation. Since these details are likely to vary among different database entities and domain object types, you can define factory objects for each translation variation. Application and middleware code can utilize these factory objects at any time. Figure 11.2 illustrates Domain Object Factory's role in domain object mapping:

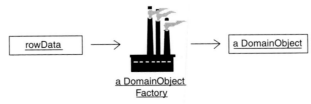

FIGURE 11.2: A Domain Object Factory maps result set row data to domain objects.

APPLICABILITY

Use the Domain Object Factory pattern when:

- You need to define a common infrastructure for translating query results to domain object attributes as part of an overall domain object mapping strategy.

- You need to define customized mapping details for individual database entities or domain object types and hide these details from both applications and generic domain object mapping infrastructure code.

STRUCTURE

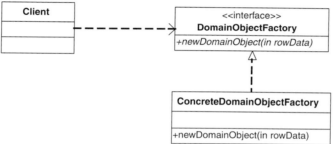

FIGURE 11.3: The static structure of the Domain Object Factory pattern.

Figure 11.3 illustrates the static structure of the Domain Object Factory pattern. The DomainObjectFactory interface defines a single operation for creating and populating new domain objects based on single rows of data. You can tailor the format for the input data based on the physical data representation that is most convenient for your middleware code. If you use a physical database driver that returns data as a result set, you can define newDomainObject to take this result set as its input parameter. If you choose to do this, you need to define and document a semantic constraint that factories only operate on a result set's current row. If you are using Layers (75) and your domain object mapping sits on top of a Data Accessor (9), then you can define newDomainObject to accept a more abstract data representation that is independent of any specific database technology.

ConcreteDomainObjectFactory implements DomainObjectFactory for a specific database entity or domain object type. Your overall domain object mapping is likely to require multiple DomainObjectFactory implementations with customized mapping details encapsulated within each of them. Client code and generic domain object mapping infrastructure code refer only to the DomainObjectFactory interface, keeping it decoupled from any specific mapping details.

INTERACTIONS

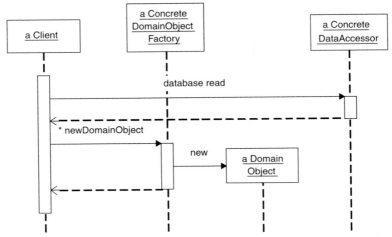

FIGURE 11.4: A client uses a ConcreteDomainObjectFactory to map a row of result set data to a DomainObject.

Figure 11.4 portrays what happens when a client requires a new domain object. It issues a database read operation and passes the results to the ConcreteDomainObjectFactory's newDomainObject operation one row at a time. newDomainObject returns a domain object that the client can use for application logic.

CONSEQUENCES

The Domain Object Factory pattern has the following benefits:

Benefits

- *Domain object mapping encapsulation*—A domain object factory encapsulates the translation of physical query result data to domain objects. This enables effective decoupling of application code from the data model and data access components.

- *Isolation of database entity and domain object details*—Translation details vary for different database entities and domain object types. You can define a different domain object factory implementation for each type of translation, keeping them isolated from each other.

- *Consistent client interface*—Domain Object Factory defines a consistent client interface that applications and other middleware code can use generically without requiring references to specific implementations. This enables you to plug in alternate implementations in later releases without requiring changes to client code.

STRATEGIES

A DomainObjectFactory implementation creates and populates specific domain objects based on data from query results. A given implementation usually requires the client to pass this data in a specific format because it depends on its contents to initialize the domain object's attributes appropriately.

A DomainObjectFactory implementation's constructor often defines parameters for any information for which it needs to create new domain objects but is not included in row data. For example, the implementation may need to report timestamps based on the current time zone. The row data includes the timestamps, but not the current time zone. It is therefore the responsibility of the code that initializes the DomainObjectFactory implementation to pass this information.

It is common for application code to issue queries that indicate that the database should return all available columns in the results. In SQL, this means using an asterisk (*) for the column list. For example:

```
SELECT * FROM CUSTOMERS WHERE CUSTID = 1594
```

It is also common for DomainObjectFactory implementations to discard columns that they do not need to include in the domain object, since client code does not require them. This means that data is fetched from the database, but never used. This superfluous data presents an opportunity for optimizing fetch performance by limiting queries to return only the columns that a particular DomainObjectFactory implementation needs.

Since a concrete DomainObjectFactory implementation is the primary consumer of the result set data, it makes sense for it to publish the columns it requires. You can incorporate this optimization by defining an additional operation in the DomainObjectFactory interface that provides this information. Generic data access code can use this information to refine queries to include only the columns that are needed to populate domain objects. Figure 11.5 shows the modified sequence. The client calls the new operation, getColumnNames, and uses this information when it issues the subsequent database query operation.

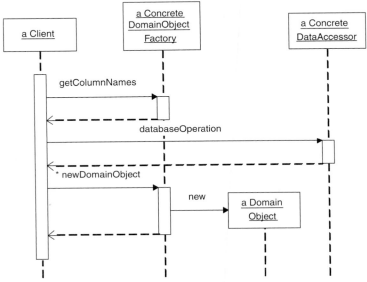

FIGURE 11.5: A client calls getColumnNames to determine the set of columns required for populating a domain object. It uses this information to refine the database query operation.

In the DomainObjectFactory implementation that populates Customer objects, this operation returns the exact set of columns required to populate Customer object attributes. The client can use this information to refine the SQL statement like this:

```
SELECT CUSTID, LAST, FIRST, ADDRESS, CITY, STATE, COUNTRY, ZIP
FROM CUSTOMERS WHERE CUSTID = 1594
```

If you find that there are many similarities among DomainObjectFactory implementations and few exceptions, consider defining a generic implementation that handles mappings declaritively. A generic implementation can infer domain object mapping details based on a consistent convention of attribute, table, and column names. Alternately, it can reference mapping metadata stored in a configuration file or system database. This approach is also useful when you want to define new domain objects without writing additional mapping code.

SAMPLE CODE

The first interface in this example is DomainObjectFactory. This interface defines the semantics for all concrete DomainObjectFactory implementations and includes the getColumnNames operation that the "Strategies" section of this chapter described. This example uses a java.util.Map object to represent a single row of data. Each map stores a collection of column name and value pairs.

```
public interface DomainObjectFactory {

    /**
    Creates and returns a new domain object
    that corresponds to the contents of a
    single row from database query results.
    */
    Object newDomainObject(Map rowData);

    /**
    Returns an array of column names that
    this factory expects to see in the
    row data that gets passed to
    newDomainObject.
    */
    String[] getColumnNames();

}
```

The "Context" section of this chapter introduced the Customer class. This class defines domain objects that represent customer information that is stored physically in the CUSTOMERS table. One of its attributes is an Address object, which also corresponds to data in the CUSTOMERS table.

```
public class Customer {

    // The properties that make up customer data.
    private int id;
    private String name;
    private Address address;
```

```java
    public int getId() {
        return id;
    }

    public void setId(int id) {
        this.id = id;
    }

    public String getName() {
        return name;
    }

    public void setName(String name) {
        this.name = name;
    }

    public Address getAddress() {
        return address;
    }

    public void setAddress(Address address) {
        this.address = address;
    }

}

public class Address
{
    private String address1 = null;
    private String address2 = null;
    private String address3 = null;
    private String cityState = null;
    private String country = null;
    private String postalCode = null;

    public String getAddress1() {
        return address1;
    }

    public void setAddress1(String address1) {
        this.address1 = address1;
    }

    // Repeat for the rest of the attributes
    // this class defines.
    // ...
}
```

CustomerFactory is a DomainObjectFactory implementation that populates new Customer objects based on row data from the CUSTOMERS table. It extracts the information it needs from the input row data and uses it to initialize a new Customer object's attributes.

```
public class CustomerFactory
implements DomainObjectFactory {

    public Object newDomainObject(Map rowData) {

        int id = ((Integer)rowData.get("CUSTID")).intValue();
        String last = (String)rowData.get("LAST");
        String first = (String)rowData.get("FIRST");
        String address1 = (String)rowData.get("ADDRESS");
        String city = (String)rowData.get("CITY");
        String state = (String)rowData.get("STATE");
        String country = (String)rowData.get("COUNTRY");
        String zip = (String)rowData.get("ZIP");

        Address address = new Address();
        address.setAddress1(address1);
        address.setCityState(city + ", " + state);
        address.setCountry(country);
        address.setPostalCode(zip);

        Customer customer = new Customer();
        customer.setId(id);
        customer.setName(last + ", " + first);
        customer.setAddress(address);

        return customer;
    }

    public String[] getColumnNames() {
        return COLUMN_NAMES;
    }

    private static final String[] COLUMN_NAMES
        = { "CUSTID", "LAST", "FIRST", "ADDRESS",
            "CITY", "STATE", "COUNTRY", "ZIP" };
}
```

Next is some client code that initializes a CustomerFactory and then issues a query that requests information for all customers who reside in Colorado. Next, it uses CustomerFactory to populate a list of Customer objects that correspond to the result set data. Notice that the majority of this code does not depend on a specific DomainObjectFactory implementation or domain object type.

```java
// Initialize the domain object factory.
DomainObjectFactory domainObjectFactory
    = new CustomerFactory();

// Get the column names that the domain
// object factory requires and build a
// string suitable for the SELECT statement.
String[] columnNames
    = domainObjectFactory.getColumnNames();
StringBuffer buffer = new StringBuffer();
for(int i = 0; i < columnNames.length; ++i) {
    if (i > 0)
        buffer.append(",");
    buffer.append(columnNames[i]);
}

// Issue the query.
ResultSet resultSet
    = statement.executeQuery(
    "SELECT " + buffer
    + " FROM CUSTOMERS WHERE STATE = 'CO'");

// Iterate through the rows of the result
// set, building a list of customer domain
// objects.
ResultSetMetaData rsmd = resultSet.getMetaData();
int columnCount = rsmd.getColumnCount();
List customers = new LinkedList();
while(resultSet.next()) {

    // Store the current row as a map, since this
    // is what the domain object factory is expecting.
    Map rowData = new HashMap();
    for(int i = 1; i <= columnCount; ++i) {
        rowData.put(rsmd.getColumnName(i),
                    resultSet.getObject(i));
    }

    // Use the domain object factory to populate the
    // new customer domain object and add it to the list.
    Object customer
        = domainObjectFactory.newDomainObject(rowData);
    customers.add(customer);
}
```

RELATED PATTERNS AND TECHNOLOGY

- Domain Object Factory specializes Abstract Factory [Gamma 1995], which describes the generic application of factory interfaces.

- Domain Object Factory is similar to Data Mapper [Fowler 2002] and Value Object Assembler [Alur 2001]. The primary difference is that these patterns also take responsibility for issuing database query operations.

- As an alternative to referencing a particular database technology, you can design Domain Object Factory's input row data representation to use logical database concepts that are defined as part of a Data Accessor (9) implementation.

- Domain Object Factory is useful for implementing the Active Domain Object (33) and Object/Relational Map (53) patterns.

- Consider isolating an entire set of Domain Object Factory implementations within a single middleware layer among other Layers (75).

- You can use Domain Object Factory in conjunction with Selection Factory (191) and Update Factory (215) to build a comprehensive domain object mapping solution.

- Domain Object Factory is a fundamental component of the framework that Domain Object Assembler (227) defines.

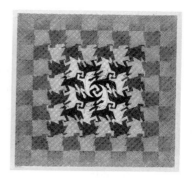

Update Factory

DESCRIPTION

Generates update operations based on modified domain object attributes.

CONTEXT

Still another function of domain object mappings is updating physical data based on new and changed domain object attributes. This is essentially the reverse of what Domain Object Factory (203) describes. Each domain object that an application references corresponds to one or more tables whose data must be updated when the analogous domain object's attributes change. In some cases, this operation is as simple as copying data directly from the domain object's attributes to tables. However, it is also common to require additional mapping and translation.

215

To illustrate a mapping from domain objects to physical data, revisit the vehicle inventory table. The VEHICLES table contains a row for every automobile that a dealer has available for sale and the dealer's applications use Vehicle objects to interact with it. Using Vehicle objects decouples the applications from the physical data model and data access details.

The domain object mapping is responsible for translating new and changed domain objects into update operations. In this discussion, an update means an operation that changes the contents of the physical database. In SQL, an update corresponds to either an INSERT or UPDATE operation, depending on whether the domain object is new or changed. In this example, the mapping inspects a domain object's attributes and creates an update that represents these attributes in terms of the VEHICLES table. Figure 12.1 illustrates this translation:

FIGURE 12.1: The domain object mapping uses a Vehicle object's attributes to create a corresponding update operation in terms of the VEHICLES table.

The Update Factory pattern describes a strategy for encapsulating the details of translating domain object changes to update operations using a single factory object. Since these details are likely to vary among different domain object types and target database entities, you can define factory objects for each translation type. Application and middleware code can utilize these factory objects at any time. Figure 12.2 illustrates Update Factory's role in domain object mapping:

FIGURE 12.2: An Update Factory maps domain objects to update operations.

APPLICABILITY

Use the Update Factory pattern when:

- You need to define a common infrastructure for translating domain object changes to updates as part of an overall domain object mapping strategy.

- You need to define customized mapping details for individual domain object types or database entities and hide these details from both applications and generic domain object mapping infrastructure code.

STRUCTURE

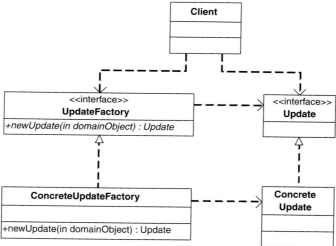

FIGURE 12.3: The static structure of the Update Factory pattern.

Figure 12.3 illustrates the static structure of the Update Factory pattern. The Update interface defines the update operation representation for your system and Concrete-Update implements it. If your domain object mapping interacts directly with a physical database that supports SQL, you can use string values to represent SQL INSERT and UPDATE operations. If you are using Layers (75) and your domain object mapping sits on top of a Data Accessor (9), then you can define an update operation representation that is independent of any specific database technology.

The UpdateFactory interface defines a single operation for generating a new Update object based on a domain object. ConcreteUpdateFactory implements this interface for a specific domain object type or target database entity. Your overall domain object mapping is likely to require multiple UpdateFactory implementations with customized mapping details encapsulated within each of them. Client code and generic domain object mapping infrastructure code refer only to the UpdateFactory and Update interfaces, keeping them decoupled from any specific mapping details.

INTERACTIONS

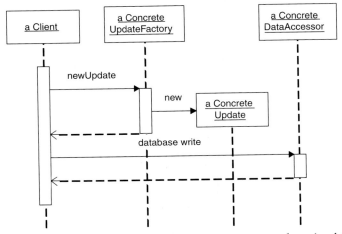

FIGURE 12.4: A client uses a ConcreteUpdateFactory to map a domain object to a ConcreteUpdate.

Figure 12.4 portrays what happens when a client requires a new update operation for a domain object. It passes the domain object to the ConcreteUpdateFactory's newUpdate operation. newUpdate returns a ConcreteUpdate, which the client can use to issue a database write operation.

CONSEQUENCES

The Update Factory pattern has the following benefits:

Benefits

- *Domain object mapping encapsulation*—An update factory encapsulates the translation of domain object changes that are defined using domain concepts to update operations that identify data using data model details. This enables effective decoupling of application code from the data model and data access components.

- *Isolation of domain object and database entity details*—Translation details vary for different domain object types and database entities. You can define a different update factory implementation for each type of translation, keeping them isolated from each other.

- *Consistent client interface*—Update Factory defines a consistent client interface that application and other middleware code can use generically, without requiring references to specific implementations. This enables you to plug in alternate implementations in later releases without requiring changes to client code.

STRATEGIES

An UpdateFactory implementation generates database update operations based on domain object attributes. A given implementation usually requires the client to pass a specific domain object type because it depends on its attribute values to build the appropriate update operation.

Some domain objects record attribute changes in addition to maintaining attribute values. UpdateFactory implementations can use this information to generate more granular update operations that include only the columns that correspond to changed attributes. Granular update operations only touch a precisely defined portion of a row and can reduce the frequency that concurrent update problems occur.

An UpdateFactory implementation's constructor often defines parameters for any information that it needs to create update operations but is not defined as domain object attributes. For example, an implementation may need to access a centralized web service that calculates the list price for an automobile. It is the responsibility of the code that initializes the UpdateFactory implementation to pass this service's connection information.

If you find that there are many similarities among UpdateFactory implementations and few exceptions, consider defining a generic implementation that handles mappings declaratively. A generic implementation can infer domain object mapping details based on a consistent convention of attribute, table, and column names. Alternately, it can reference mapping metadata stored in a configuration file or system database. This approach is also useful when you want to define new domain objects without writing additional mapping code.

SAMPLE CODE

The first interface in this example is UpdateFactory. This interface defines the semantics for all concrete UpdateFactory implementations. This example uses java.util.Map objects to represent update operations. Each Map instance contains the column names and values to be updated in terms of the physical data model.

You can use SQL SET clauses to represent update operations, but these only work for SQL UPDATE operations, and SQL UPDATE operations apply only when the data already exists in the database. However, you may want to issue SQL INSERT operations to handle writing data for the first time. SQL INSERT operations designate column values differently. Using a Map keeps the representation generic and enables common domain object mapping infrastructure code to generate the appropriate SQL operation depending on its knowledge of whether the data exists.

```
public interface UpdateFactory {

    /**
    Returns a Map that contains the column names
    and values to be updated based on the
    attributes of the specified domain object.
    */
    Map newUpdate(Object domainObject);

}
```

The "Context" section of this chapter introduced the Vehicle class. This class defines domain objects that correspond to rows in the VEHICLES table.

```
public class Vehicle {

    private String vin;
    private String color;
    private String make;
    private String model;
    private int year;
    private int price;

    public String getVin() {
```

```java
            return vin;
        }

    public void setVin(String vin) {
        this.vin = vin;
    }

    public String getColor() {
        return color;
    }

    public void setColor(String color) {
        this.color = color;
    }

    public String getMake() {
        return make;
    }

    public void setMake(String make) {
        this.make = make;
    }

    public String getModel() {
        return model;
    }

    public void setModel(String model) {
        this.model = model;
    }

    public int getYear() {
        return year;
    }

    public void setYear(int year) {
        this.year = year;
    }

    public int getPrice() {
        return price;
    }

    public void setPrice(int price) {
        this.price = price;
    }
}
```

VehicleUpdateFactory is an UpdateFactory implementation that generates update operations based on a Vehicle's attributes.

```
public class VehicleUpdateFactory
implements UpdateFactory {

    public Map newUpdate(Object domainObject) {
        Vehicle vehicle = (Vehicle)domainObject;

        Map update = new HashMap();
        update.put("VIN", vehicle.getVin());
        update.put("COLOR", vehicle.getColor());
        update.put("MAKE", vehicle.getMake());
        update.put("MODEL", vehicle.getModel());
        update.put("YEAR", new Integer(vehicle.getYear()));
        update.put("PRICE", new Integer(vehicle.getPrice()));

        return update;
    }
}
```

Next is some client code that initializes a VehicleUpdateFactory and uses it to generate an update operation that corresponds to a brand new Vehicle object. It builds the SQL INSERT operation and issues it using JDBC. Other than the initialization of the VehicleUpdateFactory and Vehicle objects, this code is generic and works the same for any UpdateFactory implementation.

```
// Initialize the update factory.
UpdateFactory updateFactory
    = new VehicleUpdateFactory();

// Create a new Vehicle domain object.
Vehicle vehicle = new Vehicle();
vehicle.setVin("NKWDE6764SD171396");
vehicle.setColor("Green");
vehicle.setMake("Honda");
vehicle.setModel("Accord");
vehicle.setYear(1994);
vehicle.setPrice(4500);

// Use the update factory to determine the
// updated column information for the new
// Vehicle domain object.
Map update = updateFactory.newUpdate(vehicle);

// Build the corresponding INSERT operation.
```

```
StringBuffer columnNames = new StringBuffer();
StringBuffer columnValues = new StringBuffer();
boolean firstExpression = true;
for(Iterator i = update.entrySet().iterator();i.hasNext();){
    Map.Entry entry = (Map.Entry)i.next();
    String columnName = (String)entry.getKey();
    Object columnValue = entry.getValue();

    if (firstExpression) {
        firstExpression = false;
    }
    else {
        columnNames.append(", ");
        columnValues.append(", ");
    }

    columnNames.append(columnName);
    if (!(columnValue instanceof Number))
        columnValues.append("'");
    columnValues.append(columnValue);
    if (!(columnValue instanceof Number))
        columnValues.append("'");
}

StringBuffer buffer = new StringBuffer();
buffer.append("INSERT INTO VEHICLES (");
buffer.append(columnNames);
buffer.append(") VALUES (");
buffer.append(columnValues);
buffer.append(")");

// Issue the INSERT operation.
statement.executeUpdate(buffer.toString());
```

Next is a similar client code example that changes the price of a Vehicle object that represents a car already stored in the database. This code uses the VehicleUpdateFactory to generate another update operation and builds and issues an analogous SQL UPDATE operation. Again, this code works with any UpdateFactory implementation.

```
// Change the domain object.
vehicle.setPrice(4100);

// Use the update factory to determine the
// updated column information for the changed
// Vehicle domain object.
Map update = updateFactory.newUpdate(vehicle);
```

```
// Build the corresponding UPDATE operation.
StringBuffer buffer = new StringBuffer();
buffer.append("UPDATE VEHICLES SET ");

boolean firstExpression = true;
for(Iterator i = update.entrySet().iterator();i.hasNext();){
    Map.Entry entry = (Map.Entry)i.next();
    String columnName = (String)entry.getKey();
    Object columnValue = entry.getValue();

    if (firstExpression)
        firstExpression = false;
    else
        buffer.append(", ");

    buffer.append(columnName);
    buffer.append(" = ");
    if (!(columnValue instanceof Number))
        buffer.append("'");
    buffer.append(columnValue);
    if (!(columnValue instanceof Number))
        buffer.append("'");
}

buffer.append("WHERE VIN = '");
buffer.append(vehicle.getVin());
buffer.append("'");

// Issue the UPDATE operation.
statement.executeUpdate(buffer.toString());
```

RELATED PATTERNS AND TECHNOLOGY

- Update Factory specializes Abstract Factory [Gamma 1995], which describes the generic application of factory interfaces.

- As an alternative to referencing a particular database technology, you can design Update and ConcreteUpdate using logical database concepts that are defined as part of a Data Accessor (9) implementation.

- Update Factory is useful for implementing Active Domain Object (33) and Object/Relational Map (53).

- Consider isolating an entire set of Update Factory implementations within a single middleware layer among other Layers (75).

- You can use Update Factory in conjunction with Selection Factory (191) and Domain Object Factory (203) to build a comprehensive domain object mapping solution.

- Update Factory is a fundamental component of the framework that Domain Object Assembler (227) defines.

Domain Object Assembler

DESCRIPTION

Populates, persists, and deletes domain objects using a uniform factory framework.

CONTEXT

Domain object mapping implementations, such as those described in Active Domain Object (33) and Object/Relational Map (53), define data access operations in terms of domain concepts. A domain object mapping enables you to decouple application logic that refers exclusively to domain objects from the underlying data model and data access details. As applications create new domain object instances and read their attributes, their domain object mapping imple-

227

mentations issue analogous database read operations. Similarly, when applications change domain object attributes, the mappings update the database accordingly.

Within the context of a domain object mapping implementation, input and output operations translate between domain objects and relational data in both directions. Here are some examples of input and output operations that a mapping implementation might provide:

- *Populate a domain object*—Populating a domain object entails finding the relevant data and creating a corresponding domain object instance. In data access terms, you need to issue one or more database read or query operations and copy their results into the attributes of a new domain object instance.

- *Persist a domain object*—Persisting a domain object involves inserting or updating a row of data corresponding to the domain object's attributes. To implement this, you need to issue the appropriate database insert or update operations, copying the domain object's attributes to their corresponding table columns.

- *Delete a domain object*—Deleting a domain object entails deleting the data that corresponds to a domain object instance. In data access terms, you need to issue the analogous database delete operations.

Selection Factory (191), Domain Object Factory (203), and Update Factory (215) describe factory interfaces that address isolated aspects of implementing domain object mapping operations. Each of these patterns succeeds in decoupling code that is specific to a particular combination of domain object type and database entity from generic domain object mapping infrastructure code.

The Domain Object Assembler pattern combines these factories into a fully functioning and customizable domain object mapping framework. A key feature of Domain Object Assembler is that it encapsulates the common mapping infrastructure within one component, while allowing you to plug in any combination of factory implementations that define specific mapping details. Figure 13.1 shows the relationship between an application, a domain object assembler, its factory implementations, and a physical database driver:

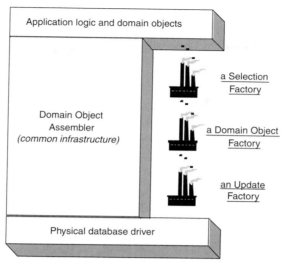

FIGURE 13.1: The relationship between an application, a domain object assembler, its factory implementations, and a physical database driver.

Domain Object Assembler defines a common, generic infrastructure for data access logic that promotes a consistent, reusable implementation for all domain object types and database entities. A domain object assembler acts as the access point for clients and hides all underlying mapping and data access details. It isolates common complexity, such as managing physical database resources, generating database operations, and incorporating caching and other optimization strategies.

This infrastructure employs factory implementations for any mapping aspects it can not handle generically. Consider the three domain object mapping operations described earlier. Populating a domain object requires finding the relevant data, creating the correct type of object, and setting its attributes. Domain Object Assembler's common infrastructure implements this by querying the database. It uses its selection factory to generate the appropriate query selection and its domain object factory to populate domain objects based on query results.

Persisting a domain object involves inserting or updating a row of data corresponding to the attributes of a domain object instance. Domain Object Assembler's common infrastructure implements this by issuing a database insert or update operation. It uses its update factory to generate the appropriate operation and its selection factory to select the rows in the database to update.

Deleting a domain object entails deleting the data that corresponds to a domain object instance. Domain Object Assembler's common infrastructure implements this by issuing a database delete operation and using its selection factory to select the rows in the database to delete.

In practice, the code required to implement each factory interface is small and focused, while Domain Object Assembler's common infrastructure isolates the majority of the mapping complexity in one place.

APPLICABILITY

Use the Domain Object Assembler pattern when:

- You need to define a common domain object mapping infrastructure that is responsible for populating, persisting, and deleting domain objects.

- You need to define customized mapping details for individual domain object types or database entities and decouple these details from both applications and generic domain object infrastructure code.

STRUCTURE

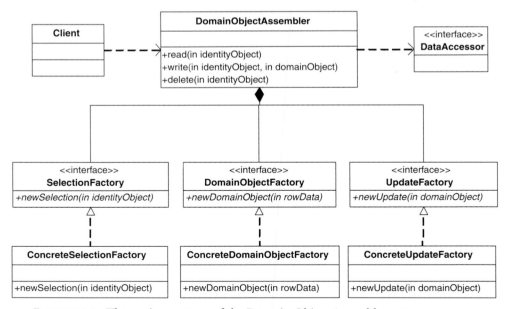

FIGURE 13.2: The static structure of the Domain Object Assembler pattern.

Figure 13.2 illustrates the static structure of the Domain Object Assembler pattern. The DomainObjectAssembler class defines the entry point for all domain object mapping operations. Client code uses a DomainObjectAssembler instance to initiate read, write, and delete operations. DomainObjectAssembler implements the majority of the common, generic implementation for these operations.

DomainObjectAssembler references a set of pluggable factories that it uses to delegate any implementation features that are specific to a particular domain object type or database entity. SelectionFactory, DomainObjectFactory, and UpdateFactory define these factories generically, while concrete factory implementations fill in the details at runtime. See each respective pattern definition, Selection Factory (191), Domain Object Factory (203), and Update Factory (215), for more details.

DomainObjectAssembler manages all direct database interaction. Figure 13.2 shows this as a relationship with a DataAccessor. The DataAccessor can either be a physical database driver or a Data Accessor (9) instance that defines database operations using logical concepts that are independent of any particular database technology.

This pattern defines a clear decoupling between generic domain object mapping infrastructure code and that which is specific to a particular domain object type or database entity. DomainObjectAssembler is responsible for generic infrastructure code like database resource management, SQL statement generation, and simple data translation, while concrete factory implementations facilitate customization. Isolating common code within a single component makes it more amenable to incorporating new features and optimizations that apply to all mapping types. At the same time, adding a new set of custom factory implementations requires minimal effort, especially for straightforward translations.

INTERACTIONS

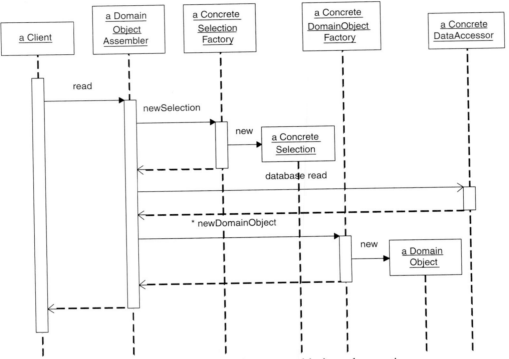

FIGURE 13.3: A client calls a DomainObjectAssembler's read operation.

Figure 13.3 portrays what happens when a client calls a DomainObjectAssembler's read operation. The DomainObjectAssembler uses its assigned SelectionFactory implementation to create a Selection based on the input identity object. The DomainObjectAssembler issues a database read operation and passes each row of result set data to its DomainObjectFactory implementation, which instantiates of set of new domain objects based on this data. Finally, the DomainObjectAssembler returns these domain objects to the client.

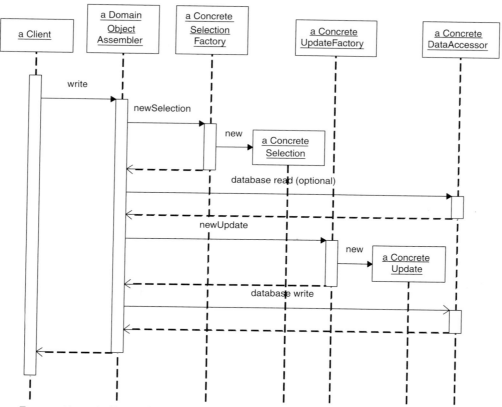

FIGURE 13.4: A client calls a DomainObjectAssembler's write operation.

Figure 13.4 illustrates the sequence of operations that occurs when a client calls a DomainObjectAssembler's write operation. First, the DomainObjectAssembler uses its assigned SelectionFactory implementation to create a Selection based on the input identity object. This Selection identifies the existing rows to be updated, if any.

Some DomainObjectAssembler implementations need to query the database at this point to determine whether the corresponding physical data already exists. This is necessary to decide which type of database write operation to issue, an insert or an update. However, this additional read operation can measurably degrade performance. Incorporating a persistence state flag in every domain object can circumvent the requirement for this operation. When a DomainObjectAssembler populates a domain object, it sets this flag to indicate that the domain object does indeed have corresponding physical data. On the other hand, when applications create new domain objects, they do not set this flag.

Finally, the DomainObjectAssembler uses its UpdateFactory implementation to create an Update object based on the input domain object's changed attributes. It issues a database write operation to ensure that the physical data reflects these changes.

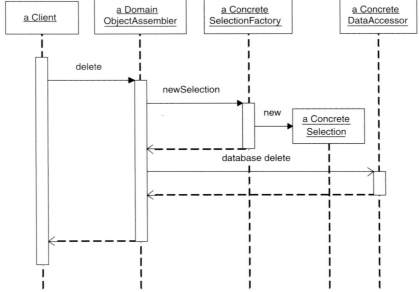

FIGURE 13.5: A client calls a DomainObjectAssembler's delete operation.

Figure 13.5 shows a client calling a DomainObjectAssembler's delete operation. Again, the DomainObjectAssembler uses its SelectionFactory implementation to create a Selection based on the input identity object. This time, it issues a database delete operation, which ensures that the corresponding physical data no longer exists.

CONSEQUENCES

The Domain Object Assembler pattern has the following benefits:

Benefits

- *Exposure to persistence operations using domain concepts*—Domain Object Assembler hides domain object mapping operations behind abstract primitive operations. These operations enable applications to interact with their data using only domain concepts.

- *Isolation of common mapping infrastructure*—Domain Object Assembler encapsulates domain object mapping within a single component. It isolates common, generic infrastructure code that encourages the incorporation of new features and optimizations that apply immediately to all domain object types and database entities.

- *Isolation of domain object and database entity details*—Mapping details vary for different domain object types and database entities. You can define a different set of factory implementations for each type of translation, keeping them isolated from each other and the generic domain object mapping infrastructure code.

STRATEGIES

Domain Object Assembler dictates a strict decoupling between common, generic domain object mapping infrastructure code and that which applies only to specific domain object types or database entities. The DomainObjectAssembler class contains the majority of the common infrastructure code such as database resource management, SQL statement generation, and default data translation. It relies on factory implementations for any specific, customizable details.

You do not need to create a subclass of DomainObjectAssembler to map a specific domain object type. Instead, you define implementations of its three factory interfaces, SelectionFactory, DomainObjectFactory, and UpdateFactory, and plug instances of these factory implementations into a new DomainObjectAssembler when you initialize it. This pluggability style is usually effective, since the overall set of factory implementations that an application requires is not likely to change at runtime.

It is common for applications to read data frequently without ever needing to write it. This is especially true for configuration and system control tables that are only updated by administration console applications. To accommodate read-only data like this, you can define DomainObjectAssembler to allow the UpdateFactory implementation to be optional. If a client does not plug in an UpdateFactory implementation, then the DomainObjectAssembler disables its write and delete operations.

The generic nature of the DomainObjectAssembler class circumvents compile-time type checking to some extent. For example, a client can initialize a Domain-ObjectAssembler with an inconsistent set of factory implementations. Clients can also pass identity or domain object types that are different from what factory implementations expect. A straightforward solution to problems like these is to create small wrapper classes that manage single DomainObjectAssembler instances along with a valid combination of concrete factory implementations. These wrappers encapsulate a significant amount of the DomainObjectAssembler's initialization complexity, enforce type checking, and handle casting for specific identity and domain object types.

SAMPLE CODE

The first set of classes in this example defines the generic infrastructure portion of a domain object mapping implementation that is based on Domain Object Assembler. The DomainObjectAssembler class implements its mapping in terms of the factory interfaces introduced in the "Sample Code" sections of the Selection Factory (191), Domain Object Factory (203), and Update Factory (215) patterns.

In this example, DomainObjectAssembler interacts directly with the database using a JDBC Connection. It represents selections using SQL WHERE clause strings and update operations using java.util.Map objects that contain the names and values of columns to update.

When a client initializes a DomainObjectAssembler object, it is responsible for plugging in specific factory implementations, a database connection, and the name of the table where the physical data resides. The constructor stores private references to each of these values.

```
public class DomainObjectAssembler {

    private Connection connection;
```

```
private String tableName;
private SelectionFactory selectionFactory;
private DomainObjectFactory domainObjectFactory;
private UpdateFactory updateFactory;

/**
Constructs a new DomainObjectAssembler object.
This assigns all the factory implementations.
*/
public DomainObjectAssembler(
    Connection connection,
    String tableName,
    SelectionFactory selectionFactory,
    DomainObjectFactory domainObjectFactory,
    UpdateFactory updateFactory) {

    this.connection = connection;
    this.tableName = tableName;
    this.selectionFactory = selectionFactory;
    this.domainObjectFactory = domainObjectFactory;
    this.updateFactory = updateFactory;
}
```

DomainObjectAssembler exposes its domain object mapping capabilities using three public operations: read, write, and delete. Each of these operations' implementations use assigned factory implementations to resolve any information that might be specific to a particular domain object type or database entity being mapped.

```
/**
Reads all domain objects that correspond to
the specified identity object.  This returns
an empty list if there are none.
*/
public List read(Object identityObject)
    throws DomainObjectException {

    try {
        List domainObjects = new LinkedList();

        // Issue the query for rows that match the
        // specified identity object.
        Statement statement
            = connection.createStatement();
        ResultSet resultSet
            = issueQuery(statement, identityObject);
```

```
                      // Iterate through the result set and create
                      // a new domain object for each row.
                      while (resultSet.next()) {

                          // Get the row data and build it into a Map
                          // suitable for the domain object factory.
                          Map rowData = new HashMap();
                          ResultSetMetaData rsmd
                              = resultSet.getMetaData();
                          int columnCount = rsmd.getColumnCount();
                          for(int i = 1; i <= columnCount; ++i) {
                              rowData.put(rsmd.getColumnName(i),
                                          resultSet.getObject(i));
                          }

                          // Use the domain object factory to create
                          // and populate a new domain object based
                          // on the row data.
                          Object domainObject
                              = domainObjectFactory
                              .newDomainObject(rowData);
                          domainObjects.add(domainObject);
                      }

                      // Close the database resources.
                      resultSet.close();
                      statement.close();

                      return domainObjects;
                  }
                  catch(SQLException e) {
                      throw new DomainObjectException(e);
                  }
          }

          /**
          Writes a domain object that corresponds to
          the specified identity object.
          */
          public void write(Object identityObject,
                            Object domainObject)
                            throws DomainObjectException {
                  try {

                      // Query the table to see if any existing rows
                      // match the specified identity object.  This
                      // fact helps to determine whether an insert or
                      // update operation is in order.
                      Statement statement
```

```
                = connection.createStatement();
            ResultSet resultSet
                = issueQuery(statement, identityObject);
            boolean rowExists = resultSet.next();
            resultSet.close();

            // If a row exists, then issue an update
            // operation.  Otherwise, issue an insert
            // operation.
            if (rowExists) {
                issueUpdate(statement,
                            identityObject,
                            domainObject);
            }
            else {
                issueInsert(statement,
                            domainObject);
            }

            // Close the database resource.
            statement.close();
        }
        catch(SQLException e) {
            throw new DomainObjectException(e);
        }
    }

    /**
    Deletes any domain objects that correspond to
    the specified identity object.
    */
    public void delete(Object identityObject)
        throws DomainObjectException {

        try {
            Statement statement
                = connection.createStatement();
            issueDelete(statement, identityObject);

            // Close the database resource.
            statement.close();
        }
        catch(SQLException e) {
            throw new DomainObjectException(e);
        }
    }
```

DomainObjectAssembler's last three private operations are responsible for generating SQL operations and sending them to the JDBC Connection.

```
/**
Queries the table for rows that match the
specified identity object.  It is the caller's
responsibility to close the returned result set.
*/
private ResultSet issueQuery(Statement statement,
                             Object identityObject)
                             throws SQLException {

    // Use the selection factory to generate the
    // selection.
    String selection
        = selectionFactory
        .newSelection(identityObject);

    // Generate the query operation.
    StringBuffer buffer = new StringBuffer();
    buffer.append("SELECT * FROM ");
    buffer.append(tableName);
    if (selection.length() > 0) {
        buffer.append(" WHERE ");
        buffer.append(selection);
    }

    // Issue the query operation.
    return statement.executeQuery(buffer.toString());
}

/**
Updates the rows that match the specified
identity object using the attributes from
the specified domain object.
*/
private void issueUpdate(Statement statement,
                         Object identityObject,
                         Object domainObject)
                         throws SQLException {

    // Use the selection factory to generate the
    // selection.
    String selection
        = selectionFactory
        .newSelection(identityObject);

    // Use the update factory to generate the
```

```
            // update.
            Map update = updateFactory.newUpdate(domainObject);

            // Generate the update operation.
            StringBuffer buffer = new StringBuffer();
            buffer.append("UPDATE ");
            buffer.append(tableName);
            buffer.append(" SET ");
            for(Iterator i = update.entrySet().iterator();
                i.hasNext(); ) {

                Map.Entry mapEntry = (Map.Entry)i.next();
                String columnName = (String)mapEntry.getKey();
                buffer.append(mapEntry.getKey());
                buffer.append(" = ");
                Object columnValue = mapEntry.getValue();
                if (!(columnValue instanceof Number))
                    buffer.append("'");
                buffer.append(columnValue);
                if (!(columnValue instanceof Number))
                    buffer.append("'");
                if (i.hasNext())
                    buffer.append(", ");
            }

        if (selection.length() > 0) {
            buffer.append(" WHERE ");
            buffer.append(selection);
        }

        // Issue the update operation.
        statement.executeUpdate(buffer.toString());
    }

    /**
    Inserts a new row using the attributes of the
    specified domain object.
    */
    private void issueInsert(Statement statement,
                             Object domainObject)
                             throws SQLException {

        // Use the update factory to generate the
        // update.
        Map update = updateFactory.newUpdate(domainObject);

        // Generate the insert operation.
        StringBuffer buffer = new StringBuffer();
        buffer.append("INSERT INTO ");
```

```
        buffer.append(tableName);
        buffer.append(" (");
        Set columnNames = update.keySet();
        for(Iterator i=columnNames.iterator();i.hasNext();) {
            buffer.append(i.next()); // The column name.
            if (i.hasNext())
                buffer.append(",");
        }
        buffer.append(") VALUES (");
        for(Iterator i=columnNames.iterator();i.hasNext();) {
            Object columnValue = update.get(i.next());
            if (!(columnValue instanceof Number))
                buffer.append("'");
            buffer.append(columnValue);
            if (!(columnValue instanceof Number))
                buffer.append("'");
            if (i.hasNext())
                buffer.append(", ");
        }
        buffer.append(")");

        // Issue the insert operation.
        statement.executeUpdate(buffer.toString());
    }

    /**
    Deletes the rows that match the specified
    identity object.
    */
    private void issueDelete(Statement statement,
                             Object identityObject)
                             throws SQLException {

        // Use the selection factory to generate the
        // selection.
        String selection
            = selectionFactory
            .newSelection(identityObject);

        // Generate the delete operation.
        StringBuffer buffer = new StringBuffer();
        buffer.append("DELETE FROM ");
        buffer.append(tableName);
        if (selection.length() > 0) {
            buffer.append(" WHERE ");
            buffer.append(selection);
        }

        // Issue the delete operation.
```

```
        statement.executeUpdate(buffer.toString());
    }
}
```

DomainObjectException defines a specific exception type that indicates domain object mapping errors. For simplicity, it contains only a chained cause exception, but in practice, you can add more information to it such as the domain object and database entity being mapped.

```
public class DomainObjectException
extends Exception {

    DomainObjectException(Throwable cause) {
        super(cause);
    }
}
```

All the sample code up to this point has been generic. It works entirely in terms of the SelectionFactory, DomainObjectFactory, and UpdateFactory interfaces and does not make any reference to domain object types or database entities. The next set of classes define the mapping details for a specific domain object type.

Consider a table that maintains direct deposit account information. This table, DIRECT_DEPOSIT_ACCOUNTS, is part of an extensive company payroll database. Since employees can designate multiple bank accounts for direct deposit of their paychecks, this table can contain multiple rows for each employee. The employee identifier and account identifier columns make up the table's primary key. The remaining columns contain the necessary details for the company to automatically transfer payments to each account.

DirectDepositAccount defines the primary domain object for this example. Each DirectDepositAccount instance corresponds to a row of data in the DIRECT_DEPOSIT_ACCOUNTS table. There is also a DirectDepositAccountKey class whose instances correspond to the primary key values for the table. DirectDepositAccountKey acts as the identity object for this example. Any payroll application can use a DirectDepositAccountKey object to identify a specific account. Figure 13.6 illustrates how the domain object mapping is responsible for translating between DirectDepositAccount and DirectDepositAccountKey objects and the data in the DIRECT_DEPOSIT_ACCOUNTS table:

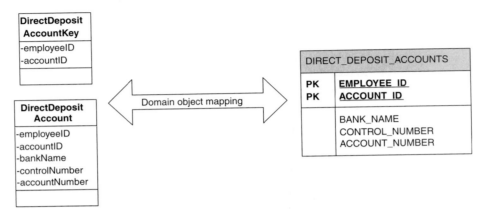

FIGURE 13.6: The domain object mapping is responsible for translating between DirectDepositAccount and DirectDepositAccountKey objects and data in the DIRECT_DEPOSIT_ACCOUNTS table.

This is the source code for these domain object classes:

```
public class DirectDepositAccountKey {

    private String employeeID;
    private String accountID;

    public DirectDepositAccountKey(String employeeID,
                                          String accountID) {
        this.employeeID = employeeID;
        this.accountID = accountID;
    }

    public String getEmployeeID() {
        return employeeID;
    }

    public String getAccountID() {
        return accountID;
    }
}

public class DirectDepositAccount {

    private String employeeID;
    private String accountID;
    private String bankName;
    private String controlNumber;
    private String accountNumber;
```

```
public String getEmployeeID() {
    return employeeID;
}

public void setEmployeeID(String employeeID) {
    this.employeeID = employeeID;
}

public String getAccountID() {
    return accountID;
}

public void setAccountID(String accountID) {
    this.accountID = accountID;
}

public String getBankName() {
    return bankName;
}

public void setBankName(String bankName) {
    this.bankName = bankName;
}

public String getControlNumber() {
    return controlNumber;
}

public void setControlNumber(String controlNumber) {
    this.controlNumber = controlNumber;
}

public String getAccountNumber() {
    return accountNumber;
}

public void setAccountNumber(String accountNumber) {
    this.accountNumber = accountNumber;
}
}
```

The next three classes define the factory implementations that plug into a DomainObjectAssembler instance to customize it for mapping DirectDepositAccount and DirectDepositAccountKey objects to the contents of the DIRECT_DEPOSIT_ACCOUNTS table. Together, these classes make up a single extension of the DomainObjectAssembler's framework. Figure 13.7 shows the relationship between these extension classes and the rest of the framework. As you examine the source code for these classes, notice that they are small, focused, and contain precisely the details that apply to mapping DirectDepositAccount domain objects.

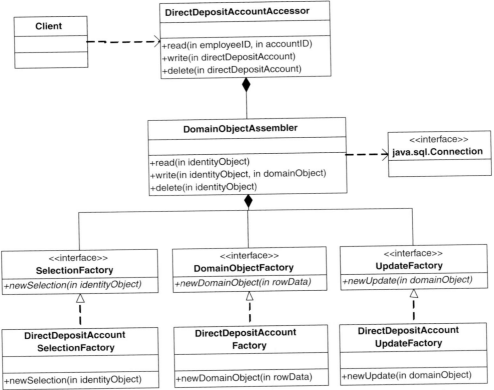

FIGURE 13.7: The relationship between the DirectDepositAccount factory implementations and the rest of the DomainObjectAssembler framework.

DirectDepositAccountSelectionFactory implements SelectionFactory and is responsible for translating a DirectDepositAccountKey identity object to a physical selection in the form of a SQL WHERE clause string:

```
public class DirectDepositAccountSelectionFactory
implements SelectionFactory {

    /**
    Returns a SQL WHERE clause that selects
    data that corresponds to the identity
    object.
```

```
      */
      public String newSelection(Object identityObject) {
          DirectDepositAccountKey directDepositAccountKey
              = (DirectDepositAccountKey)identityObject;

          StringBuffer buffer = new StringBuffer();
          buffer.append("EMPLOYEE_ID = '");
          buffer.append(
              directDepositAccountKey.getEmployeeID());
          buffer.append("' AND ACCOUNT_ID = '");
          buffer.append(
              directDepositAccountKey.getAccountID());
          buffer.append("'");
          return buffer.toString();
      }

  }
```

DirectDepositAccountFactory implements DomainObjectFactory and is responsible for translating a row of data from the DIRECT_DEPOSIT_ACCOUNTS table to a new DirectDepositAccount domain object. It also maintains a list of columns that it requires for populating new domain objects.

```
  public class DirectDepositAccountFactory
  implements DomainObjectFactory {

      /**
      Creates and returns a new domain object
      that corresponds to the contents of a
      single row from database query results.
      */
      public Object newDomainObject(Map rowData) {

          String employeeID
              = (String)rowData.get("EMPLOYEE_ID");
          String accountID
              = (String)rowData.get("ACCOUNT_ID");
          String bankName
              = (String)rowData.get("BANK_NAME");
          String controlNumber
              = (String)rowData.get("CONTROL_NUMBER");
          String accountNumber
              = (String)rowData.get("ACCOUNT_NUMBER");

          DirectDepositAccount directDepositAccount
              = new DirectDepositAccount();
          directDepositAccount.setEmployeeID(employeeID);
```

```
        directDepositAccount.setAccountID(accountID);
        directDepositAccount.setBankName(bankName);
        directDepositAccount.setControlNumber(controlNumber);
        directDepositAccount.setAccountNumber(accountNumber);
        return directDepositAccount;
    }

    /**
    Returns an array of column names that
    this factory expects to see in the
    row data that gets passed to
    newDomainObject.
    */
    public String[] getColumnNames() {
        return COLUMN_NAMES;
    }

    private static final String[] COLUMN_NAMES
        = { "EMPLOYEE_ID", "ACCOUNT_ID", "BANK_NAME",
            "CONTROL_NUMBER", "ACCOUNT_NUMBER" };
}
```

DirectDepositAccountUpdateFactory is an UpdateFactory implementation that is responsible for generating a map of column name and value pairs that represents the domain object's attributes in terms of the DIRECT_DEPOSIT_ACCOUNTS table's columns:

```
public class DirectDepositAccountUpdateFactory
implements UpdateFactory {

    /**
    Returns a map that contains the column names
    and values to be updated based on the
    attributes of the specified domain object.
    */
    public Map newUpdate(Object value)
    {
        DirectDepositAccount directDepositAccount
            = (DirectDepositAccount)value;

        Map update = new HashMap();
        update.put("EMPLOYEE_ID",
            directDepositAccount.getEmployeeID());
        update.put("ACCOUNT_ID",
            directDepositAccount.getAccountID());
        update.put("BANK_NAME",
            directDepositAccount.getBankName());
```

```
        update.put("CONTROL_NUMBER",
            directDepositAccount.getControlNumber());
        update.put("ACCOUNT_NUMBER",
            directDepositAccount.getAccountNumber());

        return update;
    }

}
```

DomainObjectAssembler's operations define generic parameters and return value types that circumvent compile-time type checking. This exposes opportunities for runtime errors caused by clients passing incorrect types of identity objects or plugging in inconsistent factory implementations. DirectDepositAccountAccessor is a wrapper that manages a DomainObjectAssembler instance and its concrete factory implementations. This wrapper encapsulates a significant amount of the DomainObjectAssembler's initialization complexity and handles casting for specific identity and domain object types.

```
public class DirectDepositAccountAccessor {

    private Connection connection;
    private DomainObjectAssembler domainObjectAssembler;

    /**
    Constructs a DirectDepositAccountAccessor
    object.
    */
    public DirectDepositAccountAccessor()
        throws DomainObjectException {

        // Initialize the JDBC connection.
        try {
            connection = ...;
        }
        catch(SQLException e) {
            throw new DomainObjectException(e);
        }

        SelectionFactory selectionFactory
            = new DirectDepositAccountSelectionFactory();
        DomainObjectFactory domainObjectFactory
            = new DirectDepositAccountFactory();
        UpdateFactory updateFactory
            = new DirectDepositAccountUpdateFactory();
```

```
        domainObjectAssembler = new DomainObjectAssembler(
            connection,
            "DIRECT_DEPOSIT_ACCOUNTS",
            selectionFactory,
            domainObjectFactory,
            updateFactory);
    }

    /**
    Reads a DirectDepositAccount object from
    the database.
    */
    public DirectDepositAccount read(
        String employeeID,
        String accountID)
        throws DomainObjectException {

        DirectDepositAccountKey directDepositAccountKey
            = new DirectDepositAccountKey(
            employeeID, accountID);

        List directDepositAccounts
            = domainObjectAssembler.read(
            directDepositAccountKey);

        if (directDepositAccounts.size() == 0) {
            return null;
        }
        else {
            return (DirectDepositAccount)
                directDepositAccounts.get(0);
        }
    }

    /**
    Writes a DirectDepositAccount object to
    the database.
    */
    public void write(
        DirectDepositAccount directDepositAccount)
        throws DomainObjectException {

        DirectDepositAccountKey directDepositAccountKey
            = new DirectDepositAccountKey(
            directDepositAccount.getEmployeeID(),
            directDepositAccount.getAccountID());

        domainObjectAssembler.write(
            directDepositAccountKey,
```

```
            directDepositAccount);
    }

    /**
    Deletes a DirectDepositAccount object from
    the database.
    */
    public void delete(
        DirectDepositAccount directDepositAccount)
        throws DomainObjectException {

        DirectDepositAccountKey directDepositAccountKey
            = new DirectDepositAccountKey(
            directDepositAccount.getEmployeeID(),
            directDepositAccount.getAccountID());

        domainObjectAssembler.delete(directDepositAccountKey);
    }

}
```

The next set of code blocks illustrates sample application code that uses a DirectDepositAccountAccessor. The first block initializes a DirectDepositAccount-Accessor instance and uses it to write a new DirectDepositAccount to the database:

```
DirectDepositAccountAccessor directDepositAccountAccessor
    = new DirectDepositAccountAccessor();

DirectDepositAccount directDepositAccount
    = new DirectDepositAccount();
directDepositAccount.setEmployeeID("C001");
directDepositAccount.setAccountID("A001");
directDepositAccount.setBankName("National Bank");
directDepositAccount.setControlNumber("123456789");
directDepositAccount.setAccountNumber("44332");
directDepositAccountAccessor.write(directDepositAccount);
```

The next block shows how an application reads an existing DirectDepositAccount from the database:

```
DirectDepositAccount anotherDirectDepositAccount
    = directDepositAccountAccessor.read("C002", "A002");
```

Next, the application changes the bank name for a DirectDepositAccount, and writes it back to the database:

```
anotherDirectDepositAccount.setBankName("State Bank");
directDepositAccountAccessor.write(
    anotherDirectDepositAccount);
```

Finally, the application deletes a DirectDepositAccount object from the database:

```
directDepositAccountAccessor.delete(directDepositAccount);
```

RELATED PATTERNS AND TECHNOLOGY

- Domain Object Assembler addresses the same issues as Table Data Gateway [Fowler 2002] and Data Mapper [Fowler 2002], but implements the details using a common framework.

- As an alternative to referencing a particular database technology, you can define Domain Object Assembler's database interaction in terms of a Data Accessor (9) implementation.

- Domain Object Assembler is useful for implementing Active Domain Object (33) and Object/Relational Map (53).

- Consider isolating Domain Object Assembler and its related factory implementations within a single middleware layer among other Layers (75).

- Domain Object Assembler incorporates Selection Factory (191), Domain Object Factory (227), and Update Factory (215) for plugging in customized mapping details that apply to a particular domain object type and database entity.

- Paging Iterator (253) works well for managing collections of domain objects that correspond to database query results. You can incorporate this into Domain Object Assembler's generic infrastructure code.

- Cache Accessor (271) describes a caching framework that you can incorporate within a Domain Object Assembler's generic infrastructure code.

Paging Iterator

DESCRIPTION

Iterates efficiently through a collection of domain objects that represents query results.

CONTEXT

When an application issues an arbitrary query based on search criteria that its users define, it generally has no expectation of the number of matching results. It is common for web interfaces that access enterprise data to incorporate extensive searching capabilities that can match any number of database entries.

Recall the vehicle information database that the "Context" section for the Selection Factory pattern 191 introduced. Consider a web application that includes a search form that enables potential customers to enter a variety of search criteria

253

such as a car's make, model, and price range. Buyers who know exactly what they are looking for enter specific criteria that matches only a small number of cars. Casual shoppers might enter fewer, broader criteria that return hundreds of results.

When a potential customer clicks the form's "Submit" button, the web application issues a database query operation that corresponds to the search criteria entered. Most relational database drivers return an object that represents a result set *cursor*. A cursor points to the current position within query results that are stored in the database. Applications use cursors to fetch and process query results.

The application can fetch all results immediately and store them in memory until the user requests them. When the result set is large, this strategy consumes a significant quantity of resources, both in terms of primary storage and network communication with the database. Consider how customers are likely to deal with hundreds of matching cars. They only study the details for a few of them, particularly those presented on the first or second pages, and discard the rest. When this happens, the application processes a lot of unnecessary data.

The other extreme is for the application to fetch a single result row at a time. Every fetch requires network communication between the application and the database. With a large number of concurrent users, these frequent database interactions can noticeably degrade the application's response time.

The Paging Iterator pattern describes a solution that optimizes the resources that an application uses to retrieve result set data. The primary idea is to fetch results in pages of a predefined size. A page of result set data contains a small number of rows and often corresponds to the number of rows that the application processes or presents in its user interface at one time. Paging Iterator strives to compromise between storing an entire result set in memory and incurring frequent database communication overhead. An application only keeps a page of result set data in memory at a time and only requires database interaction to fetch subsequent pages.

Another feature of Paging Iterator is that it incorporates domain object mapping into its paging functionality. A page represents a subset of the result set data, but exposes this data using domain objects. It does this in a manner similar to Domain Object Assembler (227). It encapsulates the common paging infrastructure within one component while allowing you to plug in any Domain Object Factory (203) implementation that defines specific mapping details. Figure 14.1 shows the relationship between an application, a paging iterator, its domain object factory, and a physical database driver. The common paging infrastructure employs the domain object factory for any mapping aspects it cannot handle generically.

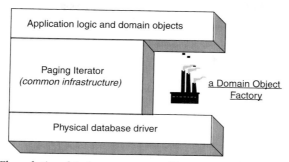

FIGURE 14.1: The relationship between an application, a paging iterator, its domain object factory, and a physical database driver.

APPLICABILITY

Use the Paging Iterator pattern when:

- You need to define a common infrastructure for fetching and iterating through a list of domain objects that corresponds to a set of query results.

- Entire result sets are potentially too large to store efficiently in memory or transmit across the network at one time.

- Entire result sets are potentially too large to efficiently transmit across the network one row at a time.

- Your application presents query results to users in small subsets or pages. Users can choose to view additional pages using interface controls.

- You need to define customized mapping details for individual domain object types or database entities and decouple these details from both applications and generic iteration infrastructure code.

STRUCTURE

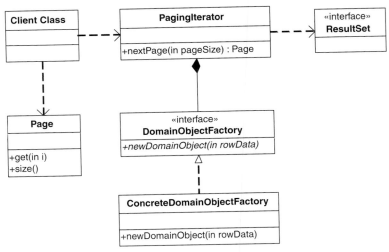

FIGURE 14.2: The static structure of the Paging Iterator pattern.

Figure 14.2 illustrates the static structure of the Paging Iterator pattern. The PagingIterator class defines the entry point for all paging and domain object mapping operations. Client code uses a PagingIterator instance to fetch a page of data from query results stored in the database. PagingIterator implements the majority of the common, generic implementation for this result set interaction.

PagingIterator returns Page objects to clients. A Page object contains zero or more domain objects, each of which corresponds to a row in the physical result set. Figure 14.2 shows a Page object exposing operations to determine its size and retrieve individual domain objects from it. In practice, it is just as effective to use a simple array or domain object list to represent a page.

This pattern defines a clear decoupling between generic iteration infrastructure code and that which is specific to a particular domain object type or database entity. PagingIterator references a pluggable factory that it uses to delegate mapping responsibilities that are specific to a particular domain object type or database entity. DomainObjectFactory defines the semantics for this delegation relationship while concrete implementations fill in the details at runtime. See the Domain Object Factory pattern (203) for more details.

PagingIterator manages all direct result set interaction. The result set can either be a physical result set returned from a database driver or a logical set of results that is defined as part of a Data Accessor (9) instance and is independent of any particular database technology.

INTERACTIONS

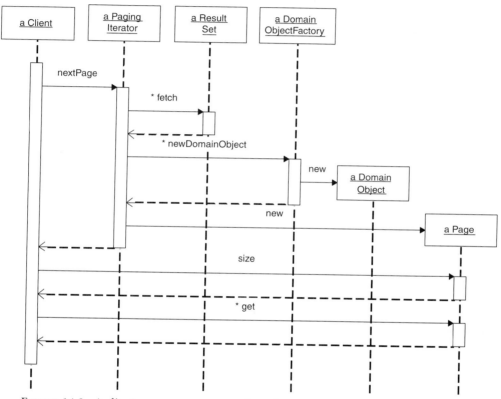

FIGURE 14.3: A client processes query results using a PagingIterator.

Figure 14.3 portrays what happens when a client processes query results using a PagingIterator. The client calls the nextPage operation, indicating how many domain objects to retrieve. This quantity is called the page size. The PagingIterator fetches this quantity of rows from the physical result set. It passes each of these rows to its assigned DomainObjectFactory implementation, which in turn creates domain objects. The PagingIterator stores these objects in a new Page object and returns the Page object to the client.

The client calls the Page object's size operation to determine how many rows the Page object contains and repeatedly calls get to retrieve its contents.

CONSEQUENCES

The Paging Iterator pattern has the following consequences:

Benefits

- *Reduced storage requirements*—Paging Iterator stores only a page of query results in memory at a time. A page often corresponds to the subset of data that an application presents to the user on a single panel or form. This subset is presumably much smaller than the size of the complete result set. When the user requests more data, Paging Iterator can usually discard the current page to make room for the next page.

- *Reduced network requirements*—Nearly every physical database interaction requires communication to the database using network resources. Retrieving a page of data with a single call is often significantly faster than fetching the same set of data one row at a time.

  In addition, Paging Iterator fetches only the data that an application presents to the user. It does not consume network and database resources retrieving data the user does not request. If an application task ends without fetching all the results, it has not incurred the overhead that retrieving potentially large result sets would require.

Drawbacks

- *Additional client complexity*—Paging Iterator imposes paging semantics on the client. Processing query results by page is more complicated than processing one row at a time.

- *Resource utilization and concurrency*—Paging Iterator interacts with a result set that the physical database manages. The result set maintains the underlying cursor that indicates the current row within the entire set of query results. To anticipate requests for subsequent pages, the result set must keep this cursor open and pointing to the first row of the next page. This consumes database resources and may also lock the affected rows depending on the database's transaction implementation and current transaction isolation level. This locking can reduce scalability for applications that access data concurrently from multiple sessions.

STRATEGIES

Consider these strategies when implementing the Paging Iterator pattern:

- *Extending the PagingIterator class to map a specific domain object type*—The Paging Iterator pattern dictates a strict decoupling between common iterator infrastructure code that applies only to specific domain object types or database entities. The PagingIterator class contains the majority of the common infrastructure code such as the result set interaction logic. It relies on DomainObjectFactory implementations for any specific, customizable domain object mapping details.

  You do not need to create a subclass of PagingIterator to map a specific domain object type. Instead, define a DomainObjectFactory implementation and plug an instance into a new PagingIterator when you initialize it.

- *Indicating the last page*—When you implement the Paging Iterator pattern, you must define and document a semantic for indicating the last page to clients. If applications use this indication primarily for signalling when to stop requesting more results, it is sufficient for PagingIterator to return an empty or incomplete page or a null value when there are no more results available.

  However, some applications also use this indication when they present data in a user interface. For example, web applications often display a "Next" button that enables users to view the next page of data. However, when there is no more data, this button should be hidden. If your applications require this, you can attach a flag to each Page object that indicates whether or not it contains the last set of result data.

- *Closing database resources*—The PagingIterator object is the best candidate for the responsibility of closing underlying database resources because it already encapsulates all other interactions with the physical result set. It also understands when it has returned the final set of results and can close the resources at that time.

  In the common case where a client stops fetching pages before reading all of the results, it is still important to ensure that resources get closed. One way is to require clients to close PagingIterators when they are finished using them. Another is to incorporate timers that close result sets after a designated period of inactivity. See the Resource Timer pattern (137) for details on implementing timers.

- *Setting the result set fetch size*—The result set semantics that many call level interfaces define only let you fetch a single row at a time. However, many also provide a mechanism to set the result set fetch size. This setting enables you to offer a suggestion to database drivers that designates how many rows to fetch at a time. Database drivers that honor this suggestion fetch pages of rows and buffer them transparently.

- *Supplying scrollable paging iterators*—The structure that this pattern describes exposes forward-only fetch semantics. In some cases, it is useful to provide other fetch options as well. For example, scrollability enables interactive applications to fetch previous pages or jump ahead arbitrarily in the result set. Implementing a scrollable paging iterator usually requires that the underlying database to support scrollable cursors.

SAMPLE CODE

The first class in this example defines the generic infrastructure portion of a Paging Iterator implementation. The PagingIterator class interacts with an existing java.sql.ResultSet object and implements its domain object mapping in terms of the DomainObjectFactory interface introduced in the "Sample Code" section of the Domain Object Factory pattern (203).

This example uses a java.util.List that contains domain objects to represent pages of data. It throws DomainObjectExceptions to indicate errors. DomainObjectException is defined in the "Sample Code" section of the Domain Object Assembler pattern (227).

```java
public class PagingIterator {

    private ResultSet resultSet;
    private ResultSetMetaData rsmd;
    private int columnCount;
    private DomainObjectFactory domainObjectFactory;

    /**
    Constructs a PagingIterator object.
    */
    public PagingIterator(
```

```
            ResultSet resultSet,
        DomainObjectFactory domainObjectFactory)
        throws DomainObjectException {

        this.resultSet = resultSet;
        this.domainObjectFactory = domainObjectFactory;

        try {
            this.rsmd = resultSet.getMetaData();
            this.columnCount = rsmd.getColumnCount();
        }
        catch(SQLException e) {
            throw new DomainObjectException(e);
        }
    }

    /**
    Fetches the next page of domain objects.  The
    list is empty when there is no more data.
    */
    public List nextPage(int pageSize)
        throws DomainObjectException {

        try {
            List domainObjects = new LinkedList();

            // Set the result set's fetch size to match
            // the page size.  Many JDBC drivers use this
            // as a hint to optimize blocked fetches.
            resultSet.setFetchSize(pageSize);

            for(int i = 0;
                i < pageSize && resultSet.next();
                ++i) {

                // Get the next row of data.
                Map rowData = new HashMap();
                for(int j = 1; j <= columnCount; ++j) {
                    rowData.put(rsmd.getColumnName(j),
                                resultSet.getObject(j));
                }

                // Use the domain object factory to initialize
                // a new domain object based on the row data.
                Object domainObject
                    = domainObjectFactory
                    .newDomainObject(rowData);

                domainObjects.add(domainObject);
```

```
            }

            return domainObjects;
        }
        catch(SQLException e) {
            throw new DomainObjectException(e);
        }
    }


    /**
    Closes the result set that this paging
    iterator manages.
    */
    public void close() throws DomainObjectException {
        try {
            resultSet.close();
        }
        catch(SQLException e) {
            throw new DomainObjectException(e);
        }
    }
}
```

PagingIterator is generic. It works entirely in terms of the DomainObjectFactory interface. The next set of classes defines the mapping details for a specific domain object type. The "Sample Code" section for the Update Factory pattern (215) described a domain object called Vehicle that represents a row of data in a vehicle inventory table that a car dealership application uses. Figure 14.4 shows the mapping between Vehicle objects and the VEHICLES table:

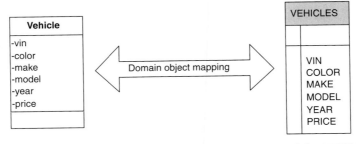

FIGURE 14.4: The mapping between Vehicle domain objects and the VEHICLES table.

VehicleFactory is a DomainObjectFactory implementation that populates new Vehicle objects based on rows from the VEHICLES table:

```
public class VehicleFactory implements DomainObjectFactory {

    /**
    Creates and returns a new domain object
    that corresponds to the contents of a
    single row from a set of database query
    results.
    */
    public Object newDomainObject(Map rowData) {

        String vin = (String)rowData.get("VIN");
        String color = (String)rowData.get("COLOR");
        String make = (String)rowData.get("MAKE");
        String model = (String)rowData.get("MODEL");
        int year
            = ((Integer)rowData.get("YEAR")).intValue();
        int price
            = ((Integer)rowData.get("PRICE")).intValue();

        Vehicle vehicle = new Vehicle();
        vehicle.setVin(vin);
        vehicle.setColor(color);
        vehicle.setMake(make);
        vehicle.setModel(model);
        vehicle.setYear(year);
        vehicle.setPrice(price);

        return vehicle;
    }

    private static final String[] COLUMN_NAMES = {
        "VIN", "COLOR", "MAKE", "MODEL", "YEAR", "PRICE"
    };

    /**
    Returns an array of column names that
    this factory expects to see in the
    row data that gets passed to
    newDomainObject.
    */
    public String[] getColumnNames() {
        return COLUMN_NAMES;
    }

}
```

Next is some sample application code that uses these classes to process query results from the VEHICLES table using paging semantics and Vehicle domain objects. It initializes a PagingIterator and fetches the first page of data. It processes the contents of this page and then closes the PagingIterator. This closes the underlying result set in turn.

```
// Initialize the DomainObjectFactory.
DomainObjectFactory domainObjectFactory
    = new VehicleFactory();

// Initialize the paging iterator.
PagingIterator pagingIterator
    = new PagingIterator(resultSet, domainObjectFactory);

// Fetch and present the first page of data.
List domainObjects = pagingIterator.nextPage(10);
for(Iterator i = domainObjects.iterator(); i.hasNext(); ) {
    Vehicle vehicle = (Vehicle)i.next();

    // Render the vehicle information ...
}

// Close the paging iterator.
pagingIterator.close();
```

RELATED PATTERNS AND TECHNOLOGY

- Paging Iterator describes nearly identical concepts to Value List Handler [Alur 2001].

- As an alternative to referencing particular database technology, you can define Paging Iterator's database interaction in terms of a Data Accessor (9) implementation.

- You can incorporate Paging Iterator into a Domain Object Assembler's (227) read operation. This integrates paging semantics with Domain Object Assembler's capabilities for generating database query operations based on identity objects.

- Consider isolating Paging Iterator and its related classes within a single middleware layer among other Layers (75).

- Paging Iterator incorporates Domain Object Factory (203) for plugging in customized domain object mapping details that apply to a particular domain object type and database entity.

- Resource Timer (137) describes a strategy for closing database resources after a designated period of inactivity. It is useful for cases when callers neglect to read all of a Paging Iterator's results or explicitly close its resources.

Part 4

Cache Patterns

Data access operations consume a significant portion of an enterprise system's resources. They are a common source of performance bottlenecks, so optimization efforts often focus on implementing data access components as efficiently as possible. Recycling database resources and creating indices goes a long way to this end, but one of the most effective strategies is to eliminate redundant data access operations altogether.

Caching enables applications to avoid issuing multiple database read operations for the same data item. After an application reads a data item for the first time, it stores it in a cache. Caches usually reside in memory and enable fast access to their contents. Applications do not need to issue subsequent database operations to access cached data. Depending on the nature of the data and how applications use it, caching can significantly improve data access performance.

267

CACHE OPERATIONS AND TRANSPARENCY

As you investigate caching, you need to consider how your application will interact with a cache. A cache starts out empty. At some point during initialization or runtime, applications or middleware components read data from the database to store in the cache. Strategies for populating caches vary, ranging from simply copying an entire set of data during initialization to making strategic, selective decisions to populate only the specific data that applications are likely to reference multiple times.

Application code is the ultimate consumer of cached data. It is common for applications to reference cached data using primary keys or identity objects, but some applications require other semantics like data handles or a query language.

The semantics that cache operations define go a long way toward achieving *cache transaparency*. Cache transparency refers to the visibility of a cache to applications and middleware code. An example of a cache that is not transparent is one where applications must explicitly interact with it. There are some advantages to a non-transparent cache, namely that applications often best judge which data should be stored in a cache. However, non-transparent caches also place a significant burden on applications, complicating their data access code with caching logic.

On the other hand, a transparent cache is one that is encapsulated within a single data access component. Applications do not interact directly with transparent caches. Cached data is accessible to applications, but the application code accesses it the same as it does when it reads directly from the database. Transparent caches encourage application code to remain focused on domain logic. In addition, you can usually update and optimize transparent caching strategies without requiring applications to change.

CACHED DATA

When you implement caching, also consider the form of the cached data. You can store data in its physical database format using software representations of tables, rows, columns, and relationships. Caching data in its raw form often requires you to implement a query mechanism as well.

Unless your applications operate directly on data in this raw form, you must repeatedly convert cached data into the domain form that your applications expect. It often makes more sense to cache data in its domain form. In other words, store populated domain objects in a cache rather than raw data.

CACHE PATTERNS

While the nature of caching depends on your applications' requirements, you can employ common caching strategies. Cache patterns define strategies for integrating caching into your applications and middleware components. These patterns concentrate on improving data access performance and resource utilization by eliminating redundant data access operations. This part of the book describes several cache patterns.

The first group of cache patterns describes strategies for integrating cache storage and retrieval operations in applications and middleware components with various degrees of transparency. These patterns address how to utilize caches rather than how to implement caches directly.

- **Cache Accessor** (271)—Decouples caching logic from the data model and data access details.

- **Demand Cache** (281)—Populates a cache lazily as applications request data. A demand cache is useful for data that is read frequently but unpredictably.

- **Primed Cache** (291)—Explicitly primes a cache with a predicted set of data. A primed cache is useful for data that is read frequently and predictably.

- **Cache Search Sequence** (305)—Inserts shortcut entries into a cache to optimize the number of operations that future searches require.

The second group of cache patterns defines various housekeeping strategies that result in more efficient caching implementations:

- **Cache Collector** (325)—Purges entries whose presence in the cache no longer provides any performance benefit.

- **Cache Replicator** (345)—Replicates operations across multiple caches.

- **Cache Statistics** (361)—Record and publish cache and pool statistics using a consistent structure for uniform presentation.

Each of these patterns is independent from the others. You can mix and match them to build as comprehensive a caching solution as your applications require. The main tradeoff to consider is the additional complexity associated with caching. Using documented caching patterns helps to manage this complexity, but it is also important to isolate specific caching decisions as much as possible. As with any software optimization, it is also important to measure the performance and resource utilization differences that caching makes. If there are no significant differences, you may not find it worth introducing the additional complexity of caching into your applications.

Cache Accessor

DESCRIPTION

Decouples caching logic from the data model and data access details.

CONTEXT

Caching enables applications to avoid issuing multiple database read operations for the same data item. While caching is an integral concept in many robust data access components, application- and middleware-level caching logic rarely relates directly to any particular data access mechanism.

Caching logic focuses on deciding when and how to access cached and physical data. As you implement a caching solution, you must determine which data is worth caching. If your application only reads a given data item once, then caching it consumes unnecessary storage overhead. However, if you expect your applica-

271

tion to reference data multiple times, then caching it will alleviate the application from having to issue identical database read operations.

Cache designs require additional attention as well. If a cache remains in use for an extended period of time, you might need to implement a manual or automated mechanism that purges expired entries. You may also want to track cache utilization or share cached data across multiple applications.

Despite the fact that caching and data access issues are mostly orthogonal, it is common to mix caching logic within data access code. When these aspects are intertwined, it is harder to debug and maintain an overall implementation. In addition, combining these features precludes you from reusing caching logic in conjunction with other data access code.

Cache Accessor decouples caching logic from the data model and data access details by defining a generic structure that promotes consistent, reusable cache utilization for all data types and database entities. Isolating caching logic into a single component enables you to incorporate sophisticated optimization, collection, replication, and administrative features that apply to multiple physical data access implementations or data types.

APPLICABILITY

Use the Cache Accessor pattern when:

- Your applications need to read a specific set of data multiple times and accessing the physical database repeatedly degrades performance.

- Cached data rarely changes. Frequent updates require additional physical database interaction, rendering caches less effective.

STRUCTURE

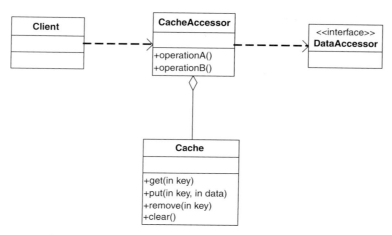

FIGURE 15.1: The static structure of the Cache Accessor pattern.

Figure 15.1 illustrates the static structure of the Cache Accessor pattern. The CacheAccessor class defines the entry point for all the client's data access operations. It manages both cache and database interactions.

Cache implements the actual cache storage mechanism. Its operations refer to cached data using unique keys. You must define keys whose instances uniquely identify each data item the cache stores. If you choose to cache data in its relational form, cache keys often mirror the structure of the underlying table's primary key. Identity objects also make appropriate keys for domain object caches.

CacheAccessor delegates database operations to a separate DataAccessor component. This separation enables you to decouple caching logic from orthogonal details such as physical database resource management and domain object mapping. In practice, the DataAccessor can be a physical database driver, a logical Data Accessor (9) implementation, or one of many domain object mapping alternatives.

You can tailor CacheAccessor's operations to match your application's requirements. The closer you define its operations to match those that the DataAccessor defines, the more transparent your CacheAccessor is to client code.

INTERACTIONS

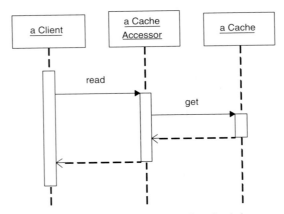

FIGURE 15.2: A client uses a CacheAccessor to read cached data.

Figure 15.2 portrays what happens when a client uses a CacheAccessor to read cached data. The CacheAccessor forms the cache key based on the read operation's parameters. It finds the data in its Cache and returns it without any physical database interaction.

Cache Accessor does not dictate how or when to populate the cache. You can populate it during application initialization or use a more focused approach like those described for the Demand Cache (281) and Primed Cache (291) patterns.

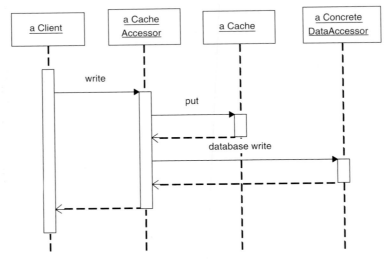

FIGURE 15.3: A client uses a CacheAccessor to write data.

Figure 15.3 shows a client issuing a write operation to a CacheAccessor. In addition to writing to the physical database, the CacheAccessor must also ensure that the Cache reflects changed data.

CONSEQUENCES

The Cache Accessor pattern has the following consequences:

Benefits

- *Cache and data access encapsulation*—When a CacheAccessor returns data to a client, the client remains unaware of whether the CacheAccessor found the data in the cache or the database. This principle keeps client code clean and efficient, and also enables you to modify caching logic without changing dependent client code.

- *Cache utilitization*—Clients assign Cache objects to CacheAccessors during initialization. This offers scoping versatility and allows you to define system-wide caches, caches that span a single application, or caches for each individual session. It also enables your system to maintain multiple caches, each for a different type of data.

  This relationship does not impose any additional burden on the client. If it proves sufficient to keep a global Cache object, then it is easy to do so. This is true in the majority of cases. However, you may want to provide system administrators with finer control of cache functionality. For example, an administrator may want to clear authorization information without also refreshing user preferences. You can implement this feature elegantly by maintaining two independently refreshable Cache objects.

Drawback

- *Opportunity for stale data*—Cached data becomes stale when the underlying physical data changes. This happens when a user or application updates data that is cached elsewhere. A common symptom of stale data is that users witness inconsistent results. Defects can also occur when an application makes calculations or updates based on stale data.

STRATEGIES

Consider these strategies when implementing the Cache Accessor pattern:

- *Multiple CacheAccessor instances*—CacheAccessor instances do not contain any cache or state data. They interact with independent Cache and DataAccessor objects. Consequently, you can create any number of CacheAccessor instances throughout the life of a system without negatively affecting caching behavior or performance.

  For example, you can declare a global CacheAccessor instance that is accessible anywhere in your application and middleware code. On the other extreme, you can instantiate a new, locally scoped CacheAccessor every time you need to read cached data. In the latter case, the Cache object must have an extended life span, since it maintains the cached data throughout the application's or session's runtime. The most common scenario falls somewhere in between these extremes: confine cached data access to a single component and manage one or more CacheAccessor instances within that component.

- *Cache implementation*—Cache performance depends heavily on the underlying data structure of the Cache object. Cache Accessor does not dictate a specific low-level storage mechanism for the cache, but it does imply that the storage mechanism provides efficient reference capabilities based on unique keys.

  A common data structure that meets this criterion is a hash table. A hash table's performance depends in turn on the distribution of key hash codes. Defining optimal hash algorithms is an extensive topic outside the scope of this book, but it is usually sufficient to come up with a marginally good hash algorithm and achieve acceptable performance. It does not really make sense to define the hash algorithm within the generic Cache or CacheAccessor classes, since neither of these classes imposes any specific key structure. Instead, the hash algorithm is usually the responsibility of the key representation. Any key representation must implement consistent hashing semantics and an efficient hash algorithm.

- *Cache administration*—Your application's users or administrators may want to explicitly refresh the cache for various reasons. One case is when cached data becomes stale. Another is when the cache grows large enough that it is affecting system resources and degrading performance. The brute-force approach is to require users or administrators to restart the application. However, this strategy is rarely acceptable, especially when system downtime is not tolerable.

A cleaner approach is to provide a manual refresh mechanism that enables a user or administrator to refresh all or part of a given Cache object. You can implement this by adding a refresh operation to either the CacheAccessor or Cache object. In practice, you also need to manifest this functionality through an administration user interface.

SAMPLE CODE

The first class in this example defines a simple CacheAccessor. It uses a java.util.Map implementation for its cache abstraction. CacheAccessor defines a single read operation that takes a Key object as input and returns a list of Row objects that represent cached data. See the "Sample Code" section of the Data Accessor pattern (9) for the Row class's source code.

```
public class CacheAccessor {

    private Map cache;

    public CacheAccessor(Map cache) {
        this.cache = cache;
    }

    /**
    Reads data from the cache.

    @param key   The key.
    @return      The data.
    **/
    public List read(Key key) {

        List data = (List)cache.get(key);

        // If no data is found, return an empty
        // list.
        if (data == null)
            data = Collections.EMPTY_LIST;

        return data;
```

```
        }
    }
```

The Key class defines the cache's key structure. It contains a sorted map of column name and value pairs. It uses a java.util.TreeMap internally because TreeMap already defines a consistent hash algorithm for itself, which is imperative for preserving key semantics.

```
public class Key {

    private Map contents = new TreeMap();

    public void set(
        String columnName,
        Object columnValue) {

        contents.put(columnName, columnValue);
    }

    public Iterator columnNames() {
        return contents.keySet().iterator();
    }

    public Object get(String columnName) {
        return contents.get(columnName);
    }

    public int hashCode() {
        return contents.hashCode();
    }

    public boolean equals(Object other) {
        if (!(other instanceof Key))
            return false;

        Key otherKey = (Key)other;
        return contents.equals(otherKey.contents);
    }

    public String toString() {
        return contents.toString();
    }
}
```

The remainder of this example implements caching for an application's user preferences. User preferences are a good candidate for caching since applications refer to them frequently, but users rarely change them.

This code initializes a cache and populates it with the entire set of user preferences stored in the database. It also initializes a CacheAccessor.

```
// Initialize the cache.
Map cache = new HashMap();

// Populate the cache with all the user
// preference data.
ResultSet resultSet
    = statement.executeQuery("SELECT * FROM PREFERENCES");

while(resultSet.next()) {

    String userName = resultSet.getString("USER_NAME");
    String locale = resultSet.getString("LOCALE");
    int gridSize = resultSet.getInt("GRID_SIZE");
    String background = resultSet.getString("BACKGROUND");

    Key key = new Key();
    key.set("USER_NAME", userName);

    Row row = new Row();
    row.addColumn("USER_NAME", userName);
    row.addColumn("LOCALE", locale);
    row.addColumn("GRID_SIZE", new Integer(gridSize));
    row.addColumn("BACKGROUND", background);

    List data = new LinkedList();
    data.add(row);

    cache.put(key, data);
}
resultSet.close();

// Initialize the CacheAccessor.
CacheAccessor cacheAccessor = new CacheAccessor(cache);
```

This is some sample application code that uses the CacheAccessor to read user preferences for a specific user:

```
key.set("USER_NAME", "george");

List data = cacheAccessor.read(key);
```

RELATED PATTERNS AND TECHNOLOGY

- Cache Accessor can improve the performance of Data Accessor (9), Active Domain Object (33), Object/Relational Map (53), and Domain Object Assembler (227) implementations.

- Consider isolating a Cache Accessor implementation within a single middleware layer among other Layers (75).

- Demand Cache (281) and Primed Cache (291) refine the concepts that Cache Accessor describes, specifically focusing on efficient cache population strategies.

- Cache Search Sequence (305) defines a strategy that optimizes cache references for search sequences that involve multiple key combinations.

- Cache Replicator (345) strives to minimize the effect of stale cache data by coordinating changes made across a set of multiple managed caches.

- Cache Statistics (361) enable you to monitor and analyze cache effectiveness at runtime.

Demand Cache

DESCRIPTION

Populates a cache lazily as applications request data. A demand cache is useful for data that is read frequently but unpredictably.

CONTEXT

Many systems maintain configuration information such as user preferences, authorization rules, and directory references in a database. Systems reference this type of information frequently, but do not modify it much during runtime. These characteristics make them good candidates for caching, but the total time and memory required to initialize a cache with a complete set of configuration data can be significant.

Consider an application where each registered user customizes the presentation details for his/her own application session. Once a user signs on, he/she can choose color and layout options as well as content filters. The application honors these preferences for his/her current session and all future sessions.

As the number of users grows, the resources required to cache all this configuration data prohibits populating the cache in full when the application initializes. An alternate strategy is to retrieve each user's preference data at sign-on. The application only incurs database and cache storage overhead for the preference data that corresponds to active users, and cache initialization is fast. Throughout each user's session, the application can retrieve this data quickly from the cache.

Demand Cache describes a strategy for populating a cache incrementally as applications request data. It refines the concepts that Cache Accessor (271) describes.

APPLICABILITY

Use the Demand Cache pattern when:

- Populating a cache with the complete data set is not feasible because it requires a significant amount of primary storage and slows system initialization.

- Populating a cache with the complete data set is not necessary because the majority of the data is unlikely to be needed at any given time or throughout a single application instance or session.

STRUCTURE

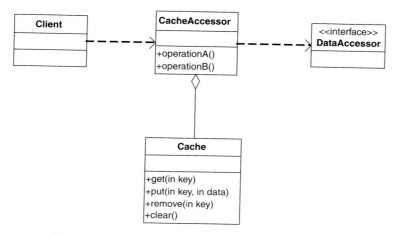

FIGURE 16.1: The static structure of the Demand Cache pattern.

Figure 16.1 illustrates the static structure of the Demand Cache pattern. This structure is identical to Cache Accessor (271). The CacheAccessor class defines the entry point for all the client's data access operations. It manages both cache and database interactions. Cache implements the cache storage mechanism, and DataAccessor is responsible for issuing physical database operations.

INTERACTIONS

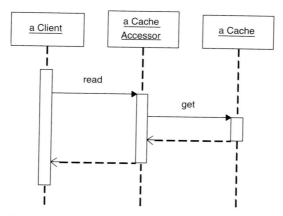

FIGURE 16.2: A client uses a CacheAccessor to read cached data.

Figure 16.2 portrays what happens when a client uses a CacheAccessor to read cached data. The CacheAccessor forms a key based on the details of the read operation, finds the data in its Cache, and returns it without any physical database interaction.

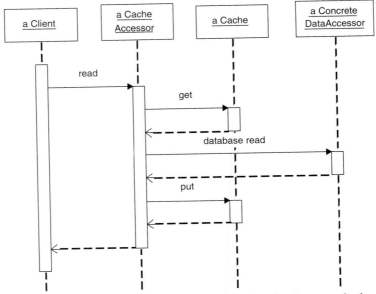

FIGURE 16.3: A client uses a CacheAccessor to read data that is not cached.

Figure 16.3 illustrates what happens when a client requests data that is not cached. The CacheAccessor discovers that its Cache does not contain the data, so it reads it from the physical database. It stores this data in the Cache before returning it to the client. Now that it is stored in the cache, the CacheAccessor can find the data quickly the next time the client requests it.

The Cache begins empty, so the first reference always requires a physical database query operation. However, as the system runs, the CacheAccessor gradually populates the Cache to contain most of the data that it references frequently. The faster scenario shown in Figure 16.2 becomes the most common.

CONSEQUENCES

The Demand Cache pattern has the following consequences:

Benefits

- *Fast initialization*—Application and system cache initialization is instantaneous since the cache begins empty. The expense of populating the cache is amortized across a series of CacheAccessor operations.

- *Minimal cached data set*—CacheAccessor only issues physical database read operations for data that its clients request. Therefore, its cache contains precisely the minimal set of data that an application or system requires.

Drawbacks

- *Slow cache population*—It can take many physical database read operations before the Demand Cache strategy improves data access performance. An application's users may notice slower response time initially with gradual improvement as a CacheAccessor populates its cache.

- *Opportunity for memory leaks*—Demand Cache does not dictate a strategy for purging cache entries when they are no longer needed. Without such a strategy, the cache grows steadily and can gradually degrade overall system performance.

STRATEGIES

Depending on the semantic details of an application and its data, it is common and valid for a caller to request data that explicitly does not exist in the database. In the user preferences example, this means that a given user has not customized their preferences. You can indicate this fact by storing a special placeholder entry in the cache that represents the notion of data that does not exist in the database. This placeholder entry prevents the CacheAccessor object from repeatedly querying the database, each time finding no matching data.

SAMPLE CODE

The structure for Demand Cache is identical to that described for Cache Accessor (271), and the sample code is similar as well. The primary difference is in the implementation of CacheAccessor's read operation. This operation implements incremental caching behavior by issuing physical database operations whenever it cannot find data in the cache.

CacheAccessor requires a DataAccessor object to read data it does not find in the cache. DataAccessor is a simple instance of Data Accessor (9), which encapsulates simple queries within a logical data access component.

```java
public class CacheAccessor {

    private DataAccessor dataAccessor;
    private String table;
    private Map cache;

    public CacheAccessor(
        DataAccessor dataAccessor,
        String table,
        Map cache) {

        this.dataAccessor = dataAccessor;
        this.table = table;
        this.cache = cache;
    }

    /**
    Reads data from the cache.

    @param key  The key.
    @return     The data.
    **/
    public List read(Key key) throws DataException {

        List data = (List)cache.get(key);

        // If the data that the caller requests
        // is not found in the cache, then read it
        // from the database.
        if (data == null) {
            data = dataAccessor.read(table, key);

            // Store the data in the cache so that it is
            // immediately accessible the next time a
            // caller requests it.  If no matching data
```

```
                // is found, then store an empty list in the
                // cache.
                cache.put(key, data);
            }

        return data;
        }
    }
```

The DataAccessor interface defines the logical read operation that CacheAccessor uses and ConcreteDataAccessor implements it using a JDBC connection. DataException is a generic exception that indicates any errors that happen along the way.

```
public interface DataAccessor {

    /**
    Reads data from a table.

    @param table        The table.
    @param key          The key.
    @return             The list of rows.
    **/
    List read(String table, Key key)
        throws DataException;

}

public class ConcreteDataAccessor
implements DataAccessor {

    private Connection connection;

    public ConcreteDataAccessor() throws DataException {
        try {
            ·connection
                = DriverManager.getConnection(...);
        }
        catch(SQLException e) {
            throw new DataException(e);
        }
    }

    public List read(String table, Key key)
        throws DataException {

        try {
```

```
// Generate the SQL SELECT statement based on
// the key.
StringBuffer buffer = new StringBuffer();
buffer.append("SELECT * FROM ");
buffer.append(table);
boolean firstColumn = true;
for(Iterator i = key.columnNames();
    i.hasNext(); ) {

    String columnName = (String)i.next();
    Object columnValue = key.get(columnName);

    if (firstColumn) {
        buffer.append(" WHERE ");
        firstColumn = false;
    }
    else {
        buffer.append(" AND ");
    }

    buffer.append(columnName);
    buffer.append(" = ");
    if (!(columnValue instanceof Number))
        buffer.append("'");
    buffer.append(columnValue);
    if (!(columnValue instanceof Number))
        buffer.append("'");
}

// Execute the read operation.
Statement statement
    = connection.createStatement();
ResultSet resultSet
    = statement.executeQuery(
    buffer.toString());
ResultSetMetaData rsmd
    = resultSet.getMetaData();
int columnCount = rsmd.getColumnCount();

// Create a list of data based on the
// contents of the result set.
List data = new LinkedList();
while(resultSet.next()) {
    Row row = new Row();
    for(int i = 1; i <= columnCount; ++i) {
        row.addColumn(
            rsmd.getColumnName(i),
            resultSet.getObject(i));
    }
```

```
            data.add(row);
        }

        // Release the database resources.
        resultSet.close();
        statement.close();

        return data;
      }
      catch(SQLException e) {
        throw new DataException(e);
      }
    }
  }

public class DataException extends Exception {

    public DataException(Throwable cause) {
        super(cause);
    }
}
```

This code initializes a cache, a DataAccessor implementation, and a CacheAccessor specifically for reading user preference data:

```
// Initialize the cache.
Map cache = new HashMap();

// Initialize the DataAccessor implementation.
DataAccessor dataAccessor
    = new ConcreteDataAccessor();

// Initialize the CacheAccessor.
CacheAccessor cacheAccessor
    = new CacheAccessor(
    dataAccessor,
    "PREFERENCES",
    cache);
```

This is some application code that uses the CacheAccessor to read user preferences for a specific user:

```
Key key = new Key();
key.set("USER_NAME", "george");

List data = cacheAccessor.read(key);
```

RELATED PATTERNS AND TECHNOLOGY

- Demand Cache is similar to Identity Map [Fowler 2002].

- Demand Cache refines the concepts that Cache Accessor (271) describes to incorporate incremental cache population.

- Primed Cache (291) defines the ability to populate a cache with a predictable subset of data using a single database read operation. This reduces the database overhead that an incremental cache population requires. You can use Demand Cache and Primed Cache within the same CacheAccessor implementation.

- Cache Collector (325) describes a strategy for cleaning up cache entries that are no longer needed. This helps to avoid the gradual storage overhead expansion that is characteristic of some Demand Cache implementations.

Primed Cache

DESCRIPTION

Explicitly primes a cache with a predicted set of data. A primed cache is useful for data that is read frequently and predictably.

CONTEXT

Consider a commercial web site management application that enables an administrator to grant and deny users authority to individual pages. The application stores its authorization data in a table with the user name and page identifier together serving as its primary key. As users navigate through the pages that it manages, the application references this table's data to enforce the configured authorization settings.

Demand Cache (281), which populates a cache incrementally as applications request data, works effectively for caching authorization data. However, one of

291

Demand Cache's drawbacks is that it can require many physical database operations to populate a cache to the point where it significantly improves data access performance.

When a user first signs on, the cache contains no authorization data. The web site management application repeatedly queries the authorization table as it presents each page to the user for the first time. Subsequent loading of each page is fast because the corresponding authorization data is now cached, but these benefits do not pay off until the user navigates to a page for a second time.

Primed Cache defines a complementary caching strategy that alleviates the problem of slow, incremental cache population. The primary difference is that your application explicitly primes the cache with an anticipated subset of data before making any requests. In this example, when a user first signs on, the web site management application can read all authorization information for that user and store it in the cache. A single comprehensive query primes the cache with a small, relevant subset of data that the application is likely to reference. Most of the time, this query operation is significantly faster than the sum of the smaller queries required to populate the cache on-demand.

Primed Cache refines the concepts that Cache Accessor (271) describes. However, Primed Cache imposes a bit more structure for its cache keys. In particular, you must define a semantic relationship between partial and specific keys. Callers use partial keys to prime a cache. A partial key usually corresponds to a discrete set of data with common characteristics. A single priming operation reads the entire set of matching data from the database and stores it in the cache.

By contrast, callers use specific keys when reading and writing data. A specific key usually corresponds to an exact data item in the cache. The caching logic must be able to infer whether a given key is a partial specification of another to determine whether referenced data has been primed.

In the web site management application, a user name and page identifier make up a key. The partial form of this key contains only a user name with no page specified. This key mirrors the priming query operation that loads all authorization information that relates to a single user. The specific form of this key contains both a user name and page identifier.

Defining key relationships in broad terms enables you to implement priming cache logic with a single, uniform framework that works with multiple data types and database entities. Maintaining a single structure reduces duplicate and inconsistent code.

APPLICABILITY

Use the Primed Cache pattern when:

- Populating the cache with a complete data set is not feasible because it requires a significant amount of primary storage and slows system initialization.

- Populating the cache with a complete data set is not necessary because the majority of the data is unlikely to be needed at any given time or throughout a single application instance or session.

- It is possible to predict a small, relevant subset of data to prime in anticipation of subsequent client requests. This subset must be small enough to make efficient use of cache storage, but large enough to include future potential requests.

STRUCTURE

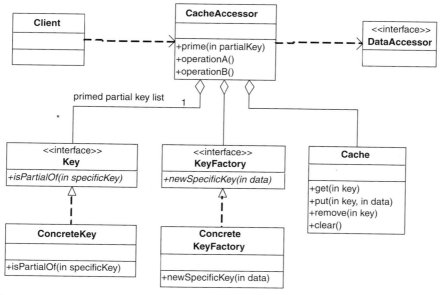

FIGURE 17.1: The static structure of the Primed Cache pattern.

Figure 17.1 illustrates the static structure of the Primed Cache pattern. This structure is similar to Cache Accessor (271). The CacheAccessor class defines the entry point for all the client's data access operations. It manages both cache and database interactions. Cache implements the cache storage mechanism, and DataAccessor is responsible for issuing physical database operations.

CacheAccessor maintains a list of partial keys that it has primed. Its uses this list to avoid repeated priming operations that involve the same partial keys. It also uses this list to discern whether a specific key should be in the cache or not. If a client requests a specific key that is not in the cache, but the key corresponds to one of the partial keys in this list, then CacheAccessor can infer that there is no matching data in the physical database.

The KeyFactory interface defines the primary customization point for this pattern. CacheAccessor uses a ConcreteKeyFactory to assign specific keys to data that it reads during a priming operation. This behavior tends to depend heavily on specific domain object types or database entities.

INTERACTIONS

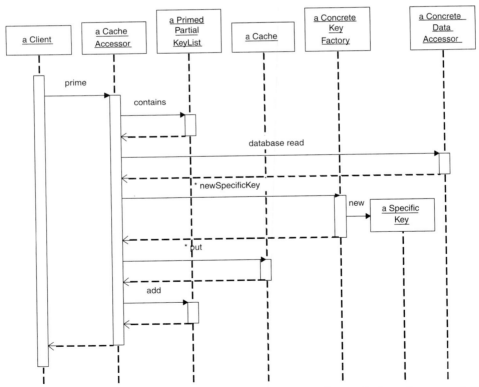

FIGURE 17.2: A client uses a CacheAccessor to prime cache entries based on a partial key.

Figure 17.2 portrays what happens when a client uses a CacheAccessor to prime cache entries based on a partial key. The CacheAccessor first checks its primed partial key list to ensure that it has not already primed the partial key. If it passes this test, then the CacheAccessor issues a database read operation that selects all the corresponding data. It sends the data items on to its ConcreteKeyFactory, which generates specific keys for each. The CacheAccessor uses these specific keys when it stores the primed data in the Cache. Finally, the CacheAccessor adds the partial key to the primed partial key list as a reference for subsequent operations.

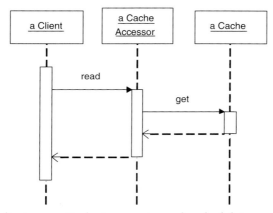

FIGURE 17.3: A client uses a CacheAccessor to read cached data.

Figure 17.3 illustrates what happens when a client uses a CacheAccessor to read cached data. The CacheAccessor forms a key based on the details of the read operation, finds the data in its Cache, and returns it without any physical database interaction.

CONSEQUENCES

The Primed Cache pattern has the following consequences:

Benefits

- *Minimal data access overhead*—Issuing a single priming operation that stores many data items in the cache is significantly faster than the analogous combination of individual read operations.

- *Optimized cached data set*—If an application can anticipate a specific set of data that it is likely to reference, then the cache should contain very few superfluous entries.

Drawbacks

- *Priming semantics*—A prime operation involves physical data access and cache storage, and it tends to be expensive. Clients initiate prime operations, so the implementation performance depends heavily on client usage. Leaving the burden of priming to the client provides many opportunities for misuse. If a client primes using a partial key that corresponds to too much data, then the Cache-Accessor reads and caches much more data than it probably needs and storage overhead can become an issue. On the other hand, if a client primes using partial keys that are too specific, it needs to prime more frequently.

- *Opportunity for memory leaks*—Primed Cache does not dictate a strategy for purging cache entries when they are no longer needed. Without such a strategy, the cache will grow steadily and gradually degrade overall system performance.

STRATEGIES

Depending on the semantic details of an application and its data, it is common and valid for a caller to request data that explicitly does not exist in the database. In the web site management application that the "Context" section described, a missing entry means that a given user does not have any authority over a specific page. You can indicate this fact by storing a special placeholder entry in the cache that represents the notion of data that does not exist in the database. This placeholder entry prevents the CacheAccessor object from repeatedly scanning the primed key list, each time finding no matching data.

If you combine Primed Cache with Demand Cache (281), then there is one additional case to address. When a client primes a partial key, the CacheAccessor stores all the corresponding data in the cache. If the client later attempts to read using a specific key that does not match any cache entries, then you have two options. The first is to immediately issue a database read operation like "Demand Cache" described. However, you may be able to avoid incurring the overhead of this operation.

You can iterate through the primed partial key list, asking each primed key if it is a partial representation of the specific key. This requires you to define an additional Key operation called isPartialOf, which strictly defines the relationship between partial and specific keys. If you find a primed key that is a partial representation, then you can conclude that there is no physical data that corresponds to the specific key. At this point, you can also add a placeholder cache entry for the specific key to indicate that there is no matching data. This placeholder entry enables faster resolution of subsequent references to the specific key.

SAMPLE CODE

The structure for Primed Cache is similar to that of Cache Accessor (271), and the sample code follows. The primary difference is the addition of CacheAccessor's prime operation. This operation implements the priming behavior by issuing physical database read operations that correspond to partial keys.

This CacheAccessor implementation uses a JDO PersistenceManager. The PersistenceManager is responsible for database interaction and domain object mapping. PersistenceManager is an instance of Object/Relational Map (53).

```
public class CacheAccessor {

    private PersistenceManager persistenceManager;
    private Class clas;
    private Map cache;
    private Set primedKeys;
    private KeyFactory keyFactory;

    public CacheAccessor(
        PersistenceManager persistenceManager,
        Class clas,
        Map cache,
        Set primedKeys,
        KeyFactory keyFactory) {

        this.persistenceManager = persistenceManager;
        this.clas = clas;
        this.cache = cache;
        this.primedKeys = primedKeys;
        this.keyFactory = keyFactory;
```

```
    }

    /**
    Primes the cache with all entries that correspond
    to the specified partial key.

    @param partialKey The partial key.
    */
    public void prime(Key partialKey) {

        // Avoid priming the same key twice.
        // This enables the caller to prime repeatedly
        // without imposing superfluous data access.
        if (primedKeys.contains(partialKey))
            return;

        // Read the physical data that corresponds
        // to the partial key.
        Query query = persistenceManager.newQuery(
            clas, partialKey.toString());
        Collection data = (Collection)query.execute();

        // For each domain object that matches the partial
        // key, use the KeyFactory to generate a specific
        // key.  Use the specific keys to store the data
        // in the cache.
        for(Iterator i = data.iterator(); i.hasNext(); ) {

            Object domainObject = i.next();
            Key specificKey
                = keyFactory.newSpecificKey(domainObject);

            // If the cache already contains a list for this
            // specific key, then add to the list.  Otherwise,
            // initialize a new list.
            List cachedData = (List)cache.get(specificKey);
            if (cachedData == null) {
                cachedData = new LinkedList();
                cache.put(specificKey, cachedData);
            }

            cachedData.add(domainObject);
        }

        // Remember that this partial key has been primed.
        primedKeys.add(partialKey);
    }

    /**
```

```
    Reads data from the cache.

    @param key   The key.
    @return      The data.
    **/
    public List read(Key key) {


        List data = (List)cache.get(key);

        // If no data is found, return an empty
        // list.
        if (data == null)
            data = Collections.EMPTY_LIST;

        return data;
    }
}
```

The Key class defines the cache key structure. It is similar to the Key class defined in the "Sample Code" section for the Cache Accessor pattern (271), except that it adds the isPartialOf operation. It also defines toString to return a JDO query filter that represents its contents. CacheAccessor's prime operation uses this query filter when it issues database read operations.

```
public class Key {

    private Map contents = new TreeMap();

    public void set(
        String attributeName,
        Object attributeValue) {

        contents.put(attributeName, attributeValue);
    }

    /**
    Indicates whether this key is a partial
    specification of another.
    */
    public boolean isPartialOf(Key specificKey) {
        for(Iterator i = contents.keySet().iterator();
            i.hasNext(); ) {

            String attributeName = (String)i.next();

            Object partialKeyValue
```

```
                = this.get(attributeName);
            Object specificKeyValue
                = specificKey.get(attributeName);

            if (partialKeyValue != null
                && !partialKeyValue.equals(specificKeyValue))
                return false;
        }

        return true;
    }

    public Iterator attributeNames() {
        return contents.keySet().iterator();
    }

    public Object get(String attributeName) {
        return contents.get(attributeName);
    }

    public int hashCode() {
        return contents.hashCode();
    }

    public boolean equals(Object other) {
        if (!(other instanceof Key))
            return false;

        Key otherKey = (Key)other;
        return contents.equals(otherKey.contents);
    }

    /**
    Returns a JDO query filter.  CacheAccessor uses this
    when it issues database read operations.
    */
    public String toString() {

        StringBuffer buffer = new StringBuffer();
        boolean isFirstAttribute = true;
        for(Iterator i = contents.entrySet().iterator();
            i.hasNext(); ) {

            if (isFirstAttribute)
                isFirstAttribute = false;
            else
                buffer.append(" & ");

            Map.Entry entry = (Map.Entry)i.next();
```

```
        String attributeName = (String)entry.getKey();
        Object attributeValue = entry.getValue();

        buffer.append(attributeName);
        buffer.append(" == ");
        if (!(attributeValue instanceof Number))
            buffer.append("'");
        buffer.append(attributeValue);
        if (!(attributeValue instanceof Number))
            buffer.append("'");
    }

        return buffer.toString();
    }
}
```

CacheAccessor uses a KeyFactory to generate specific keys when it stores primed data in its cache. Defining KeyFactory as an interface enables you to reuse a single CacheAccessor class for a variety of data types and database entities.

```
public interface KeyFactory {

    /**
    Returns a specific key based on a domain object.
    */
    Key newSpecificKey(Object domainObject);

}
```

AuthorizationData defines the domain object representation of the web site management application's authorization information. AuthorizationKeyFactory generates specific keys that correspond to AuthorizationData instances.

```
public class AuthorizationData {

    private String userName;
    private String pageIdentifier;
    private String accessLevel;
    private String grantedBy;
    private Date grantedOn;

    public String getUserName() {
        return userName;
    }

    public void setUserName(String userName) {
        this.userName = userName;
```

```
    }

    public String getPageIdentifier() {
        return pageIdentifier;
    }

    public void setPageIdentifier(String pageIdentifier) {
        this.pageIdentifier = pageIdentifier;
    }

    public String getAccessLevel() {
        return accessLevel;
    }

    public void setAccessLevel(String accessLevel) {
        this.accessLevel = accessLevel;
    }

    public String getGrantedBy() {
        return grantedBy;
    }

    public void setGrantedBy(String grantedBy) {
        this.grantedBy = grantedBy;
    }

    public Date getGrantedOn() {
        return grantedOn;
    }

    public void setGrantedOn(Date grantedOn) {
        this.grantedOn = grantedOn;
    }
}

public class AuthorizationKeyFactory
implements KeyFactory {

    public Key newSpecificKey(Object domainObject) {

        AuthorizationData authorizationData
            = (AuthorizationData)domainObject;

        Key specificKey = new Key();
        specificKey.set(
            "userName",
            authorizationData.getUserName());
        specificKey.set(
            "pageIdentifier",
```

```
        authorizationData.getPageIdentifier());

    return specificKey;
    }

}
```

This code initializes a cache, a primed keys list, a concrete KeyFactory, a PersistenceManager, and a CacheAccessor specifically for reading authorization data:

```
// Initialize the cache, primed key set, and
// KeyFactory implementation.
Map cache = new HashMap();
Set primedKeys = new HashSet();
KeyFactory keyFactory = new AuthorizationKeyFactory();

// Initialize the PersistenceManager.
PersistenceManager persistenceManager
    = pmFactory.getPersistenceManager();

// Initialize the CacheAccessor.
CacheAccessor cacheAccessor
    = new CacheAccessor(
    persistenceManager,
    AuthorizationData.class,
    cache,
    primedKeys,
    keyFactory);
```

In the next block, an application primes the CacheAccessor using a partial key that corresponds to all the authorization information corresponding to a specific user:

```
Key partialKey = new Key();
partialKey.set("userName", "george");
cacheAccessor.prime(partialKey);
```

This is some application code that uses the CacheAccessor to read authorization information using a specific key:

```
Key specificKey = new Key();
specificKey.set("userName", "george");
specificKey.set("pageIdentifier", "PAYROLL001");

List data = cacheAccessor.read(specificKey);
```

RELATED PATTERNS AND TECHNOLOGY

- Primed Cache refines the concepts that Cache Accessor (271) describes to incorporate a targeted cache population.

- Demand Cache (281) defines the ability to populate a cache incrementally as applications request data. This offers a complementary strategy for resolving data that cannot be primed effectively. You can use Demand Cache and Primed Cache within the same CacheAccessor implementation.

- Cache Collector (325) describes a strategy for cleaning up cache entries that are no longer needed. This helps avoid the gradual storage overhead expansion that is characteristic of some Primed Cache implementations.

Cache Search Sequence

DESCRIPTION

Inserts shortcut entries into a cache to optimize the number of operations that future searches require.

CONTEXT

System administration information stored in a database enables fast access from console applications and runtime systems. You can store preference, tracking, and security information for each user. Tables like these often include a user name column that serves as the primary key. The majority of entries contain default values since customization is rare. In addition, sometimes it is more convenient to assign users to groups so that configuration is not as granular.

Consider a badge reader system for a corporate office building. An administrator can configure specific classes of door access for any employee, but most of the time, he/she assigns them to entire departments or areas. The system is tied to the company's employee and department tables, which keep track of the organizational department hierarchy. In addition, the badge access table contains access information that is assigned to specific departments and users. Since employees expect badge readers to react quickly, the system caches BadgeAccessRecord domain objects for fast resolution.

Figure 18.1 illustrates a fictional company's organizational hierarchy and its corresponding BadgeAccessRecord cache. When an employee presents his/her badge to a reader, the system checks its cache for a BadgeAccessRecord that is assigned specifically to him/her. If it does not find one, then it looks for a BadgeAccessRecord that is assigned to his/her department. If it still turns up nothing, then it checks the next higher level department in the company's organizational hierarchy. It continues until it finds an assigned BadgeAccessRecord or it reaches the highest level department in the company.

This is an example of a *search sequence*, where a single logical read operation requires a sequence of one or more cache read operations to find a matching entry. You can measure the performance of a search sequence based on the number of cache read operations that it requires. In some applications, cache operations are fast enough that their optimization is negligible in the big picture. However, the badge reader system warrants this level of optimization since its users consider any delay in unlocking a door to be a defect.

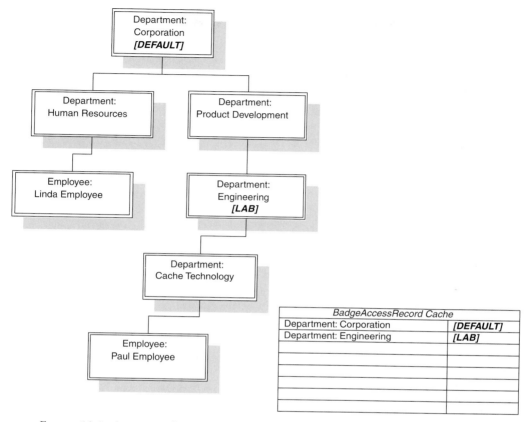

FIGURE 18.1: A company's organizational hierarchy and its corresponding BadgeAccess-Record cache. Employees in the Engineering department have access to labs, while the rest of the corporation has default access.

In most installations, administrators grant default badge access to whole areas at a time, while only select employees have access to restricted areas. Figure 18.1 shows an example of this configuration. Employees in the Engineering department have access to labs, while the rest of the corporation has default access. Most badge reader operations require the same sequence of cache read operations to resolve to the default entry. In other words, performance suffers for the majority of the users. Employees that have been granted special access get into doors the fastest, since the system only issues a single cache read operation to find their entry.

The Cache Search Sequence pattern defines a strategy for inserting *shortcut entries* into a cache to optimize the number of cache read operations that later sequences require. For example, once you determine that Paul Employee's applicable entry is the one that is explicitly defined for the entire Engineering area, you can add shortcut entries that correspond to all the keys involved in that discovery. The same holds true for Linda Employee and the default entry that is defined for the entire corporation. Figure 18.2 shows these additional entries:

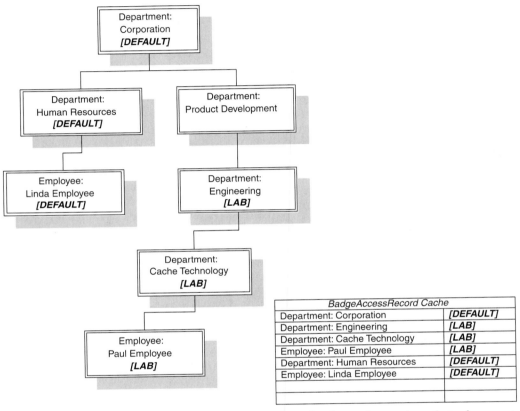

FIGURE 18.2: Shortcut entries reduce the number of cache read operations that subsequent requests require.

With the shortcut entries in place, subsequent requests for these employees' entries require only a single cache read operation. In addition, requests for other employees in their departments also get a boost, since there is now a shortcut entry for the departments as well.

APPLICABILITY

Use the Cache Search Sequence pattern when:

- A single logical read operation requires a sequence of multiple cache read operations, mirroring either a hierarchical relationship or a step-by-step search that starts with specific criteria and ends with a default criteria.

- Search sequences that require multiple cache read operations must be optimized to the degree where reducing the number of cache operations measurably improves a system's performance.

STRUCTURE

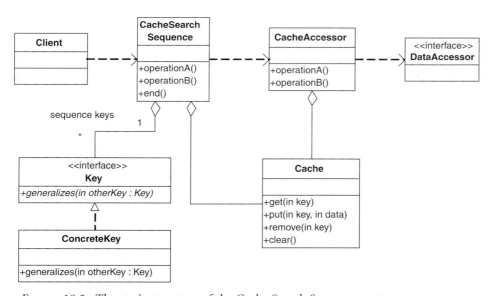

FIGURE 18.3: The static structure of the Cache Search Sequence pattern.

Figure 18.3 illustrates the static structure of the Cache Search Sequence pattern. This structure is similar to Cache Accessor (271). The primary difference is the addition of the CacheSearchSequence class. CacheSearchSequence maintains the state of a single sequence of associated cache read operations. It keeps a collection of the keys that make up the sequence and uses them to add shortcut entries to the Cache when the sequence ends.

The Key interface defines an operation called generalizes, which ConcreteKey implements to indicate whether it is a generalization of another key. The "Strategies" section defines what generalization means in this context and describes how CacheSearchSequence uses this information.

Clients use CacheSearchSequence to issue cache operations rather than interacting directly with the CacheAccessor or Cache.

INTERACTIONS

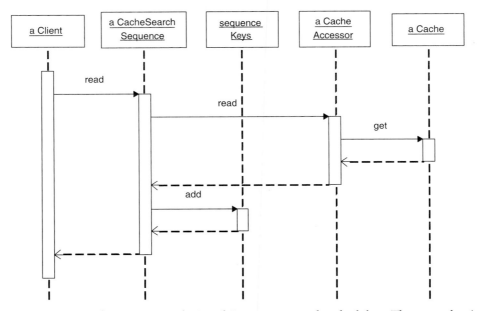

FIGURE 18.4: A client uses a CacheSearchSequence to read cached data. The entry that it requests does not exist.

Figure 18.4 shows what happens when a client uses a CacheSearchSequence to read cached data and the entry that it requests does not exist. CacheSearchSequence adds the key to its collection of those that make up the sequence.

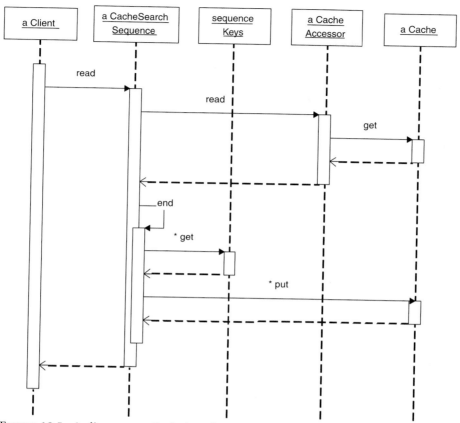

FIGURE 18.5: A client uses a CacheSearchSequence to read cached data. This time, the entry that it requests does exist.

Figure 18.5 illustrates what happens when a client uses a CacheSearchSequence to read cached data and the entry that it requests does exist. This condition indicates the end of the sequence, so the CacheSearchSequence adds shortcut entries to the Cache for each key in its collection. The next time a client issues a search sequence that involves any of these keys, it finds these shortcut entries and resolves its logical read operation faster.

If a client finishes its search sequence without finding an entry, it calls CacheSearchSequence's end operation explicitly. CacheSearchSequence adds shortcut entries just like it does when it finds an entry, but the shortcut entries are simply placeholders that indicate no matches. These shortcut entries enable subsequent client requests to conclude that no entries exist without repeating the entire sequence.

CONSEQUENCES

The Cache Search Sequence pattern has the following consequences:

Benefits

- *Optimizes cache operations*—The shortcut entries that CacheSearchSequence adds to the cache optimize subsequent operations that reference a search sequence's keys.

- *Encapsulates optimization logic*—CacheSearchSequence encapsulates the search sequence and shortcut entry optimization logic so that client code only needs to define the keys for the search sequence.

Drawback

- *Increases cache size*—CacheSearchSequence can add a significant number of shortcut entries to the cache, which substantially increases its size. Depending on the cache's implementation, this can degrade its operational performance.

STRATEGIES

Sometimes, a linear list of a search sequence's keys does not adequately represent the set of shortcut entries that provides accurate semantic results for future search sequences. Consider a variation of the badge reader system where you can assign any employee a list of roles that give him/her special door access that is not necessarily granted to other employees in his/her department. For example, suppose asset managers are spread throughout the organization. When an employee presents his/her badge, the modified system looks for his/her entry followed by any entries defined for his/her assigned roles. If the system does not find any of these entries, the search sequence continues up the company's organizational hierarchy.

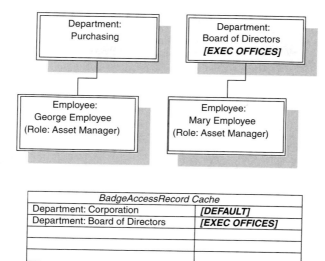

FIGURE 18.6: Mary Employee is both an asset manager and a member of the Board of Directors. She requires access to the executive offices.

You can run into trouble if you use a linear list to keep track of this search sequence. Figure 18.6 illustrates a case where this happens. Suppose there are no cache entries defined for the asset manager role. However, Mary Employee is an asset manager and also a member of the Board of Directors, which gains her access to the executive offices. If the system uses a linear search sequence implementation and finds her badge access record using these rules, then it adds an incorrect short-cut entry that unintentionally grants all asset managers access to the executive offices. Figure 18.7 shows the result of this defect:

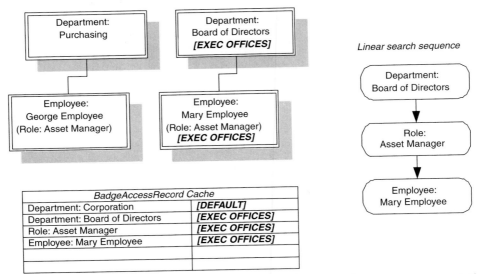

FIGURE 18.7: When the badge reader system uses a linear search sequence representation, it unintentionally grants all asset managers access to the executive offices.

A solution to this problem is to use directed graphs to represent search sequences. A directed graph defines a sequence's keys along with its generalization relationships. Each key programmatically indicates if its applicable cache entries also apply to another key. In the badge reader system, a department generalizes each of its employees and the departments under it in the organizational hierarchy. The same relationship holds true for a role and employees assigned to it. However, there is no generalization relationship between departments and roles.

CacheSearchSequence uses this information to build its directed graph. When CacheSearchSequence adds shortcut entries, it does so for all the keys that are specifications of the last key in the directed graph. Figure 18.8 portrays how the directed graph solves this problem:

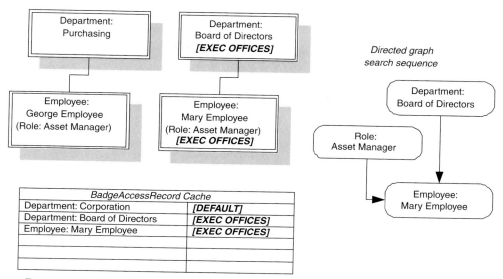

FIGURE 18.8: When the badge reader system uses a directed graph search sequence representation, it no longer grants all asset managers access to the executive offices.

SAMPLE CODE

This example illustrates a generic CacheSearchSequence implementation. It depends on CacheAccessor, which is nearly identical to the example in the "Sample Code" section for the Cache Accessor pattern (271). The primary difference is that CacheSearchSequence expects CacheAccessor to return null rather than a special placeholder to indicate that it cannot find a requested entry.

```
public class CacheSearchSequence {

    private CacheAccessor cacheAccessor;
    private Map cache;
    private DirectedGraph sequenceKeys = new DirectedGraph();
    private boolean done = false;
    private Key lastKey = null;

    public CacheSearchSequence(
        CacheAccessor cacheAccessor,
        Map cache) {

        this.cacheAccessor = cacheAccessor;
        this.cache = cache;
    }
```

```java
/**
Reads data from the cache.

@param key   The key.
@return      The data.
**/
public List read(Key key) {

    if (done)
        throw new IllegalStateException("done");

    // Add this key to the list of those
    // in this sequence.
    sequenceKeys.add(key);
    lastKey = key;

    // Get the values using the cache accessor.
    List values = cacheAccessor.read(key);

    // If values are found, then implicitly end
    // this sequence.
    if(values != null)
        end(values);

    return values;
}

/**
Marks the sequence as done.  Call this if no values
are found after trying every key in the sequence.
*/
public void end() {

    // Mark the end of the sequence with an
    // empty list to indicate that no values were
    // found.
    if (!done)
        end(Collections.EMPTY_LIST);
}

/**
Marks the sequence as done.
*/
private void end(List values) {
    if (lastKey != null) {

        // Place a shortcut entry in the cache for
        // each key that the last key in the sequence
```

```
            // generalizes.
            Set specifications
                = sequenceKeys.getSpecifications(lastKey);
            for(Iterator i = specifications.iterator();
                i.hasNext(); ) {
                Object key = i.next();
                cache.put(key, values);
            }

        }

        done = true;
    }
}
```

The Key interface defines the generalization operation for keys. Employee, Department, and Role are Key implementations that the badge reader system uses. These keys define generalization relationships between each other based on the following rules:

- An Employee object does not generalize any other key.

- A Role object generalizes any Employee object assigned to it.

- A Department object generalizes all Employee and Department objects below it in the organizational hierarchy.

```
public interface Key {

    /**
    Indicates if cache entries that apply to
    this key also apply to the specified key.
    */
    boolean generalizes(Key otherKey);

}

public class Employee implements Key {

    private String name;
    private Department department;
    private List roles;

    public Employee() {
    }
```

```java
    public String getName() {
        return name;
    }

    public void setName(String name) {
        this.name = name;
    }

    public Department getDepartment() {
        return department;
    }

    public void setDepartment(Department department) {
        this.department = department;
    }

    public List getRoles() {
        return roles;
    }

    public void setRoles(List roles) {
        this.roles = roles;
    }

    /**
    Always returns false.
    */
    public boolean generalizes(Key otherKey) {
        return false;
    }

    public String toString() {
        return name;
    }
}

public class Role implements Key {

    private String name;

    public Role() {
    }

    public String getName() {
        return name;
    }

    public void setName(String name) {
        this.name = name;
```

```java
        }

        /**
        Returns true if and only if the key is an
        employee who is assigned this role.
        */
        public boolean generalizes(Key otherKey) {
            if (otherKey instanceof Employee) {
                List roles = ((Employee)otherKey).getRoles();
                return roles.contains(this);
            }
            else {
                return false;
            }
        }

        public String toString() {
            return name;
        }
}

public class Department implements Key {

    private String name;
    private Department nextLevel;
    private List employees;
    private List departments;

    public Department() {
    }

    public String getName() {
        return name;
    }

    public void setName(String name) {
        this.name = name;
    }

    public Department getNextLevel() {
        return nextLevel;
    }

    public void setNextLevel(Department nextLevel) {
        this.nextLevel = nextLevel;
    }

    public List getEmployees() {
        return employees;
```

```
    }

    public void setEmployees(List employees) {
        this.employees = employees;
    }

    public List getDepartments() {
        return departments;
    }

    public void setDepartments(List departments) {
        this.departments = departments;
    }

    /**
    Returns true if and only if the key is an
    employee that is a member of this department
    or a department that is under this one in
    the organizational hierarchy.
    */
    public boolean generalizes(Key otherKey) {

        if (employees.contains(otherKey))
            return true;

        if (departments.contains(otherKey))
            return true;

        for(Iterator i = departments.iterator();
            i.hasNext(); ) {
            Department department = (Department)i.next();
            if (department.generalizes(otherKey))
                return true;
        }

        return false;
    }

    public String toString() {
        return name;
    }
}
```

DirectedGraph is a data structure class that assembles the generalization and specification relationships among the keys in a search sequence:

```
public class DirectedGraph {
```

```java
private Map contents = new HashMap();

/**
Adds a key to the directed graph.
*/
public void add(Key key) {

    // Resolve the collection of specifications that
    // applies to the key.  Create it if one does not
    // already exist.
    Set specifications = (Set)contents.get(key);
    if (specifications == null) {
        specifications = new HashSet();
        contents.put(key, specifications);
    }

    // Iterate through each of the keys in the graph.
    for(Iterator i = contents.entrySet().iterator();
        i.hasNext(); ) {

        Map.Entry entry = (Map.Entry)i.next();
        Key existingKey = (Key)entry.getKey();
        Set existingSpecifications
            = (Set)entry.getValue();

        // Update the specification relationships for
        // the keys.
        if (existingKey.equals(key))
            ;
        else {
            if (existingKey.generalizes(key))
                existingSpecifications.add(key);
            if (key.generalizes(existingKey))
                specifications.add(existingKey);
        }
    }
}

/**
Returns the collection of keys that are specifications
of the given key.
*/
public Set getSpecifications(Key key) {
    Set specifications = (Set)contents.get(key);
    if (specifications != null)
        return specifications;
    else
        return Collections.EMPTY_SET;
```

```
        }
    }
```

Finally, this is some client code that uses CacheSearchSequence to find the appropriate BadgeAccessRecord for an employee:

```
CacheSearchSequence cacheSearchSequence
        = new CacheSearchSequence(cacheAccessor, cache);

// First, try getting the badge access records for the
// employee.
List badgeAccessRecords
        = cacheSearchSequence.read(employee);

// If none are found, then check to see if any are set
// for the employee's roles.
if (badgeAccessRecords == null) {

    List roles = employee.getRoles();
    for(Iterator i = roles.iterator();
        i.hasNext() && badgeAccessRecords == null; ) {

        Role role = (Role)i.next();
        badgeAccessRecords
            = cacheSearchSequence.read(role);

    }
}

// If none are found, then check to see if any are set
// for the employee's department.  Go up the deparment
// chain until you find some.
if (badgeAccessRecords == null) {

    Department department = employee.getDepartment();
    do {
        badgeAccessRecords
            = cacheSearchSequence.read(department);
        department = department.getNextLevel();
    }
    while(badgeAccessRecords == null && department != null);
}

// Mark the end of the sequence.  This places shortcut
// entries for all keys in the sequence so that
// the access records are found faster on subsequent
// references.
cacheSearchSequence.end();
```

RELATED PATTERNS AND TECHNOLOGY

- Cache Search Sequence optimizes cache operations for and can integrate with any Cache Accessor (271), Demand Cache (281), or Primed Cache (291) implementation.

- Cache Statistics (361) enable you to monitor the effectiveness of the shortcut entries that Cache Search Sequence adds to a cache.

Cache Collector

DESCRIPTION

Purges entries whose presence in the cache no longer provides any performance benefit.

CONTEXT

Applications that employ caching strategies like Demand Cache (281) and Primed Cache (291) store data in response to or in anticipation of user requests. Consider a marketing representative who studies pricing data for a particular product set. The application caches this data to optimize response time for subsequent requests. When the marketing representative leaves to make a sales call, the application no longer needs to access this pricing data, but it still occupies cache storage. The cache entries for this data have *expired*, because their presence in the cache no longer provides any performance benefit to the application.

A *cache collection strategy* is a set of rules for identifying and removing expired entries from a cache. You may prefer different collection strategies depending on the nature of your application's data and usage patterns. Some common cache collection strategies are:

- *Fixed expiration*—Entries expire after being in the cache for a fixed time interval. This strategy works well when the physical data that backs a cache changes frequently. Fixed expiration requires an application to reload data after a fixed interval.

- *Inactive expiration*—Entries expire after not having been accessed for a fixed time interval. This strategy applies to data that an application accesses frequently within a small period, and then not again for a long interval after that. The pricing data described earlier falls into this category.

- *Least recently used expiration*—When the cache exceeds a preset size, entries that were used least recently expire. This strategy is useful when you need to keep the size of a cache bounded.

Cache Collector enables you to incorporate a cache collection strategy within a Cache Accessor (271) implementation. You can decouple collection logic from other orthogonal aspects of caching. In addition, Cache Collector accommodates multiple collection strategies by defining its operations in terms of pluggable abstractions. You can incorporate a specific collection strategy by implementing each of these abstractions and plugging them into a CacheAccessor object.

APPLICABILITY

Use the Cache Collector pattern when:

- The size of a cache continuously increases until it consumes a significant quantity of storage. The impact of using too much storage for caching is that it can hinder system performance to the point where caching is no longer effective.

- An application references specific cache entries frequently within a finite time period and then does not reference them for a longer interval afterward. Purging these entries once their presence in the cache is no longer effective makes room for more relevant data.

- You need to implement multiple collection strategies depending on the nature of your applications' data or usage patterns.

STRUCTURE

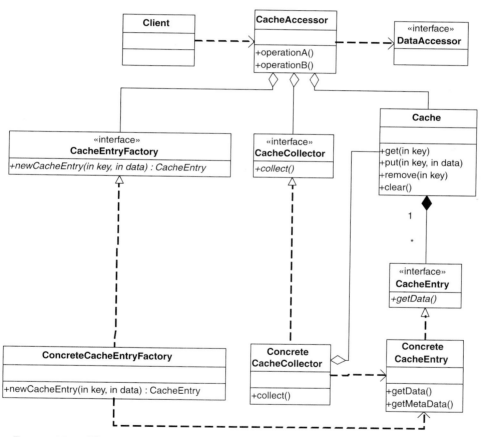

FIGURE 19.1: The static structure of the Cache Collector pattern.

Figure 19.1 illustrates the static structure of the Cache Collector pattern. Cache-Collector, CacheEntry, and CacheEntryFactory are interfaces that define various abstractions for cache collection strategies without dictating specific algorithms or rules. These interfaces enable you to plug multiple collection strategies into the same CacheAccessor implementation. More importantly, they enable you to isolate collection logic within its own component.

CacheCollector defines a collection algorithm. A ConcreteCacheCollector implements its collect operation by making a single pass or iteration through all or part of the Cache's contents, identifying and removing expired entries.

A ConcreteCacheEntry implementation associates a single data item with any cache-related metadata that the corresponding ConcreteCacheCollector requires to determine the ConcreteCacheEntry's expiration status. For example, a ConcreteCacheCollector that implements a fixed expiration strategy must identify the time when each entry was stored in the cache. ConcreteCacheEntry maintains this timestamp. Since most ConcreteCacheCollectors require ConcreteCacheEntries to store specific metadata, the two implementations tend to be tightly coupled.

CacheEntryFactory defines a generic factory mechanism that CacheAccessor uses to create new ConcreteCacheEntries when it stores data in the cache. ConcreteCacheEntryFactory implementations are also tightly coupled with their corresponding ConcreteCacheEntry classes.

CacheAccessor pulls these concrete implementations together to form a complete cache collection solution. CacheAccessor employs its concrete implementations whenever it needs to interact with the cache. Just as in Cache Accessor (271), the CacheAccessor class defines the entry point for all client data access operations. This effectively hides all of the cache collection design and complexity from clients.

INTERACTIONS

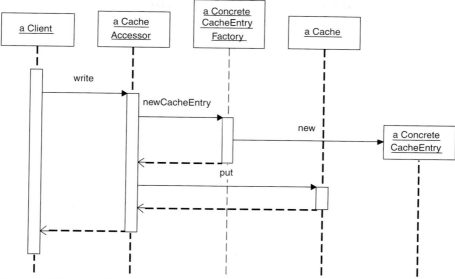

FIGURE 19.2: A CacheAccessor writes a new cache entry.

Figure 19.2 portrays what happens when a CacheAccessor writes a new cache entry. The CacheAccessor uses its ConcreteCacheEntryFactory to wrap the data in a ConcreteCacheEntry object. It stores the ConcreteCacheEntry in the cache rather than the original data so it can maintain any cache-related metadata that its ConcreteCacheCollector requires.

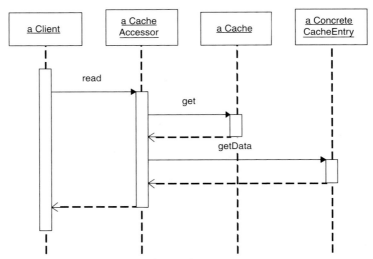

FIGURE 19.3: A CacheAccessor reads a cache entry.

Figure 19.3 shows what happens when a CacheAccessor reads a cache entry. It gets the corresponding ConcreteCacheEntry object from the cache. Instead of returning this ConcreteCacheEntry to the client, CacheAccessor retrieves and returns the original data that the ConcreteCacheEntry wraps.

This has three positive effects. First, the concept of ConcreteCacheEntries remains hidden from clients, which reduces their dependency on a specific cache collection strategy. Second, CacheAccessor's read and write operations are symmetrical so that clients read and write data in the same form. Finally, it gives ConcreteCacheEntries an opportunity to update their metadata. For example, a ConcreteCacheEntry that participates in an inactive expiration collection strategy implementation updates its last access timestamp whenever CacheAccessor calls getData.

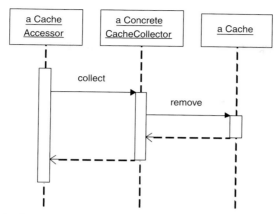

FIGURE 19.4: A CacheAccessor instructs its ConcreteCacheCollector to collect expired entries.

When a CacheAccessor initializes, it starts a low-priority daemon thread that is dedicated to collecting expired cache entries at regular intervals. Figure 19.4 illustrates what happens when it initiates a single collection operation. CacheAccessor periodically calls its assigned ConcreteCacheCollector's collect operation. The ConcreteCacheCollector responds by carrying out the rules for its cache collection strategy and removing expired entries from the Cache along the way.

CONSEQUENCES

The Cache Collector pattern has the following consequences:

Benefits

- *Manages cache size*—Cache Collector reduces the effect of memory leak symptoms that stem from caches growing indefinitely.

- *Has configurable cache collection strategies*—Different collection strategies are more effective than others depending on the nature of the cached data and its usage. Cache Collector accommodates the integration of multiple collection strategies within the same CacheAccessor implementation.

- *Isolates cache collection strategies*—Cache collection details are encapsulated within their own components. They remain isolated from general caching logic, client code, and each other.

Drawback

- *Cache collection degrades performance*—Depending on the cache collection strategy you choose, the process of identifying expired entries may be computationally intensive. Even when a collection runs in a low-priority thread, the process still consumes resources and usually requires synchronized access to the cache structure and its entries, which affects response time for foreground cache operations.

STRATEGIES

To minimize the performance overhead that collecting expired cache entries requires, collection operations usually run periodically in a low-priority daemon thread. However, this introduces concurrent cache access from multiple threads and requires additional synchronization involving the cache structure and its entries. Without synchronization, concurrent access is likely to cause inconsistent and unpredictable results.

The most straightforward approach for synchronization is to place all code that accesses the cache within critical sections. The runtime environment ensures that only one thread accesses these critical sections at a time. Consequently, when a collect operation is running in the background, foreground applications may block while waiting to access cached data. If the collection strategy takes a long time to run or runs frequently, this can significantly degrade concurrency and response time for foreground cache operations. When you implement a collection strategy, try to minimize the interval when you define its critical sections that lock the cache structure or its entries.

Another alternative is to integrate a collection with the cache implementation so that it gets invoked as part of some or all cache operations. This works particularly well with least recently used expiration. Synchronization becomes less of an issue since the cache operation implementations normally already account for it.

SAMPLE CODE

The overall structure for Cache Collector is consistent with that of Cache Accessor (271). In this case, CacheAccessor maintains references to CacheCollector and CacheEntryFactory implementations that it assigns when it is initialized.

CacheAccessor starts a daemon thread to perform collections on regular intervals. This thread awakens periodically to call CacheCollector's collect operation. CacheAccessor synchronizes using the cache object whenever it reads or writes cache entries. This is a precaution to ensure that the cache remains consistent when being referenced concurrently in multiple threads. CacheCollector implementations must also synchronize using the same cache object to preserve consistent semantics.

```
public class CacheAccessor {

    private Map cache;
    private long collectionInterval;
    private CacheCollector cacheCollector;
    private CacheEntryFactory cacheEntryFactory;
    private CollectorThread collectorThread;

    public CacheAccessor(
        Map cache,
        long collectionInterval,
        CacheCollector cacheCollector,
        CacheEntryFactory cacheEntryFactory) {

        this.cache = cache;
        this.collectionInterval = collectionInterval;
        this.cacheCollector = cacheCollector;
        this.cacheEntryFactory = cacheEntryFactory;

        // Start the collector thread.
        Thread collectorThread
            = new CollectorThread();
        collectorThread.start();
    }

    /**
    When this object is no longer needed, stop the
    collector thread.
    */
    protected void finalize() throws Throwable {
        collectorThread.safeStop();
    }

    /**
    Reads data from the cache.  This returns
    null if the key the caller requests does
    not exist in the cache.
    **/
```

```java
public Object read(Object key) {
    synchronized(cache) {
        CacheEntry entry = (CacheEntry)cache.get(key);
        if (entry != null)
            return entry.getData();
        else
            return null;
    }
}

/**
Writes data to the cache.
*/
public void write(Object key, Object data) {
    CacheEntry entry
        = cacheEntryFactory.newCacheEntry(key, data);
    synchronized(cache) {
        cache.put(key, entry);
    }
}

/**
The cache collector thread, which repeatedly
invokes the collect operation.
*/
private class CollectorThread extends Thread {

    private boolean done = false;

    CollectorThread() {
        setDaemon(true);
    }

    public void run() {
        sleep();
        while(!done) {
            cacheCollector.collect();
            sleep();
        }
    }

    private void sleep() {
        try {
            Thread.sleep(collectionInterval);
        }
        catch(InterruptedException ignore) {
        }
    }
}
```

```
            void safeStop() {
                done = true;
                this.interrupt();
            }
        }
    }
```

CacheAccessor is defined in abstract terms without referring to details that are specific to any particular cache collection strategy. It depends on three interfaces whose implementations fill the holes that dictate specific collection rules. The CacheEntry interface defines the wrapper for cached data and any associated metadata that the corresponding CacheCollector implementation requires. It does not define operations for this metadata. Those details are left for the specific implementation instead.

```
public interface CacheEntry {

    /**
    Returns the cached data.
    */
    Object getData();
}
```

CacheEntryFactory defines an abstract factory that assists the CacheAccessor when it needs to instantiate a new CacheEntry object as part of a write operation:

```
public interface CacheEntryFactory {

    /**
    Returns a new CacheEntry object.
    */
    CacheEntry newCacheEntry(
        Object key,
        Object data);
}
```

CacheCollector defines the collect operation. CacheAccessor calls this operation to instruct the implementation to make a single pass through the cache and remove its expired entries. A CacheCollector implementation defines the algorithmic aspect of a cache collection strategy.

```
public interface CacheCollector {

    /**
```

```
    Make a single pass through the cache,
    collecting expired entries where possible.
    **/
    void collect();
}
```

Coupled implementations of the CacheEntry, CacheEntryFactory, and Cache-Collector interfaces cooperate to form a complete cache collection strategy. The following sections present three common strategies:

Fixed Expiration

The first example is a simple implementation of a fixed expiration strategy. Each FixedExpirationCacheEntry maintains its creation timestamp, which the Fixed-ExpirationCacheCollector uses to decide when it expires.

These classes also maintain a queue that lists the keys in their creation order. This queue enables FixedExpirationCacheCollector to avoid iterating through the entire cache's contents to identify expired entries. Instead, it checks only the keys on the front of this queue. Once it finds a key that has not expired, it safely assumes the rest of the keys in the queue follow suit.

```java
class FixedExpirationCacheEntry
implements CacheEntry {

    private Object data;
    private long creationTime;

    FixedExpirationCacheEntry(Object data)
    {
        this.data = data;
        creationTime = System.currentTimeMillis();
    }

    public Object getData()
    {
        return data;
    }

    long getCreationTime()
    {
        return creationTime;
    }
}

public class FixedExpirationCacheEntryFactory
```

```
implements CacheEntryFactory {

    private List keyCreationQueue;

    public FixedExpirationCacheEntryFactory(
        List keyCreationQueue) {

        this.keyCreationQueue = keyCreationQueue;
    }

    public CacheEntry newCacheEntry(
        Object key,
        Object data) {

        // Add this key to the front of the list.
        // If it already exists, remove the old
        // entry, since the corresponding cache
        // entry is replaced as well.
        synchronized(keyCreationQueue) {
            keyCreationQueue.remove(key);
            keyCreationQueue.add(key);
        }

        return new FixedExpirationCacheEntry(data);
    }

}

public class FixedExpirationCacheCollector
implements CacheCollector {

    private Map cache;
    private List keyCreationQueue;
    private long expirationInterval;

    public FixedExpirationCacheCollector(
        Map cache,
        List keyCreationQueue,
        long expirationInterval) {

        this.cache = cache;
        this.keyCreationQueue = keyCreationQueue;
        this.expirationInterval = expirationInterval;
    }

    public void collect() {

        // Compute the expiration time.
        long expirationTime
```

```
                    = System.currentTimeMillis()
                    - expirationInterval;

            synchronized(cache) {
                synchronized(keyCreationQueue) {

                    // Find the list of keys to remove.
                    List keysToRemove = new LinkedList();
                    for(Iterator i = keyCreationQueue.iterator();
                        i.hasNext(); ) {

                        Object key = i.next();
                        FixedExpirationCacheEntry entry
                            = (FixedExpirationCacheEntry)
                            cache.get(key);

                        if (entry.getCreationTime()
                            < expirationTime)
                            keysToRemove.add(key);
                        else
                            break;
                    }

                    // Remove the expired cache entries.
                    for(Iterator i = keysToRemove.iterator();
                        i.hasNext(); ) {

                        Object key = i.next();
                        keyCreationQueue.remove(key);
                        cache.remove(key);
                    }
                }
            }
        }
    }
```

Inactive Expiration

The next set of classes implements an inactive expiration cache collection strategy. Every InactiveExpirationCacheEntry maintains its last access timestamp, which it updates every time a client refers to its data. InactiveExpirationCacheCollector uses this timestamp to identify expired entries.

These classes also maintain a queue that lists the keys in their access order. This queue enables InactiveExpirationCacheCollector to avoid iterating through the entire cache's contents to identify expired entries. Instead, it checks only the keys on the front of this queue. Once it finds a key that has not expired, it safely assumes the rest of the keys in the queue are also not expired.

```
class InactiveExpirationCacheEntry
implements CacheEntry {

    private List keyAccessQueue;
    private Object key;
    private Object data;
    private long lastAccessTime;

    InactiveExpirationCacheEntry(
        List keyAccessQueue,
        Object key,
        Object data) {

        this.keyAccessQueue = keyAccessQueue;
        this.key = key;
        this.data = data;
        lastAccessTime = System.currentTimeMillis();
    }

    public Object getData() {

        // Move the key to the front of the queue
        // to indicate that it was accessed.
        synchronized(keyAccessQueue) {
            keyAccessQueue.remove(key);
            keyAccessQueue.add(0, key);
        }

        lastAccessTime = System.currentTimeMillis();
        return data;
    }

    long getLastAccessTime() {
        return lastAccessTime;
    }
}

public class InactiveExpirationCacheEntryFactory
implements CacheEntryFactory {

    private List keyAccessQueue;

    public InactiveExpirationCacheEntryFactory(
        List keyAccessQueue) {
```

```
            this.keyAccessQueue = keyAccessQueue;
    }

    public CacheEntry newCacheEntry(Object key, Object data) {

        return new InactiveExpirationCacheEntry(
            keyAccessQueue,
            key,
            data);
    }

}

public class InactiveExpirationCacheCollector
implements CacheCollector {

    private Map cache;
    private List keyAccessQueue;
    private long expirationInterval;

    public InactiveExpirationCacheCollector(
        Map cache,
        List keyAccessQueue,
        long expirationInterval) {

        this.cache = cache;
        this.keyAccessQueue = keyAccessQueue;
        this.expirationInterval = expirationInterval;
    }

    public void collect() {

        // Compute the expiration time.
        long expirationTime
            = System.currentTimeMillis()
            - expirationInterval;

        synchronized(cache) {
            synchronized(keyAccessQueue) {

                // Find the list of keys to remove.
                List keysToRemove = new LinkedList();
                for(Iterator i = keyAccessQueue.iterator();
                    i.hasNext(); ) {

                    Object key = i.next();
                    InactiveExpirationCacheEntry entry
                        = (InactiveExpirationCacheEntry)
                        cache.get(key);
```

```
                    if (entry.getLastAccessTime()
                        < expirationTime)
                        keysToRemove.add(key);
                    else
                        break;
                }

                // Remove the expired cache entries.
                for(Iterator i = keysToRemove.iterator();
                    i.hasNext(); ) {

                    Object key = i.next();
                    keyAccessQueue.remove(key);
                    cache.remove(key);
                }
            }
        }
    }
}
```

Least Recently Used Expiration

The last example is a least recently used expiration cache collection strategy implementation. It also maintains a queue that lists the keys in the order that clients access them. When a client accesses a key, the corresponding LRUCacheEntry moves it to the front of the queue. If the queue size exceeds a designated threshold, LRUCacheCollector removes all cache entries that correspond to the keys at the back of the queue.

```
class LRUCacheEntry implements CacheEntry {

    private List keyAccessQueue;
    private Object key;
    private Object data;

    LRUCacheEntry(
        List keyAccessQueue,
        Object key,
        Object data) {

        this.keyAccessQueue = keyAccessQueue;
        this.key = key;
        this.data = data;

        // Add the key to the front of the queue.
        synchronized(keyAccessQueue) {
```

```
                keyAccessQueue.add(0, key);
            }
        }

        public Object getData() {

            // Move the key to the front of the queue
            // to indicate that it was accessed.
            synchronized(keyAccessQueue) {
                keyAccessQueue.remove(key);
                keyAccessQueue.add(0, key);
            }

            return data;
        }
    }

public class LRUCacheEntryFactory
implements CacheEntryFactory {

    private List keyAccessQueue;

    public LRUCacheEntryFactory(List keyAccessQueue) {
        this.keyAccessQueue = keyAccessQueue;
    }

    public CacheEntry newCacheEntry(Object key, Object data) {
        return new LRUCacheEntry(keyAccessQueue, key, data);
    }
}

public class LRUCacheCollector
implements CacheCollector
{
    private Map cache;
    private List keyAccessQueue;
    private int queueSizeThreshold;

    public LRUCacheCollector(
        Map cache,
        List keyAccessQueue,
        int queueSizeThreshold) {

        this.cache = cache;
        this.keyAccessQueue = keyAccessQueue;
        this.queueSizeThreshold = queueSizeThreshold;
    }

    public void collect() {
```

```
            synchronized(cache) {
                synchronized(keyAccessQueue) {

                    if (keyAccessQueue.size()
                        > queueSizeThreshold) {

                        // Get a list of keys that correspond
                        // to the least recently used entries.
                        // These are the ones at the back of
                        // the queue.
                        List keysToRemove
                            = keyAccessQueue.subList(
                            queueSizeThreshold,
                            keyAccessQueue.size());

                        // Remove the keys from the cache's
                        // contents.
                        for(Iterator i = keysToRemove.iterator();
                            i.hasNext(); )
                            cache.remove(i.next());

                        // Remove the keys from the queue.
                        keysToRemove.clear();
                    }
                }
            }
        }
```

This block initializes an LRUCacheCollector and LRUCacheEntryFactory and plugs them into a CacheAccessor. Application code uses this CacheAccessor to interact with the cache and collection happens transparently. Initialization for other collection strategies works the same way.

```
// Initialize and plug in the LRU collection strategy.
List keyAccessQueue = new LinkedList();

CacheCollector cacheCollector = new LRUCacheCollector(
    cache,
    keyAccessQueue,
    1000); // queueSizeThreshold = 1000

CacheEntryFactory cacheEntryFactory
    = new LRUCacheEntryFactory(keyAccessQueue);

CacheAccessor cacheAccessor = new CacheAccessor(
    cache,
```

```
60000, // collectionInterval = 1 minute
cacheCollector,
cacheEntryFactory);
```

RELATED PATTERNS AND TECHNOLOGY

- Cache Collector specializes Strategy [Gamma 1995], which describes how to make families of algorithms interchangeable.

- CacheEntryFactory specializes Abstract Factory [Gamma 1995], which describes the generic application of factory interfaces.

- Demand Cache (281) and Primed Cache (291) describe how to populate a cache. Cache Collector complements these patterns by incorporating a strategy for removing expired cache entries. This helps to avoid the gradual storage overhead expansion that is characteristic of incremental caching implementations.

- Cache Statistics (361) describe a mechanism for monitoring cache size and are especially useful when configuring and debugging cache collection implementations.

Cache Replicator

DESCRIPTION

Replicates operations across multiple caches.

CONTEXT

It is common for multiple application instances to cache the same data. When one instance updates physical data, the other instance's cached copy becomes stale. This means that it no longer accurately reflects the physical data. Recall the web application user preferences example that the "Context" section for the Demand Cache pattern (281) described. Users can configure colors, page layout, and other presentation and functional aspects to tailor the user interface for their own sessions. This information persists in a database that the application accesses frequently. An application continuously reads this data while rendering its user

345

interface. Storing it in a cache within the application server's primary storage improves response time significantly because it spends less time querying the user preference data.

To meet scalability requirements, suppose that you install multiple application instances on a set of clustered servers. When a user signs on, a small front-end broker transparently migrates its session to one of these servers. The front-end application chooses a server using a scheme that balances the load evenly across the set of servers.

Each application instance maintains its own cache. Suppose that when a user first signs on, the broker initializes a session on server A. The next time the user signs on, the broker initializes a session on server B. During this second session, the user changes the menu style preference from "Basic" to "Expert." The database and server B's cache reflect this change, but server A's cache still contains a copy of the user's old preferences. If the user signs on a third time, there is a chance that the broker will initialize a session on server A again, which honors the user's original preferences.

This is an application defect because it appears to the user, who knows nothing about the clustered servers, that the application simply forgot or ignored the preference change. The semantics that the caching strategy imposes manifest as a user interface limitation. A drastic solution is to eliminate caching of user preference data altogether, but this may have a worse impact on usability, since performance degrades for all scenarios.

Another solution is to replicate cached data changes to other cache instances in the system. Whenever an application updates cached data, a replicated cache duly notifies the other caches in the system with the primary, cooperative goal of keeping all copies consistent. This is sometimes called maintaining *cache coherency*. Applicable cache update operations include adding, replacing, and removing cache entries. When the user in this example changes the preferences in one session, the active application session updates the database, its own cache, and then notifies all other caches in the system so that they update themselves to reflect the same changes.

Here are some terms that are useful when describing cache replication strategies:

- *Replicated cache*—A cache instance that notifies others when its contents change.

- *Notification*—A mechanism that caches use to replicate changes. Notification can take the form of system events, messages sent across the network, or through a reliable, distributed queuing mechanism.

- *Topology*—A layout that describes how multiple replicated caches connect with and notify each other.

Your system configuration may dictate the topology that you use. Alternately, you can define a topology that fits most conveniently and efficiently with other aspects of your system's environment. Some common topologies are:

- *Peer cache replicator*—Each replicated cache notifies every other cache instance when its contents change. This topology requires exactly $n - 1$ notifications per update, where n is the number of caches in the system. It does not readily adapt when instances are dynamically added or removed from the system, because every other cache instance must be cognizant of the change and adjust accordingly. Figure 20.1 shows a peer cache replication topology that involves five cache instances:

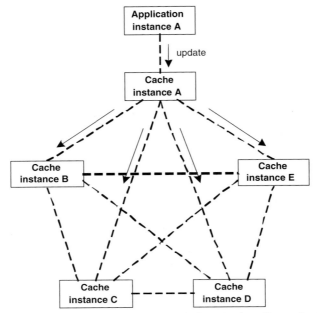

FIGURE 20.1: A peer cache replication topology that involves five cache instances. A single update operation to cache instance A requires four notifications.

- *Centralized cache replicator*—Each replicated cache notifies a central cache instance when its contents change. The central cache is dedicated to dispatching update notifications to all other cache instances in the system. This topology also requires $n - 1$ notifications per update operation. A central cache is more amenable to topology changes, since it is the only instance that maintains a complete cache list. Figure 20.2 illustrates a centralized cache replication topology, again with five cache instances:

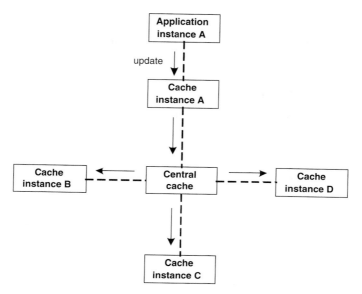

FIGURE 20.2: A centralized cache replication topology that involves five cache instances with one designated as the central cache. A single update operation to cache instance A again requires four notifications.

It is beneficial to manage cache replication in a generic fashion outside your application and data access code. This enables you to build a versatile and reusable system that is not tied to a particular application or topology. Cache Replicator describes such a strategy that not only decouples replication logic from application and data access code, but also from the local cache implementation. It is entirely self-contained and you can even employ it to coordinate replication among heterogeneous cache implementations.

APPLICABILITY

Use the Cache Replicator pattern when:

- Multiple application instances or sessions update cached data and it is important for other instances to consistently reflect the changes.

- You need the versatility to arrange replicated caches in varying topologies to accommodate multiple system structures.

STRUCTURE

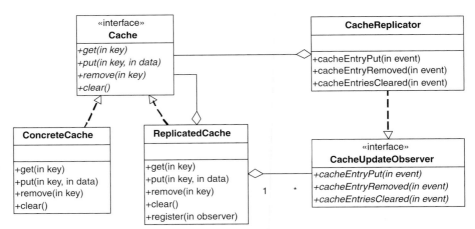

FIGURE 20.3: The static structure of the Cache Replicator pattern.

Figure 20.3 illustrates the static structure of the Cache Replicator pattern. This structure shows the Cache split into an interface and a concrete implementation. The design requires this division because ReplicatedCache acts as a Decorator [Gamma 1995]. It implements the Cache interface and delegates all operations to any other Cache implementation. In addition, it maintains a list of registered CacheUpdateObservers that it notifies whenever it delegates a put or remove operation.

You can implement CacheUpdateObserver to do anything related to cache update operations. For example, if you simply want to log these operations, you can register a CacheUpdateObserver implementation that issues messages whenever the ReplicatedCache notifies it. CacheReplicator is a special CacheUpdateObserver implementation that updates another Cache instance when a ReplicatedCache notifies it. This structure defines the primary cache replication mechanism.

INTERACTIONS

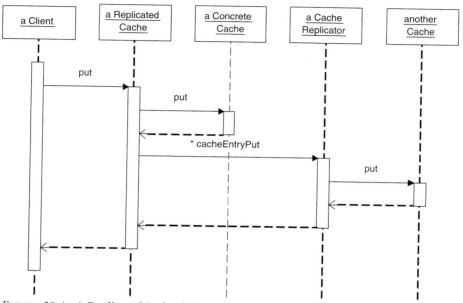

FIGURE 20.4: A ReplicatedCache delegates a put operation to its local ConcreteCache and notifies each registered CacheReplicator as well.

Figure 20.4 portrays what happens when a client issues a ReplicatedCache put operation. The ReplicatedCache delegates the put operation to its local Concrete-Cache. Next, it notifies each registered CacheReplicator object by calling its cacheEntryPut operation. Each CacheReplicator responds by invoking the analogous put operation on another Cache instance.

CONSEQUENCES

The Cache Replicator pattern has the following consequences:

Benefits

- *Replicates operations across multiple caches*—This is the pattern's description and also its primary benefit. Replicated caches can make caching a feasible solution when it is imperative for changes to be reflected across a distributed system.

- *Has configurable cache replication topologies*—Different replication topologies are more effective depending on the nature of the cached data and the systems that share it. Cache Replicator accommodates the integration of multiple replication topologies dynamically because you can wire its participants together in nearly any combination.

- *Isolates cache replication strategies*—Cache replication details are encapsulated within their own components. They remain isolated from general caching logic, client code, and each other.

Drawbacks

- *Chatty protocol*—The system notifies every participating cache instance whenever cached data changes. If these notifications occur across a network, and cache updates happen frequently, the replication overhead can subsume the performance benefit of caching the data in the first place. Buffering cache operations can alleviate this to some degree, but it also adds considerable complexity to the design.

- *Potential for redundant notifications*—In a centralized cache replication topology, most cache instances get notified of changes that they initiate unless you build a mechanism to explicitly prevent it. This is not a significant drawback unless cache updates are frequent and notification is expensive. You must also carefully consider this phenomenon when setting up your cache relationships to avoid infinite loops where two or more replicated caches continuously notify each other regarding the same cache operation.

- *Potential for inconsistent data*—Timing scenarios, race conditions, delivery and reliability constraints, and concurrent updates to the same cached data can surface as inconsistent data across multiple caches.

STRATEGIES

The CacheReplicator's role in this pattern is to serve as the notification channel from a *source* cache to a *target* cache. If the participating caches exist entirely within a single process space, then you can implement notification using synchronized shared memory or system events. If this channel crosses process or machine boundaries, then your CacheReplicator implementation requires the ability to communicate using interprocess mechanisms or a distributed networking facility such as a reliable messaging system. It is also feasible for replicated caches to exist on heterogeneous platforms, provided that the CacheReplicator implementation takes care of the appropriate conversions for cached data.

The source cache must always be a ReplicatedCache that issues update notifications, but the target can be any Cache implementation. If the target is responsible for delegating changes to other caches, like the central cache instance in Figure 20.2, attach the CacheReplicator to the target's ReplicatedCache. If the target is not responsible for delegating changes, then you can attach the CacheReplicator directly to the appropriate ConcreteCache.

SAMPLE CODE

This example uses the java.util.Map interface for its cache abstraction and java.util.HashMap as its concrete implementation. ReplicatedCache implements a Map by delegating all of its operations to another Map implementation that you assign during initialization. It also maintains a list of CacheUpdateListeners using the standard Java event idiom. Anytime it delegates an update operation, specifically put, putAll, remove, and clear, it notifies all registered listeners accordingly.

```java
public class ReplicatedCache implements Map {

    private Map cache;
    private List listeners = new LinkedList();

    public ReplicatedCache(Map cache) {
        this.cache = cache;
    }

    /**
    Adds a cache update listener to be notified
    when any cache update operation occurs.
    */
```

```java
public void addCacheUpdateListener(
    CacheUpdateListener listener) {
    listeners.add(listener);
}

/**
Removes a cache update listener.
*/
public void removeCacheUpdateListener(
    CacheUpdateListener listener) {
    listeners.remove(listener);
}

/**
Puts a new cache entry and notifies all
cache update listeners.
*/
public Object put(Object key, Object value) {

    // Delegate the put operation to the
    // underlying cache.
    Object previousValue = cache.put(key, value);

    // Notify all cache update listeners.
    CacheUpdateEvent event
        = new CacheUpdateEvent(this, key, value);
    for(Iterator i = listeners.iterator();
        i.hasNext(); ) {

        ((CacheUpdateListener)i.next())
            .cacheEntryPut(event);
    }

    return previousValue;
}

/**
Puts all entries from a Map into the cache and
notifies all cache update listeners.
*/
public void putAll(Map otherMap)
{
    // Iterate through the map, calling put for
    // each entry.  The put operation takes care of the
    // rest.
    for(Iterator i = otherMap.entrySet().iterator();
        i.hasNext(); )   {

        Map.Entry mapEntry = (Map.Entry)i.next();
```

```
            this.put(mapEntry.getKey(), mapEntry.getValue());
        }
    }

    /**
    Removes a cache entry and notifies all cache update
    listeners.
    */
    public Object remove(Object key) {

        // Delegate the remove operation to the cache.
        Object previousValue = cache.remove(key);

        // Notify all cache update listeners.
        CacheUpdateEvent event
            = new CacheUpdateEvent(this, key);
        for(Iterator i = listeners.iterator();
            i.hasNext(); ) {

            ((CacheUpdateListener)i.next())
                .cacheEntryRemoved(event);
        }

        return previousValue;
    }

    /**
    Clears the cache's contents and notifies all cache update
    listeners.
    */
    public void clear() {

        // Delegate the clear operation to the cache.
        cache.clear();

        // Notify all cache update listeners.
        CacheUpdateEvent event = new CacheUpdateEvent(this);
        for(Iterator i = listeners.iterator();
            i.hasNext(); ) {

            ((CacheUpdateListener)i.next())
                .cacheEntriesCleared(event);
        }
    }

    //
    // Implement the rest of the java.util.Map operations
    // by simply delegating to the cache's contents.
    //
```

```java
public boolean containsKey(Object key) {
    return cache.containsKey(key);
}

public boolean containsValue(Object value) {
    return cache.containsValue(value);
}

public Set entrySet() {
    return cache.entrySet();
}

public boolean equals(Object other) {
    if (!(other instanceof ReplicatedCache))
        return false;
    ReplicatedCache otherReplicatedCache
        = (ReplicatedCache)other;
    return otherReplicatedCache.cache.equals(
        this.cache);
}

public Object get(Object key) {
    return cache.get(key);
}

public int hashCode() {
    return 37 * cache.hashCode();
}

public boolean isEmpty() {
    return cache.isEmpty();
}

public Set keySet() {
    return cache.keySet();
}

public int size() {
    return cache.size();
}

public Collection values() {
    return cache.values();
}
}
```

CacheUpdateEvent extends java.util.EventObject and represents the details of a cache update notification. CacheUpdateListener extends java.util.EventListener and is the interface for any object that requires cache update notifications. Cache-UpdateListener serves the same purpose as the CacheUpdateListener that the "Structure" section described. The name is different in this example to conform to the Java convention for events and listeners.

```java
public class CacheUpdateEvent
extends EventObject {

    private Object key;
    private Object value;

    public CacheUpdateEvent(
        Object source,
        Object key,
        Object value) {

        super(source);
        this.key = key;
        this.value = value;
    }

    public CacheUpdateEvent(
        Object source,
        Object key) {

        super(source);
        this.key = key;
        this.value = null;
    }

    public CacheUpdateEvent(Object source) {
        super(source);
        this.key = null;
        this.value = null;
    }

    public Object getKey() {
        return key;
    }

    public Object getValue() {
        return value;
    }
}
```

```
public interface CacheUpdateListener
extends EventListener {

    void cacheEntryPut(CacheUpdateEvent event);
    void cacheEntryRemoved(CacheUpdateEvent event);
    void cacheEntriesCleared(CacheUpdateEvent event);

}
```

CacheReplicator implements CacheUpdateListener by delegating all update operations to another cache instance within the same JVM.

```
public class CacheReplicator
implements CacheUpdateListener {

    private Map cache;

    public CacheReplicator(Map cache) {
        this.cache = cache;
    }

    public void cacheEntryPut(
        CacheUpdateEvent event) {

        cache.put(event.getKey(), event.getValue());
    }

    public void cacheEntryRemoved(
        CacheUpdateEvent event) {

        cache.remove(event.getKey());
    }

    public void cacheEntriesCleared(
        CacheUpdateEvent event) {

        cache.clear();
    }
}
```

The following code block initializes a central cache instance and five replicated caches that participate in a complete centralized replication solution:

```
// Initialize the central cache.
ReplicatedCache centralCache
    = new ReplicatedCache(new HashMap());
```

```
// Initialize five replicated caches.
ReplicatedCache[] replicatedCaches = new ReplicatedCache[5];
for(int i = 0; i < replicatedCaches.length; ++i)
{
    Map cache = new HashMap();
    replicatedCaches[i] = new ReplicatedCache(cache);

    // Attach a cache replicator so that the replication
    // cache notifies the central cache of all updates
    // to it.
    replicatedCaches[i].addCacheUpdateListener(
        new CacheReplicator(centralCache));

    // Attach a cache replicator so that the central
    // cache notifies this cache when other
    // replicated caches are updated.
    centralCache.addCacheUpdateListener(
        new CacheReplicator(cache));
}
```

At this point, the system delegates any cache update operation to all participating cache instances.

RELATED PATTERNS AND TECHNOLOGY

- ReplicatedCache is an instance of Decorator [Gamma 1995] since it attaches additional replication behavior to any Cache implementation without subclassing.

- ReplicatedCache and CacheReplicator together form an instance of Observer [Gamma 1995]. They take on the roles of subject and observer, respectively.

- You can incorporate Cache Replicator in conjunction with Cache Accessor (271), Demand Cache (281), and Primed Cache (291). If you use Demand Cache exclusively, then you do not need to replicate the actual details of every cache update operation. Instead, it is sufficient to simply indicate that a particular cache entry changed. Other cache instances respond to notifications by removing the corresponding cache entry altogether. This has the effect of forcing subsequent local cache operations to read the updated value from the database. One benefit of this scheme is that it simplifies the Cache Replicator protocol. In addition, it minimizes the problems that result from two instances sending inconsistent or contradictory update notifications.

Cache Statistics

DESCRIPTION

Record and publish cache and pool statistics using a consistent structure for uniform presentation.

CONTEXT

Systems that make heavy use of caching and pooling facilities significantly reduce database overhead. These optimizations improve performance, but debugging and administering them sometimes requires custom monitoring tools over and above those provided by commercial database products. Developers and administrators need to inspect key system attributes regarding cache and pool utilization. These details provide a measure of how effective these optimizations are and provide clues for further configuration changes and debugging.

Developers use various statistics to analyze the efficiency of their cache implementations. A common statistic is the number of cache "hits," that is, the number of times applications find their data in a cache without requiring additional database operations.

Developers use pool statistics to ensure that their code has not introduced any resource leaks. They can identify major leaks by watching pool sizes change as applications run. Under normal usage, a pool should not grow continuously.

System administrators monitor pool sizes to understand hardware requirements based on concurrent database usage. They also use cache and pool statistics to make decisions regarding configuration options such as minimum and maximum sizes and expiration intervals.

During development, it is sufficient to dump this information to a log file, but ultimately, system administrators require access by way of a GUI. In some cases, providing multiple console interfaces can serve different needs. A full graphical interface works well at the office, while a scaled down servlet interface enables administrators to access basic information remotely with only a browser or mobile phone. Figure 21.1 shows an administration console servlet displaying a set of cache and pool statistics:

System Statistics

Description	Hits	Accesses	Hit Ratio	Size
Connection pool	1056	1079	98%	35
General purpose cache	9334	9446	99%	112
Configuration cache	423	431	98%	8

FIGURE 21.1: A sample administration console servlet displaying a set of cache and pool statistics.

Cache Statistics define a common interface that enables multiple cache and pool implementations to record and publish their details using a consistent structure. This pattern also enables you to decouple the presentation of cache and pool statistics from their contents.

APPLICABILITY

Use the Cache Statistics pattern when:

- You need to record and publish cache or pool statistics to enable system monitoring or debugging.

- You want to decouple the presentation of cache and pool statistics from their contents.

STRUCTURE

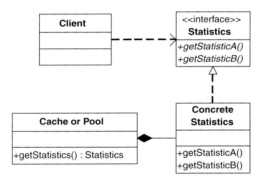

FIGURE 21.2: The static structure of the Cache Statistics pattern.

Figure 21.2 illustrates the static structure of the Cache Statistics pattern. The Statistics interface represents a single set of cache or pool statistics. It defines get operations that clients call to retrieve specific statistical values.

ConcreteStatistics implements this interface and is directly coupled to a specific cache or pool instance. It is the cache or pool's responsibility to maintain the accuracy and currency of ConcreteStatistics' data.

INTERACTIONS

Cache and pool implementations normally define specific ConcreteStatistics objects that directly reflect the relevant information. Clients interact with these generically through the Statistics interface. This enables clients to build a single-user interface component that presents statistics for any structure that publishes them.

CONSEQUENCES

The Cache Statistics pattern has the following benefits:

Benefits

- *Consistent structure*—Multiple cache and pool facilities use the same format to publish statistics.

- *Consistent presentation*—Defining a consistent Statistics interface promotes a uniform presentation for multiple sets of cache or pool statistics.

- *Separation between statistics and presentation*—The Statistics interface decouples the structure of the statistics from their presentation. This enables you to vary presentations and statistics data independently.

STRATEGIES

When you publish cache or pool statistics, you can designate them as either current or snapshot statistics. *Current statistics* always represent the current cache or pool state and reflect changes immediately. Clients only need to retrieve this type of Statistics object once and refer to it repeatedly for updated, accurate information. A current Statistics implementation often refers directly to some internal cache or pool data structure. Current statistics are convenient when you want to constantly monitor statistical information, such as in an interactive, graphical administration console.

By contrast, *snapshot statistics* represent the cache or pool's state at a single instant. Clients must repeatedly retrieve a new snapshot Statistics instance to refresh its values. Snapshot statistics are convenient when you want to compare or measure information such as pool size growth within a defined interval. In addition, snapshots work better for transmitting statistics across a network connection to a remote administration console.

If clients require both current and snapshot statistics, consider using the modified structure shown in Figure 21.3. SnapshotStatistics is a default, immutable Statistics implementation whose attributes are assigned during initialization. The CurrentStatistics interface extends the Statistics interface, adding getSnapshot, an operation that returns a SnapshotStatistics object on request.

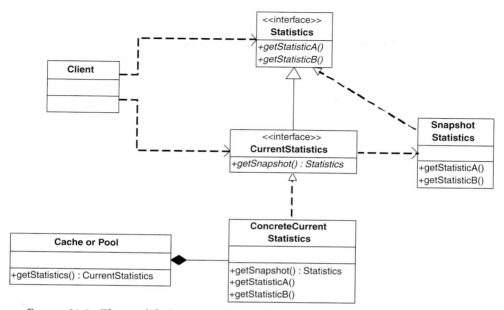

FIGURE 21.3: The modified structure for Cache Statistics, where a CurrentStatistics implementation returns a new SnapshotStatistics object on request.

SAMPLE CODE

This is a simple definition of the Statistics interface, which publishes the number of hits, number of accesses, and the size of a cache or pool. It also returns a description that comes in handy when you process multiple Statistics instances within the same analysis logic or user interface component.

```
public interface Statistics {

    /**
    Returns a description for the statistics.
    */
    String getDescription();

    /**
    Returns the number of hits.
    */
    long getHits();

    /**
    Returns the total number of accesses.
```

```
*/
long getAccesses();

/**
Returns the cache size.
*/
long getSize();
}
```

SnapshotStatistics is a default, immutable Statistics implementation:

```
public class SnapshotStatistics
implements Statistics {

    private String description;
    private long hits;
    private long accesses;
    private long size;

    public SnapshotStatistics(
        String description,
        long hits,
        long accesses,
        long size) {

        this.description = description;
        this.hits = hits;
        this.accesses = accesses;
        this.size = size;
    }

    public String getDescription() {
        return description;
    }

    public long getHits() {
        return hits;
    }

    public long getAccesses() {
        return accesses;
    }

    public long getSize() {
        return size;
    }
}
```

The CurrentStatistics interface extends the Statistics interface and adds get-Snapshot, an operation that clients call to get a snapshot of the information at a particular instant:

```
public interface CurrentStatistics
extends Statistics {

    /**
    Returns a snapshot of the statistics.
    */
    Statistics getSnapshot();
}
```

CollectionStatistics is a concrete CurrentStatistics implementation for use by both caches and pools. It is the owning cache or pool's responsibility to maintain its notion of hits and accesses by calling its markHit and markAccess operations when appropriate.

In Java, many cache and pool implementations define their internal contents using java.util.Collection implementations. The CollectionStatistics implementation relates its size directly to an underlying Collection object. This is a cleaner alternative than trying to keep the collection's and statistics' size synchronized though mutator operations, especially when automated collection or timers are in effect.

```
public class CollectionStatistics
implements CurrentStatistics {

    private long hits = 0;
    private long accesses = 0;
    private String description;
    private Collection collection;

    public CollectionStatistics(
        String description,
        Collection collection) {

        this.description = description;
        this.collection = collection;
    }

    public String getDescription() {
        return description;
    }

    public long getHits() {
```

```
            return hits;
        }

        public long getAccesses() {
            return accesses;
        }

        public long getSize() {
            return collection.size();
        }

        public Statistics getSnapshot() {
            return new SnapshotStatistics(
                description,
                hits,
                accesses,
                collection.size());
        }

        public void markHit() {
            ++hits;
            ++accesses;
        }

        public void markMiss() {
            ++accesses;
        }
    }
```

Next is a CacheAccessor implementation that uses a CollectionStatistics object to keep track of hits, misses, and its size:

```
public class CacheAccessor {

    private Map cache = new HashMap();
    private CollectionStatistics statistics
        = new CollectionStatistics("Generic cache",
        cache.keySet());

    /**
    Returns the cache statistics.
    */
    public CurrentStatistics getStatistics() {
        return statistics;
    }

    /**
    Reads data from the cache.
```

```
@param key    The key.
@return       The data.
**/
public List read(Object key) {

    List data = (List)cache.get(key);

    // If the value was found in the cache,
    // then mark this operation as a hit.
    if (data != null) {
        statistics.markHit();
    }

    // Otherwise, mark this operation as a miss
    // and return an empty list.
    else {
        statistics.markMiss();
        data = Collections.EMPTY_LIST;
    }

    return data;
}
}
```

StatisticsServlet generates the graphical console interface that is shown in Figure 21.1:

```
public class StatisticsServlet
extends HttpServlet
{
    private Statistics[] statistics;

    public StatisticsServlet(Statistics[] statistics)  {
        this.statistics = statistics;
    }

    protected void doGet(
        HttpServletRequest request,
        HttpServletResponse response)
        throws ServletException, IOException {

        // Write the title and table header.
        response.setContentType("text/html");
        PrintWriter out = response.getWriter();
        out.println("<title>System statistics</title>");
        out.println("<body>");
        out.println("<h1>System Statistics</h1>");
```

```
out.println("<table border>");
out.println("<tr><th>Description</th>");
out.println("<th>Hits</th>");
out.println("<th>Accesses</th>");
out.println("<th>Hit Ratio</th>");
out.println("<th>Size</th></tr>");

// Write a row for each statistics object.
for(int i = 0; i < statistics.length; ++i) {
    long hits = statistics[i].getHits();
    long accesses = statistics[i].getAccesses();
    out.println("<tr><td>");
    out.println(statistics[i].getDescription());
    out.println("</td><td>");
    out.println(hits);
    out.println("</td><td>");
    out.println(accesses);
    out.println("</td><td>");
    out.println(NumberFormat.getPercentInstance()
        .format((double)hits/(double)accesses));
    out.println("</td><td>");
    out.println(statistics[i].getSize());
    out.println("</td></tr>");
}

// Write the table and page footer.
out.println("</table></body>");
out.close();
    }
}
```

RELATED PATTERNS AND TECHNOLOGY

- The separation of statistics content from its presentation within a user interface is indicative of Model-View-Controller [Buschmann 1996].

- The information that Cache Statistics maintain comes in handy for administering instances of Resource Pool (117), Cache Accessor (271), Demand Cache (281), and Primed Cache (291).

- The information that Cache Statistics maintain is helpful when debugging issues that arise when implementing Cache Collector (325).

Part 5

Concurrency Patterns

When multiple application instances and sessions share data, they must cooperate to ensure that they do not make contradictory updates. In addition, they must consistently reflect changes that each instance makes. This chapter presents some problems that stem from concurrent database access. It also describes characteristics of common solutions and introduces patterns for implementing them.

UNITS OF WORK

In all but the simplest enterprise applications, database update operations are not isolated. They are often preceded by read operations and grouped with other updates. A *unit of work* is a group of related database operations that form a logical operation from an application's perspective.

A common unit of work in interactive enterprise applications that enables users to find and update data includes these steps:

1. An end-user selects a table entry to update.

2. The application renders the selected entry's contents in an editable form.

3. The user edits one or more of the form's fields and applies the changes.

4. The application applies the user's changes to the database.

For example, a project manager uses a planning application to search a work items table to find all entries for which a specific individual is responsible. He or she selects one of the matching work items and updates its status from "in progress" to "on hold." These steps define a single unit of work.

A more generic form for this common unit of work designation is:

- *Read*—Read data from the database and keep it in a working copy in primary storage.

- *Calculate*—Perform a calculation based on the working copy of the data.

- *Update*—Write the calculated data back to the database.

In batch applications such as a report or in automated conversions, calculations involve automated, programmatic processes. In interactive applications like the project planning application example, calculations are really update operations that end-users drive. The project manager makes decisions based on the data that the application presents and changes the data accordingly.

WORKING COPIES

Applications rarely perform direct calculations on physical data. Instead, they usually keep a *working copy* of the data in primary storage. One form that a working copy takes is a domain object that your application creates as a mechanism for encapsulating physical data. Even if you do not explicitly create a working copy, it is likely that your GUI library components or prefabricated driver data structures do this on your behalf.

A working copy represents a snapshot of a data set at the precise moment when a single application instance or session reads it from the database. An application depends on a working copy's contents as a basis for logical decisions and subsequent update operations. Normally, this dependency lasts until the end of the unit of work for which it was created.

When a project manager selects a specific work item to edit, the project planning application reads the work item's data and creates a working copy that serves as the basis for the changes. The application uses this working copy until explicitly instructed to apply or cancel the changes.

CONCURRENCY PROBLEMS

Working copies are the root of many concurrency problems. Multiple application instances create distinct working copies as starting points for their own individual calculations and updates. If there are no concurrency strategies in place, each application instance applies its own changes without any regard for the others.

Longer units of work significantly increase the window of opportunity for concurrency problems. Batch applications tend to read and update data quickly, using working copies for only brief intervals. On the other hand, interactive applications operate on working copies for as long as end-users are required to enter changes.

In the project planning application, it does not necessarily take a long time to change the status of a work item. However, updating a work item's detailed description usually does extend a unit of work's duration. To make matters worse, there is typically nothing to prevent a user from taking an extended break in the middle of an extensive edit. In these cases, the application uses a working copy of data for a long interval, and is therefore more prone to concurrency problems.

Concurrency problems that involve critical data like project work items, inventory, and customer call entries can significantly affect productivity and budgets. The following sections characterize some common concurrency problems in terms of the project planning application example.

Missing Updates

When two application instances make calculations based on individual working copies that represent the same data set, the resulting database update operations can conflict with each other. Suppose that two project managers are updating the same work item. The first is simply updating its date to reflect a recently completed task. The second project manager is going through an entire component's work items and moving the deadline for each uncompleted task back one week.

When the first project manager applies his/her changes, the application flushes them from the working copy to the database. Shortly afterward, the second project manager applies his/her changes and the application duly overwrites those made by the first project manager. Whichever application instance updates the database last overwrites some or all of the changes made by the first instance. This is called a *missing update* because the changes that the first user made are effectively gone.

Dirty Reads

Consider what happens when an application issues a database update operation in the middle of a unit of work. A project manager uses the planning application to change the status of a work item to "on hold," but has second thoughts before closing the work item update form. If the application flushes this tentative update operation to the database, then other users that read the table see the work item's new status.

When the project manager finally cancels the operation, his/her application instance resets the original work item's status. However, other instances now have working copies based on inaccurate, uncommitted data. This condition is commonly known as a *dirty read*.

Non-Repeatable Reads

Most applications expect consistent results when they issue identical read operations multiple times within a single unit of work. Suppose that a project manager inspects a work item's description to decide its status. At the same time, a system architect updates the description, adding a key issue that was not previously identified.

The project manager navigates to another form to gather additional information. When he/she returns to the description page, it is changed to reflect the system architect's update. This condition requires the project manager to reconsider the information gathered during the unit of work before making a decision on the work item's new status. This is called a non-repeatable read and causes problems when an application or business process depends on query results remaining consistent throughout a unit of work.

Phantom Reads

Phantom reads occur when query results change within a single unit of work. This happens when one application instance queries a particular table while another inserts data into it. If the original application instance reissues the query within the same unit of work, its results now include additional data.

A common project management task is retrieving a list of all work items assigned to a particular employee. This list enables the project manager to quickly assess the employee's workload before assigning additional work items. Suppose that the project manager does this at the same time that one of his/her colleagues performs a similar duty. When the list is refreshed, the employee has more work items than originally intended.

CONCURRENCY SOLUTIONS

Here are some simple strategies that can reduce the potential for concurrency problems:

- *Reduce unit of work durations*—Applications that involve shorter units of work use the working copies that they create for shorter intervals, and consequently, allow fewer opportunities for concurrency problems to arise. In most cases, it is not feasible to restrict the duration that an application can use a working copy, but you can employ timers to avoid leaving important resources open while a user takes an extended break or a calculation takes longer than expected. See Resource Timer (137) for one such strategy. You can also tune batch applications to carry out units of work as efficiently as possible.

- *Reduce the quantity of working copies*—In the interest of consistency and code reuse, many applications use identical logic to read data regardless of whether an end-user plans to edit it or simply view it. This results in the creation of working copies even when users do not intend to update the data.

  Applications that are able to indicate their intent for data can distinguish read-only working copies from those that are likely to be updated. Most batch applications can specify this programmatically, but interactive applications have to determine this based on context and user selections.

  In many applications, the number of working copies that correspond to update operations is significantly less than the total number of working copies overall. Isolating these updatable copies reduces the potential for concurrency problems since the chance that multiple contradictory units of work will overlap decreases.

- *Serialize working copies*—If you ensure that no two application instances or sessions use working copies for the same data at the same time, then you can eliminate concurrency problems.

One way to implement this is to utilize native database support for updatable cursors. When an application creates a working copy, the underlying database locks the corresponding rows. Subsequent attempts to create a working copy for the same data result in blocking or errors.

Serializing working copies solves many concurrency problems, but this strategy can have an enormous negative impact on your system's usability and scalability. The database often locks any physical data that relates to an active working copy, so batch processes and other interactive applications may not function as expected. Worse, end-users attempting to update locked data may experience long delays or terse database error messages. Taken to the extreme, serialization can result in deadlock between instances that are waiting for each other to release their locks.

- *Validate working copies*—Before you update data from a working copy, verify that the underlying data has not changed since the working copy was created and issue an error or warning message to the end-user if it has.

It is important to address potential concurrency issues throughout an application's design and implementation phases. The problems that your customers face are often difficult to recreate within your own development environment and automated testing. Scalability and multiple user simulation testing can be invaluable for identifying concurrency problems before they affect customers.

CONCURRENCY PATTERNS

This part of the book describes patterns that address concurrency problems at the application or middleware level. Each pattern approaches concurrency issues differently. This part contains chapters for each of the following patterns:

- **Transaction** (379)—Executes concurrent units of work in an atomic, consistent, isolated, and durable manner. Nearly every database platform supports native transactions.

- **Optimistic Lock** (395)—Maintains version information to prevent missing database updates. Optimistic locking uses application semantics to validate a working copy's version before updating the database.

- **Pessimistic Lock** (405)—Attaches lock information to data to prevent missing database updates. Explicit pessimistic locking often offers better application diagnostics than native transaction support.

- **Compensating Transaction** (417)—Defines explicit compensating operations to roll back units of work that are not part of a native database transaction.

As you consider the alternatives that these patterns define, pay close attention to the description and applicability designation for each of them. Some patterns are substantially better suited for specific scenarios, depending on the way an application uses and shares its data.

Transaction

DESCRIPTION

Executes concurrent units of work in an atomic, consistent, isolated, and durable manner. Nearly every database platform supports native transactions.

CONTEXT

A unit of work in enterprise software rarely comprises just a single database operation. Transactions usually span multiple tables, and sometimes multiple data sources. As business logic gets more complex, units of work grow, and so does the potential for concurrent data access problems.

Consider a video rental store's point-of-sale (POS) application. There is an entry in the INVENTORY table for every item in the store. Each of these entries indicates whether an item is currently rented and if so, when it is due back. There

379

is also a TITLES table that acts as a quick reference for checking to see if a given title is in stock. Finally, the CUSTOMERS table maintains customer information, including each customer's address, phone number, and a tally of how many times they have rented from the store.

When a customer rents an item, the POS application updates each of these tables in succession. It marks the item's rented state in the INVENTORY table, decrements the title's availability in the TITLES table, and logs the customer's rental activity in the CUSTOMERS table. These update operations form a single unit of work. Since this unit of work requires multiple update operations, there is a window of opportunity for concurrency problems to arise.

Transactions provide a mechanism for serializing units of work like this, so that applications can ensure that other concurrent update operations do not conflict with its own. A transaction satisfies the following properties:

- *Atomicity*—The operations within a unit of work are carried out logically as a single, atomic operation. If any component operation fails, every other component operation is rolled back. The net effect is that either all or none of the component operations are executed.

- *Consistency*—The system is left in a consistent state when the unit of work is complete. A *consistent state* means that the net effect of the component operations makes semantic sense to applications.

- *Isolation*—Each unit of work runs independently of other concurrent units of work. This means that a transaction has the same effect regardless of other transactions' states.

- *Durability*—Once committed, the effect of completed units of work remains intact.

Transaction semantics are difficult to implement yourself because they involve system- or database-level locking. Fortunately, most database products provide native transactional functionality, of which you can readily take advantage.

In most native transaction facilities, you indicate where transactions begin and end using transaction primitives. This is known as *demarcating* transaction boundaries. Demarcation enables you to group your application's database operations into logical transactions. Some common transaction primitives include:

- *begin*—Designates the beginning of a transaction.

- *commit*—Designates the end of a transaction and instructs the database to commit all the transaction's operations. Call this when all the operations run successfully.

- *rollback*—Designates the end of a transaction and instructs the database to roll back, or undo, all the transaction's operations. Call this when one or more of the operations fail.

- *setRollbackOnly*—Designates a failure within a transaction, but does not immediately roll it back. Instead, this primitive sets a flag within the transaction implementation. When the application later commits, this flag instructs the transaction implementation to roll its operations back instead. setRollbackOnly provides a way for applications to signal an error without interrupting program flow. Not all transaction facilities expose this primitive.

Databases implement transactions using diverse strategies, but they nearly always incur locking overhead. Transaction implementations lock either single rows or entire tables. As a result, large transactions leave a greater number of locks in place and can prevent other concurrent transactions from accessing data. This behavior can manifest to applications as long pauses that are caused by program flow blocking until the database releases the corresponding locks at the ends of transaction boundaries. Users perceive these symptoms as poor performance or response time on the part of affected applications. A general guideline is to keep transactions as small and fast as possible so that single applications do not hold locks for a significant duration.

The three operations in the video rental example make up a logical unit of work and can be implemented using a single transaction. The transaction ensures that the updates are made consistently, and that if any of them fail, all of them are rolled back.

APPLICABILITY

Use transactions when:

- You require applications to serialize units of work so that you can safely depend on the data they reference throughout all concurrent data access scenarios.

- You want to take advantage of native database and system locking mechanisms to enforce transaction semantics without introducing platform-dependent application or middleware code.

- The data involved in your applications' units of work are not likely to be accessed concurrently in high-traffic scenarios where native locking would unacceptably degrade performance and scalability.

STRUCTURE

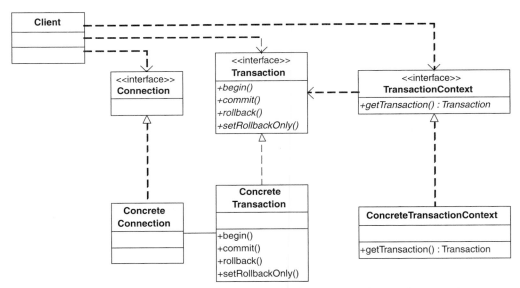

FIGURE 22.1: A common static structure for database connections and transactions.

Figure 22.1 illustrates a common static structure for database connections and transactions. The Connection interface represents the primary resource that clients use to issue database operations. ConcreteConnection is the native database driver's Connection implementation.

Likewise, the Transaction interface is a handle that clients use to issue transaction primitives. The native database driver usually associates its ConcreteTransactions with ConcreteConnections. This association is important because clients use ConcreteTransaction to demarcate transaction boundaries that apply to the database operations that they issue using the related ConcreteConnection. Clients use a ConcreteTransactionContext to resolve new ConcreteTransaction objects.

Many call-level interfaces merge the operations and behavior defined for Transaction and TransactionContext into the Connection interface. This simplifies client operations that issue both database operations and transaction primitives using the same object.

INTERACTIONS

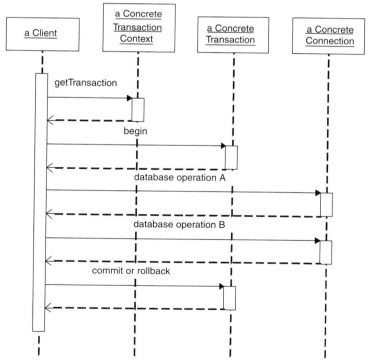

FIGURE 22.2: A client issues database operations that make up a single transaction.

Figure 22.2 portrays what happens in a typical transaction. The client first resolves the ConcreteTransaction by invoking ConcreteTransactionContext's getTransaction operation. Next, it demarcates the beginning of a new transaction by calling ConcreteTransaction's begin primitive.

At this point, a transaction is active. The native database driver carries out any database operations the client issues, but it executes them within the scope of this transaction. When the client finishes issuing database operations, it demarcates the end of the transaction boundary by calling either commit or rollback.

CONSEQUENCES

Transactions have the following consequences:

Benefits

- *Native database support*—Nearly every database supports native transactions. It is straightforward to take advantage of native transaction support, especially when the database implements a common transactional model like that described in this chapter.

- *Serialized units of work*—Transactions reliably serialize units of work. You can confidently issue database operations within transactions, knowing that they do not conflict unpredictably with database interactions in other concurrent applications.

- *Configuration*—You can configure each transaction's isolation level to trade off concurrency for transaction isolation. See the "Strategies" section for more information on isolation levels.

Drawback

- *Locking semantics hinder concurrency.* Databases usually implement transactions using system- or database-level object locking that imposes concurrency. Consequently, the more transactions your system carries out, the fewer that are able to run concurrently. End-users perceive this characteristic as slow response time.

STRATEGIES

This section describes some additional strategies to consider when you implement application data access logic using transactions.

Local Transactions

Local transactions confine operations to a single data source. A single database implementation manages all required locking and concurrency mechanisms. Most database drivers provide simplified application semantics for local transactions that merge a subset of the concepts that TransactionContext and Transaction define into the Connection interface. There is usually a one-to-one correspondence between database connections and transactions. A connection begins a new transaction as soon as the application commits or rolls back the previous one. Figure 22.3 illustrates this modified structure:

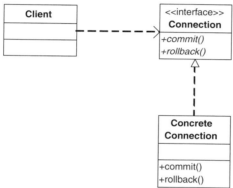

FIGURE 22.3: A common, simplified, static structure for local transactions. This structure merges a subset of the concepts that TransactionContext and Transaction define into the Connection interface.

This is a template for application code that carries out a single local transaction using JDBC:

```
try {
    // Issue the database operations.
    // ...

    // Mark the transaction boundary.
    connection.commit();
}
catch(Exception e) {
    // In case of an error, rollback.
    connection.rollback();

    // Dispatch the error to the client.
    // (Optional)
    throw e;
}
```

Distributed Transactions

Distributed transactions are transactions whose operations span multiple data sources. Distributed transaction systems are complex because they require multiple database implementations to cooperate to manage uniform transaction semantics.

Since distributed transactions often involve heterogeneous databases, it is important for each database to communicate using standard protocols. The following software entities work together to implement a complete distributed transaction management system:

- *Transaction processing monitor*—A transaction processing monitor controls the overall distributed transaction. It exposes fundamental transaction primitives to applications, while encapsulating their implementation.

- *Transaction managers*—A transaction processing monitor sends orders to one or more transaction managers that carry out transaction operations in turn. There is usually one transaction manager for each server or environment that participates in a distributed transaction. Transaction managers communicate with each other to coordinate their operations. OMG's Object Transaction Service (OTS) is a common protocol used for transaction manager communication. Transaction processing monitors and transaction managers are often packaged within commercial middleware products or standards. In Java, the Java Transaction API (JTA) and Java Transaction Service (JTS) specifications define these concepts. J2EE compliant application servers provide implementations for these specifications.

- *Resource managers*—There is a resource manager in charge of implementing each data source's part of a transaction. Resource managers take orders from transaction managers, usually by way of yet another standard protocol like the Open Group's XA Specification. Each resource manager interacts directly with its data source and is often packaged as a feature of a native database product.

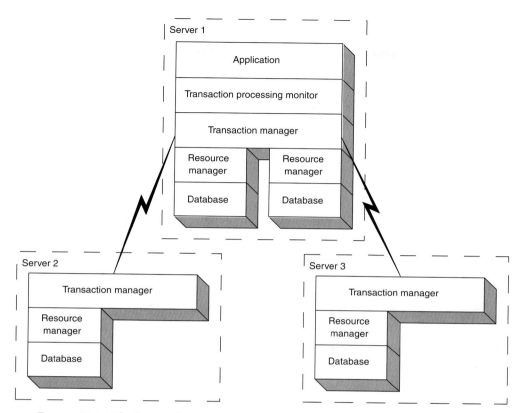

FIGURE 22.4: The interactions between a transaction processing monitor, transaction managers, and resource managers. In this figure, the distributed transaction spans four databases on three servers.

Figure 22.4 shows the interactions between these entities. A transaction processing monitor, transaction managers, and resource managers cooperate to implement a *two-phase commit*. The two-phase commit protocol guarantees that either all or none of the database operations that comprise a distributed transaction get committed to their respective data sources. As its name suggests, this protocol involves two phases. In the first phase, each resource manager prepares to commit its part of the transaction. The resource manager indicates to the transaction manager whether it can guarantee successful committal without actually carrying out the commit. The second phase begins when all the participating resource managers successfully complete this preparation. At this point, the transaction managers instruct their resource managers to commit the transaction's database operations.

This is a template for application code that carries out a single distributed transaction using JTA. Notice that JTA encapsulates the interactions between the transaction processing monitor, transaction managers, and resource managers, so that the application's sole responsibility is demarcating the transaction boundary.

```
// Get the current transaction object from the container.
UserTransaction transaction = ejbContext.getUserTransaction();

// Mark the transaction boundary.
transaction.begin();

try {
    // Issue the database operations.
    // ...
}
catch(Exception e) {
    // In case of an error, set the transaction
    // to rollback only.
    transaction.setRollbackOnly();
}

// Either commit or rollback the transaction, depending
// on whether it is set to rollback only.
transaction.commit();
```

Isolation Levels

Most transaction implementations allow you to configure an *isolation level* for each transaction. Isolation levels define the degree to which units of work are isolated from each other. Common isolation levels are:

- *Read uncommitted*—Prevents missing updates, but allows dirty reads, non-repeatable reads, and phantom reads. Changes that have not been committed are visible to other transactions. If you roll back these changes, subsequent reads in other transactions reflect the original data.

- *Read committed*—Prevents missing updates and dirty reads, but allows non-repeatable reads and phantom reads. Other transactions cannot view uncommitted data, but you may see inconsistent results if you issue the same query repeatedly within your transaction, assuming another transaction updates the same data.

- *Repeatable read*—Prevents missing updates, dirty reads, and non-repeatable reads, but allows phantom reads. Your transaction cannot see uncommitted or committed data that is modified by other transactions.

- *Serializable*—Prevents missing updates, dirty reads, non-repeatable reads, and phantom reads. Serializable transactions are completely isolated from the effects of other transactions.

Databases implement serializable isolation by locking a significant quantity of database resources. With these locks in place, applications that access a lot of data concurrently suffer significant performance degradation. This is where the concept of transaction isolation levels comes in handy. Each successive level trades off strict attention to transaction properties with the benefit of higher concurrency. Compare the criteria for each isolation level and select the most appropriate one based on your isolation and concurrency requirements.

Declarative Transactions

Declarative transactions are part of another common transaction model that enables you to declare higher level transaction semantics for any application module. You can declare a *transaction attribute* for each module, and the application environment takes care of issuing transaction primitives. Transaction attributes indicate whether a module must run in the context of a transaction and how they interact with the calling module's active transaction, if at all.

The advantage of declarative transactions is that they are much easier to modify and configure transaction attributes for using graphical administration or development tools. Otherwise, you would need to change the corresponding application code. Another advantage is that they hide potential low-level and platform-dependent transactional operations from applications.

EJBs support a form of declarative transaction called container-managed transaction demarcation. You can associate any of the following transaction attributes with each of an EJB's methods, and the EJB container manages the transaction semantics accordingly:

- *Required*—The method must always run within a transaction. If a transaction is already active, then the method's operations apply to it. Otherwise, the container begins a new transaction when the method is called and commits it when the method returns. This is the most common transaction attribute for methods that do transactional work.

- *RequiresNew*—The container always begins a new transaction when the method is called and commits it when the method returns. If another transaction is already active, the container suspends it for the duration of the method call. Use this transaction attribute when you want to force a commit without allowing the caller to rollback your changes.

- *NotSupported*—The method never runs within a transaction. If a transaction is active when this method is called, the container suspends it for the duration of the method call. Use this transaction attribute if the method uses a data source that does not support or participate in distributed transactions.

- *Supports*—If a transaction is already active, the method runs within it. Otherwise, it does not run within a transaction at all. The method essentially inherits its transactional behavior from its caller.

- *Mandatory*—The method must run within a transaction. The container throws an exception if there is no active transaction when this method is called. This transaction attribute limits the method's usability since it places the burden of transaction management on its callers.

- *Never*—The method must never run within a transaction. This time, the container throws an exception if a transaction is active when this method is called. This transaction attribute also limits the method's usability.

Even though methods that declare transaction attributes relinquish much of their transactional control, they are still able to throw exceptions that indicate failed operations so that the container rolls back affected transactions accordingly.

Savepoints

Some transaction implementations allow you to define *savepoints* within your application code. A savepoint is an intermediate step within a transaction that represents the transaction's state at a given instant. At any point within the transaction, your application can roll back to any savepoint within that transaction, effectively unwinding the transaction to a previous state. Keep in mind that savepoints are purely a convenience for applications and do not affect a transaction's boundaries or implementation.

SAMPLE CODE

Recall the video rental store POS application that the "Context" section described? This block of code issues the three database operations for a single rental transaction using a local transaction:

```
// Initialize the database connection.
Connection connection
    = DriverManager.getConnection(url, user, password);

// Turn auto commit off, since we plan to use
// transactions.
connection.setAutoCommit(false);

// Set the isolation level to read uncommitted. This
// allows dirty reads, which is desirable since we want
// queries for title availability to reflect current
// rental transactions that are in progress.
connection.setTransactionIsolation(
    Connection.TRANSACTION_READ_UNCOMMITTED);

// Prepare statements for updating the INVENTORY,
// TITLES, and CUSTOMERS tables.
PreparedStatement inventoryUpdate
    = connection.prepareStatement(
    "UPDATE INVENTORY "
    + "SET RENTED_BY = ?, RENTED_ON = ? "
    + "WHERE ITEM_ID = ?");

PreparedStatement titleAvailabilityDecrement
    = connection.prepareStatement(
    "UPDATE TITLES "
    + "SET QUANTITY_AVAILABLE = QUANTITY_AVAILABLE - 1 "
    + "WHERE TITLE = "
    + "(SELECT TITLE FROM INVENTORY WHERE ITEM_ID = ?)");

PreparedStatement customerActivityIncrement
    = connection.prepareStatement(
    "UPDATE CUSTOMERS "
    + "SET ACTIVITY = ACTIVITY + 1, LAST_ACTIVITY = ? "
    + "WHERE CUSTOMER_ID = ?");

// Assume that customerID and itemID have been initialized
// using barcodes.  Update the INVENTORY, TITLES, and
// CUSTOMERS table to reflect a rental transaction.  If all
// updates are successful, then commit the transaction.
// Otherwise, roll it back.
try {
```

```
        Timestamp rightNow
            = new Timestamp(System.currentTimeMillis());

        inventoryUpdate.setInt(1, customerID);
        inventoryUpdate.setTimestamp(2, rightNow);
        inventoryUpdate.setInt(3, itemID);
        inventoryUpdate.executeUpdate();

        titleAvailabilityDecrement.setInt(1, itemID);
        titleAvailabilityDecrement.executeUpdate();

        customerActivityIncrement.setTimestamp(1, rightNow);
        customerActivityIncrement.setInt(2, customerID);
        customerActivityIncrement.executeUpdate();

        connection.commit();
    }
    catch(Exception e) {
        connection.rollback();
    }
```

This is a similar block of code that issues the same database operations using a distributed transaction within the context of an EJB. ejbContext represents an EJB container's transaction context and UserTransaction is the transaction handle class.

```
    // Get the current transaction object from
    // the container.
    UserTransaction transaction
        = ejbContext.getUserTransaction();

    // Assume that the customerID and itemID have been
    // initialized using barcodes.  Update the INVENTORY,
    // TITLES, and CUSTOMERS tables to reflect a rental
    // transaction.  If any of the updates are not
    // successful, then set the transaction to rollback
    // only.
    try {
        Timestamp rightNow
            = new Timestamp(System.currentTimeMillis());

        inventoryUpdate.setInt(1, customerID);
        inventoryUpdate.setTimestamp(2, rightNow);
        inventoryUpdate.setInt(3, itemID);
        inventoryUpdate.executeUpdate();

        titleAvailabilityDecrement.setInt(1, itemID);
        titleAvailabilityDecrement.executeUpdate();
```

```
        customerActivityIncrement.setTimestamp(1, rightNow);
        customerActivityIncrement.setInt(2, customerID);
        customerActivityIncrement.executeUpdate();
    }
    catch(Exception e) {
        transaction.setRollbackOnly();
    }

    // Either commit or rollback the transaction, depending
    // on whether it is set to rollback only.
    transaction.commit();
```

RELATED PATTERNS AND TECHNOLOGY

Nearly every relational database platform and driver implements native transactions. Levels of support vary, so check your database platform's documentation for details. In addition, most drivers provide standard programmatic interfaces that you can use to check the extent of their transaction support at runtime, including supported isolation levels and specific features like two-phase commit and savepoints.

There are many commercial distributed transaction management products available as well. J2EE compliant application servers provide this as standard support.

These patterns also relate to transactions:

- Longer transactions retain native system- or database-level locks that can hinder concurrency. As a safeguard to prevent deadlock or otherwise excessively long transactions, you can use Resource Timer (137) to automatically roll back transactions after a configurable period of inactivity.

- Optimistic Lock (395) and Pessimistic Lock (405) define alternatives to native database transactions. These patterns employ application semantics with improved diagnostic information and less locking overhead.

- Compensating Transaction (417) defines a strategy for coordinating distributed transactions when no native distributed transaction support is available.

Optimistic Lock

DESCRIPTION

Maintains version information to prevent missing database updates. Optimistic locking uses application semantics to validate a working copy's version before updating the database.

CONTEXT

A fundamental feature of order processing software is keeping accurate inventory records. Salespeople depend on up-to-the-second availability quotes when they make delivery commitments to customers. Working copy representations of inventory data can create problematic scenarios, especially during the moments between the instant when a salesperson checks a product's availability and when he/she places an order for that product. If a second salesperson places a similar order during this interval, he/she runs the risk of changing the product's on-hand quantity and interfering with availability that the first salesperson has already promised.

This potential problem exists throughout the duration when the application depends on its working copy as an accurate representation of a product's inventory data. In the worst case, this interval lasts from the time the application reads the data until the salesperson processes the order. If another application instance or session changes the inventory data during this interval, the working copy's details are no longer accurate.

Locking provides one type of solution to this problem. System- or database-level locking mechanisms such as those associated with updatable cursors or transactions can prevent this situation. Depending on the transaction isolation level, locks block other sessions from reading or updating any data that is involved in a process's active working copy. If there can never be more than one active working copy at a time, then it is impossible for other application instances or sessions to change the underlying data during this interval.

Unfortunately, accessing pervasive information like inventory data using locks can significantly increase contention for the data and reduce overall system scalability. In the extreme situation, locking semantics allow only one salesperson to view a given product's availability at a time. Even worse, it slows other applications that operate on the same data set, such as warehouse restocking and daily reports.

Another solution is to attach a version to each inventory item. The most common way to achieve this is to add a version column to the inventory table. This column contains timestamp data that indicates when each row's data was most recently changed. When the order processing application creates a working copy of inventory data, it keeps track of its version as well. When a salesperson places an order, the application compares the working copy version with the copy in the database. If these versions are different, then the application notifies the salesperson immediately, giving him/her the ability to resolve inconsistencies while finalizing the order.

This strategy is called *optimistic locking*. This term is somewhat of a misnomer since the application does not actually lock the data. Instead, it simply assumes that no other application instance or session requires the same data. The term "optimistic" refers to the idea that this assumption is valid most of the time.

When this assumption does not hold true, the version test detects the potential for inconsistent updates. The application may notify the end-user or prevent the update from occurring without refreshing the working copy first. At this point in the order processing application, the salesperson can either cancel the order or re-enter it based on a refreshed working copy.

APPLICABILITY

Use the Optimistic Lock pattern when:

- Multiple processes can issue inconsistent update operations involving common data.

- An application accesses a particular data set frequently enough that locking solutions significantly impact scalability.

- You need to customize diagnostic information beyond what native database or transaction facilities provide.

STRUCTURE

FIGURE 23.1: The static structure of the Optimistic Lock pattern.

Figure 23.1 illustrates the static structure of the Optimistic Lock pattern. Clients interact with working copies of the data, shown here as the WorkingCopy class. WorkingCopy can define a domain object or any other software data representation.

Each WorkingCopy instance maintains a Version that corresponds to the analogous value in the physical table at the instant when it read WorkingCopy's data. Common Version implementations use timestamps, global counters, incremental change identifiers, or even a subset of the row data.

INTERACTIONS

When a client writes WorkingCopy's changes to the database, it carries out a version test. This test verifies that no other processes have updated the corresponding physical data since the data in WorkingCopy was read.

This SQL UPDATE operation implements optimistic locking semantics, including the version test:

```
UPDATE  tableName
SET     column1    = 'newAttributeValue1',
        column2    = 'newAttributeValue2',
        VERSION    = 'newVersion'
WHERE   keyColumn1 = 'identityAttribute1'
AND     VERSION    = 'oldVersion'
```

Notice the highlighted clauses. The first is important because it assigns a new version to the updated data. This indicates to other processes that the data has changed. The second highlighted clause is the version test. If another process has updated the physical copy of the data, this test prevents the operation from matching any existing rows in the table and the update operation ultimately fails. This mechanism prevents the current process from overwriting other processes' changes.

Client code uses the update count that this operation returns to determine whether it was successful. If it was not, then client code can throw an exception or display a suitable message to the end-user.

CONSEQUENCES

The Optimistic Lock pattern has the following consequences:

Benefits

- *Customizable diagnostic information*—Clients do not unknowingly update data inconsistently. Applications can detect consistency errors and notify clients before carrying out update operations. This notification can take the form of an exception that a batch process logs or a graphical message box presented to an end-user.
  You can tailor this notification to include whatever diagnostic information will suit clients best. For example, it may be helpful to inform users who updated

the data last and when it changed. This type of information can encourage users to be more aware of concurrency issues and remind them to refresh working copies after returning from extended breaks.

- *No locking overhead*—Applications do not actually lock physical data and therefore do not suffer the impact of associated negative scalability.

- *No potential for orphan locks*—An orphan lock occurs when an application instance or session locks a database entity and neglects to release it. Optimistic locking does not actually lock any database entities, so there is no potential for orphan locks.

Drawbacks

- *Users can lose work*—Applications do not detect inconsistent update operations until they attempt to write them to the database. If a version test fails, the user's only recourse is to refresh his/her application instance's working copy and re-enter the changes. This causes users to lose work and is a significant usability issue when the data entry process is lengthy.

- *External components do not necessarily implement the pattern*—Optimistic locking is most effective when every update to a particular data set employs the same strategy. If defective or third-party components make updates without updating or testing the version column, they prevent applications that implement optimistic locking from completely enforcing consistent updates.

STRATEGIES

The order processing application example that the Context section described uses timestamps for versions. Timestamps are effective because they are easy to generate and compare. They also convey additional diagnostic information about the corresponding data, specifically the time when it was last updated.

The downside of using timestamp versions is that they open a window, albeit extremely small, in which two processes can assign their update operations identical timestamps. The duration of this window depends on the precision to which your database platform stores timestamp data.

Some other version representation possibilities include:

- *Incremental change identifier*—Initialize the change identifier to 0 and increment it every time you update the corresponding data. You can define change identifiers that are unique within each row, table, or data set.

- *Subset of row data*—Consider a subset of the row data to be its version. When you issue update operations, include this subset of original data in the selection or WHERE clause. When another application instance or session changes any of this data, at least one of the values is different and the version test fails.
  This is an example SQL UPDATE operation that implements optimistic locking using a subset of row data. Column1 and column2 together form the version representation.

```
UPDATE  tableName
SET     column1    = 'newAttributeValue1',
        column2    = 'newAttributeValue2'
WHERE   keyColumn1 = 'identityAttribute1'
AND     column1    = 'oldAttributeValue1'
AND     column2    = 'oldAttributeValue2'
```

Some databases automatically maintain version columns that are intended specifically for implementing optimistic locking. Depending on your database platform, you can define native database triggers to do the same. Implementing optimistic locking within a database requires additional installation and portability considerations, but it has the advantage of enforcing optimistic locking semantics even when data is updated outside of your applications' control.

A single version for each row of data may be too restrictive for tables that contain several columns that are frequently updated independently. When this scenario arises, consider defining separate version data for each updatable column in the table and maintain the versions separately.

Finally, if a logical unit of work involves multiple physical updates, then it is a good idea to enclose the update operations and version tests in a Transaction (379). This hybrid approach ensures a consistent and atomic set of updates without incurring locking overhead for the entire unit of work.

SAMPLE CODE

This example illustrates optimistic locking in conjunction with the inventory table for the order processing application example described in the "Context" section. The InventoryItem class is a domain object that serves as the working copy of a single product's inventory information. Notice that it includes a java.sql.Time-stamp attribute for its version.

```
public class InventoryItem
{
    private String productID;
    private String description;
    private int onHand;
    private Timestamp version;

    public String getProductID() {
        return productID;
    }

    public void setProductID(String productID) {
        this.productID = productID;
    }

    public String getDescription() {
        return description;
    }

    public void setDescription(String description) {
        this.description = description;
    }

    public int getOnHand() {
        return onHand;
    }

    public void setOnHand(int onHand) {
        this.onHand = onHand;
    }

    public Timestamp getVersion() {
        return version;
    }

    public void setVersion(Timestamp version) {
        this.version = version;
    }

    public String toString() {
        StringBuffer buffer = new StringBuffer();
        buffer.append("Inventory item ");
        buffer.append(productID);
        return buffer.toString();
```

```
        }
}
```

This is client code that reads and populates a single InventoryItem object. Assume that the application uses this object as its working copy throughout a single unit of work.

```
StringBuffer buffer = new StringBuffer();
buffer.append("SELECT DESCRIPTION, ON_HAND, VERSION ");
buffer.append("FROM INVENTORY WHERE PRODUCT_ID = ?");
String selectStatement = buffer.toString();

PreparedStatement ps
    = connection.prepareStatement(selectStatement);
ps.setString(1, productID);
ResultSet rs = ps.executeQuery();

// Create the working copy for the
// inventory item, including its version.
InventoryItem inventoryItem = null;
if (rs.next()) {
    inventoryItem = new InventoryItem();
    inventoryItem.setProductID(productID);
    inventoryItem.setDescription(rs.getString(1));
    inventoryItem.setOnHand(rs.getInt(2));
    inventoryItem.setVersion(rs.getTimestamp(3));
}

rs.close();
ps.close();
```

The next block of client code flushes changes that the application makes from the InventoryItem to the database. The SQL UPDATE statement performs the version test to ensure that the data has not changed since the InventoryItem was read. It also updates the row's version to reflect the new version.

```
StringBuffer buffer = new StringBuffer();
buffer.append("UPDATE INVENTORY SET ");
buffer.append("ON_HAND = ?, DESCRIPTION = ?, ");
buffer.append("VERSION = ? ");
buffer.append("WHERE PRODUCT_ID = ? AND VERSION = ?");
String updateStatement = buffer.toString();

PreparedStatement ps
    = connection.prepareStatement(updateStatement);
ps.setInt(1, inventoryItem.getOnHand());
```

```
ps.setString(2, inventoryItem.getDescription());
ps.setTimestamp(3, new Timestamp(System.currentTimeMillis()));
ps.setString(4, inventoryItem.getProductID());
ps.setTimestamp(5, inventoryItem.getVersion());
int updateCount = ps.executeUpdate();
ps.close();

// If no rows are updated, then the
// corresponding data was updated with a new version
// since this working copy was read.
if (updateCount == 0)
    throw new OptimisticLockException(inventoryItem);
```

The update operation returns the number of rows that it changed. It returns zero to indicate that it did not update any rows. This condition indicates that the version test failed. When this happens, the code block throws an OptimisticLock-Exception.

When interactive applications catch this type of exception, they can present a message to the end-user. Likewise, batch applications can log exception details and continue processing. In practice, this exception can contain additional diagnostic information such as the timestamp when the data was updated and the user who made the conflicting change. This is a sample definition of Optimistic-LockException:

```
public class OptimisticLockException
extends Exception {

    public OptimisticLockException(Object workingCopy) {
        super("The data for " + workingCopy
            + " has changed.  Please refresh and try again.");
    }
}
```

RELATED PATTERNS AND TECHNOLOGY

- [Fowler 2002] refers to this pattern as Optimistic Offline Lock.

- [Marinescu 2002] describes a specific Optimistic Lock implementation called Version Number.

- Optimistic Lock prevents you from requiring a Transaction (379) to span an entire unit of work. However, you can still benefit by using a transaction that includes only the update operations at the end of a logical unit of work.

Pessimistic Lock

DESCRIPTION

Attaches lock information to data to prevent missing database updates. Explicit pessimistic locking often offers better application diagnostics than analogous native transaction support.

CONTEXT

Applications can store full documents and free-form text in relational databases using character and large object columns that correspond to tags and structured data in the same table. For example, a customer service tracking application can store call records like this. Each call record includes vital information like a customer identifier, the date and time when the customer opened and closed a call, the software version that the customer uses, and free-form text fields for the problem description and resolution.

Customer service representatives, technical support representatives, and managers use and edit these text fields to keep each other apprised of problem statuses. If all goes as planned, this shared data becomes a communication channel that leads to effective problem resolution, and ultimately, satisfied customers.

However, consider what happens when two application users make concurrent changes to the same data. The first, a customer service representative, uses the application to query the CALLS table and create a working copy for a particular call record. The application presents this working copy's contents in graphical form. The customer service representative uses this form to edit the problem description so that it reflects a recent conversation with the customer who originally raised the problem.

At the same time, a technical support representative debugs the problem and discovers its underlying cause. He/she uses the same application to edit the call record and appends this new information. His/her application instance also makes a working copy based on the same, original call record data.

At this point, both users have made changes to their individual working copies of the same call record. When the customer support representative saves the changes, the application duly updates the record in the database. Unfortunately, when the technical support representative saves the changes, the application does the same, overwriting the first set of changes without notice.

This missing update problem stems from multiple processes editing the same data concurrently. The duration when an application depends on its working copy's data to be a basis for changes defines the exposure when this type of problem can occur. When large amounts of data or free-form text are involved, this duration tends to be longer, since users require more time to edit it.

Optimistic Lock (395) describes a solution that prevents the second user from unknowingly overwriting the first user's changes. However, with optimistic locking, the application does not notify the second user of the conflict until the changes are applied. When this happens, the second user's recourse is to refresh the working copy and enter the changes again. This strategy imposes a significant burden when changes are extensive.

You can also solve this problem by employing system- or database-level locks. If the application locks single call records using a Transaction (379) or updatable cursor, then only one user can access a given call record at any time. As long as the customer support representative edits a particular call record's problem description, the technical support representative's session's attempt to edit the same call record either blocks indefinitely or times out, and ultimately displays a non-descriptive database-level error message.

Pessimistic locking works similarly to system- and database-level locks in that it locks a single row of data while one user makes changes to it. It is called "pessimistic" because it assumes that other processes will try to update the same data, and it employs locks as a precaution on every access. The difference between explicit pessimistic locking and that which databases enforce in conjunction with transactions and updatable cursors is that applications control locking semantics. When an application defines and explicitly controls the locks that it depends on, it can present semantically correct diagnostic information to users.

You can apply pessimistic locking within the customer service tracking application by adding one or more lock columns to the call records table. These lock columns store current lock information that pertains to each call record. When an application reads a call record with the intent of updating its contents, it changes the lock columns' values to include the identifier for the user who currently holds the lock and the timestamp when he/she obtained it. Similarly, the application clears these columns when it applies changes to the call record.

When other application instances attempt to read and potentially update locked data, they immediately notify the end user that the data is already in use. In the concurrent update scenario defined above, the customer service application notifies the technical service representative that another user is already editing the call record with a descriptive warning like this:

```
George Employee locked call record 99448 at Fri Oct 25 12:30:11.
You cannot update this call record now.
```

At this point, the technical service representative can choose to view the record without any update capabilities or he/she can talk to the customer service representative to find out when the call record will be available.

APPLICABILITY

Use the Pessimistic Lock pattern when:

- Multiple processes can issue inconsistent update operations that involve common data.

- You need to customize diagnostic information beyond what native database or transaction facilities provide.

- The amount of data in working copies is large, making it common for update operations to take a long time.

STRUCTURE

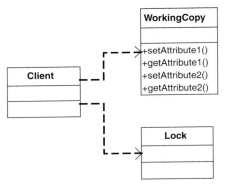

FIGURE 24.1: The static structure of the Pessimistic Lock pattern.

Figure 24.1 illustrates the static structure of the Pessimistic Lock pattern. Clients interact with working copies of data, shown here as the WorkingCopy class. WorkingCopy can define a domain object or any other software representation.

Clients also refer to Lock values that indicate whether another process is updating the corresponding physical data. Common Lock implementations store user identifiers, application names, process identifiers, timestamp values, or a combination of these.

INTERACTIONS

When a client reads data to populate a WorkingCopy, it checks its Lock values to ensure that no other process is updating the same data. If another process holds the lock, then the client throws an exception or displays a suitable error message. If the Lock values indicate that no other process holds the lock, then the client immediately updates the physical lock value to designate that it is updating the data.

This combination of read, test, and update operations must be atomic to prevent multiple processes from locking data at precisely the same time. You can achieve this atomicity by enclosing these operations within a Transaction (379) or by using an updatable cursor. These mechanisms do not impose significant native locking overhead since they only apply to the operations for populating a working copy's data and not the entire logical unit of work.

The client must release its lock as part of its final update operation. This usually amounts to setting the corresponding physical lock values to be empty or null.

CONSEQUENCES

The Pessimistic Lock pattern has the following consequences:

Benefits

- *Customizable diagnostic information*—Applications can detect conditions where multiple clients are editing the same data and can notify the second client before it attempts to enter changes. This notification can take the form of an exception that is logged by a batch process or a graphical message box presented to an end-user.

    You can tailor this notification to include whatever diagnostic information suits clients best. For example, it may be helpful to inform users who else is updating the data and when they obtained the lock. This information can encourage users to be more aware of concurrency issues and enable them to communicate with other users to negotiate turns with the data.

- *Customizable locking semantics*—Application designers can define lock value contents and semantics that enable applications to include diagnostic and administrative functions that monitor lock utilization and contention. By contrast, when you rely on system- or database-level locking like that employed by transactions and updatable cursors, the resulting diagnostic information usually describes lock utilization in terms of database concepts that provide little useful information to end-users and application administrators.

Drawbacks

- *External components do not necessarily implement the pattern*—Pessimistic locking is most effective when every update to a particular data set employs the same strategy. If defective or third-party components make updates without checking or setting the lock columns' values, they prevent applications that implement pessimistic locking from completely enforcing consistent updates.

- *Potential for orphan locks*—An orphan lock occurs when an application instance or session locks a database entity and neglects to release it. If a process ends abruptly after locking a row of data, there is no explicit mechanism for removing the lock.

STRATEGIES

The customer service tracking application that the "Context" section described stores user identifiers and timestamps for locks. User identifiers are effective because they are readily available and convey useful information about who has locked the data. Timestamp values enable users to gauge how long someone has been editing the corresponding information.

A single lock for each row of data may be too restrictive for tables that contain several columns that are frequently updated independently. When this scenario arises, consider defining separate lock columns for each updatable column in the table and maintain these locks separately.

Orphan locks create significant problems, especially when there is no mechanism to clean them up once you detect them. Without any such mechanism, data can become effectively locked forever. Consider using Resource Timer (137) to automatically release locks if an application holds them longer than a configured interval. You can also release orphan locks by running a customized batch process periodically or by way of an administrative console operation. If you use any of these strategies, you must ensure that any application's final update operation tests the lock value to verify that it still holds the lock before writing data. This additional test guards against concurrency problems that occur when an application confuses orphan locks with those that its processes hold legitimately for an extended duration.

Finally, consider implementing pessimistic locking within the database. Depending on your database platform, you may be able to define native database triggers that maintain and enforce pessimistic locking semantics. Triggers require additional installation and portability considerations, but they have the advantage of enforcing a single strategy even when data is updated outside of your application's control.

SAMPLE CODE

This example illustrates pessimistic locking in conjunction with the CALLS table for the customer service tracking application example described earlier. The Call-Record class is a domain object that serves as a working copy of a single call record's data.

```java
public class CallRecord {

    private String callID;
    private String customerID;
    private String problemDescription;
    private String problemResolution;

    public String getCallID() {
        return callID;
    }

    public void setCallID(String callID)  {
        this.callID = callID;
    }

    public String getCustomerID() {
        return customerID;
    }

    public void setCustomerID(String customerID)  {
        this.customerID = customerID;
    }

    public String getProblemDescription() {
        return problemDescription;
    }

    public void setProblemDescription(
        String problemDescription) {
        this.problemDescription = problemDescription;
    }

    public String getProblemResolution()
```

```
    {
        return problemResolution;
    }

    public void setProblemResolution(
        String problemResolution) {
        this.problemResolution = problemResolution;
    }

    public String toString() {
        StringBuffer buffer = new StringBuffer();
        buffer.append("Call record ");
        buffer.append(callID);
        return buffer.toString();
    }
}
```

This client code reads and populates a single CallRecord object. Assume that the application uses this object as its working copy throughout a single unit of work. This block checks the lock values for the data. It throws a PessimisticLock-Exception if another process already holds the lock. Otherwise, it sets the lock value with the current user identifier and timestamp before proceeding.

```
StringBuffer buffer = new StringBuffer();
buffer.append("SELECT CALL_ID, CUSTOMER_ID, ");
buffer.append("PROBLEM_DESCRIPTION, PROBLEM_RESOLUTION, ");
buffer.append("LOCK_USER, LOCK_TIMESTAMP FROM CALLS ");
buffer.append("WHERE CALL_ID = ?");
String selectStatement = buffer.toString();

PreparedStatement ps
    = connection.prepareStatement(selectStatement,
    ResultSet.TYPE_FORWARD_ONLY,
    ResultSet.CONCUR_UPDATABLE);
ps.setString(1, callID);
ResultSet rs = ps.executeQuery();

// Create the working copy for the call record.
CallRecord callRecord = null;
try {
    if (rs.next()) {
        callRecord = new CallRecord();
        callRecord.setCallID(rs.getString(1));
        callRecord.setCustomerID(rs.getString(2));
        callRecord.setProblemDescription(rs.getString(3));
        callRecord.setProblemResolution(rs.getString(4));
```

```
        // If there is already a lock on the record,
        // then throw an exception.
        String lockUser = rs.getString(5);
        Timestamp lockTimestamp = rs.getTimestamp(6);
        if (lockUser != null) {
            throw new PessimisticLockException(
                callRecord, lockUser, lockTimestamp);
        }

        // Otherwise, lock the call record.
        rs.updateString(5, userID);
        rs.updateTimestamp(6,
            new Timestamp(System.currentTimeMillis()));
        rs.updateRow();
    }
}
finally {
    rs.close();
    ps.close();
}
```

The next block of client code flushes changes that the application makes from the CallRecord to the database. The SQL UPDATE statement verifies that the application still holds the lock. This happens in the WHERE clause and is a precaution to prevent updates when an external process or timer automatically releases the lock. This might happen when an application holds it too long and an external process mistakenly identifies it as an orphan lock.

The SQL UPDATE statement also clears the lock to indicate that this process has finished updating the call record.

```
StringBuffer buffer = new StringBuffer();
buffer.append("UPDATE CALLS SET ");
buffer.append("PROBLEM_DESCRIPTION = ?, ");
buffer.append("PROBLEM_RESOLUTION = ?, ");
buffer.append("LOCK_USER = ? ");
buffer.append("LOCK_TIMESTAMP = ? ");
buffer.append("WHERE CALL_ID = ? ");
buffer.append("AND LOCK_USER = ?");
String updateStatement = buffer.toString();

// Issue the update.
PreparedStatement ps
    = connection.prepareStatement(updateStatement);
ps.setString(1, callRecord.getProblemDescription());
ps.setString(2, callRecord.getProblemResolution());
ps.setNull(3, Types.VARCHAR);
```

```
ps.setNull(4, Types.TIMESTAMP);
ps.setString(5, callRecord.getCallID());
ps.setString(6, userID);
int updateCount = ps.executeUpdate();
ps.close();

// If no rows are updated, an external
// process released the lock and we should not
// update the record.  This condition indicates
// that we left the lock open too long.
if (updateCount == 0)
    throw new PessimisticLockException(callRecord);
```

When either of these client code blocks detects pessimistic locking errors, it throws a PessimisticLockException. When interactive applications catch this type of exception, they can present its message to the end-user. Likewise, batch applications can log exception details and continue processing. This is a sample definition of PessimisticLockException:

```
public class PessimisticLockException
extends Exception {

    public PessimisticLockException(
        Object workingCopy,
        String lockUser,
        Timestamp lockTimestamp) {

        super(lockUser + " locked call record "
            + workingCopy + " at "
            + lockTimestamp + ".  You can not "
            + "currently update this call record.");
    }

    public PessimisticLockException(Object workingCopy) {

        super("Call record " + workingCopy
            + " was not updated. An external component "
            + "released its update lock.");
    }
}
```

RELATED PATTERNS AND TECHNOLOGY

- [Fowler 2002] refers to this pattern as a Pessimistic Offline Lock.

- Pessimistic Lock prevents you from requiring a Transaction (379) to span an entire unit of work. However, you can still benefit from using a transaction that includes only the read operation at the beginning of a logical unit of work and another that includes only the update operation at the end.

- Consider employing a Resource Timer (137) to automatically release locks after a configured interval. This can reduce the potential for orphan locks.

Compensating Transaction

DESCRIPTION

Defines explicit compensating operations to roll back units of work that are not part of a native database transaction.

CONTEXT

Self-service class registration applications allow university students to enroll themselves in courses for an upcoming semester. This type of application relieves registrar employees from taking on mundane tasks such as checking class statuses and updating student information. Most universities implement this type of self-service application using either a web or custom client interface.

Consider a specific registration application that lists the classes for which each student has enrolled in its ENROLLMENTS table. In addition, the application maintains a ROSTER table that keeps statistical class information such as the total number of available seats for each class and how many of those seats are still open. A typical student spends most of his/her time querying the ROSTER table, checking class times and open seats. When he/she finalizes his/her registration decision, the application updates the ENROLLMENTS and ROSTER tables. It is best to group these update operations within a Transaction 379 since they make up a logical, atomic unit of work.

Now suppose that these tables physically reside in different data sources. Many other applications such as billing, transcript generation, and scheduling use the ENROLLMENTS table, so it is stored along with other tables that relate to these core university management applications. On the other hand, the self-service registration application is the only application that requires the ROSTER table, so it is stored in a database on the same server as the application itself. Figure 25.1 illustrates the topology of this distributed system. The self-service registration transaction includes operations that update tables from two data sources.

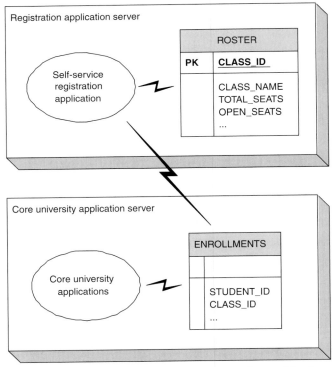

FIGURE 25.1: The self-service registration application updates tables from two data sources as part of a single logical unit of work.

A commercial transaction manager can coordinate distributed transactions and their individual components to ensure preservation of data integrity and transactional semantics. However, a transaction manager only works when all the data sources involved are able to participate in distributed transactions. It is not uncommon to find a case where either no transaction manager is available in the environment, or one or more of the database products involved do not support distributed transactions. For example, although most J2EE application servers include a distributed transaction manager, some of the most common JDBC drivers do not implement the interfaces required for participating in a distributed transaction.

When you encounter this situation, you are left to coordinate distributed transactions yourself. It is difficult to solve this problem completely and robustly, but it is feasible to approximate the results. The brute-force solution is for your application to divide a logical unit of work into distinct, local transactions and commit each local transaction in turn. However, problems occur when you commit one local transaction and then errors occur while committing another. When this happens, you have to simulate a rollback that "undoes" the operations that you have already committed.

The notion of "undoing" a committed database operation is called *compensating*. Compensation is akin to performing the reverse or opposite of a database operation to roll back its effect. Compensating enables your application to rollback changes that have already been committed in local, database-level transactions.

Compensatable operations are not simply a matter of switching data back to its original value, because this can easily result in missing updates when another process changes the same data in the same interval. Instead, you usually define compensatable operations in terms of a delta change to existing values or to a table's state. Compensatable operations must be isolated from one another and other database operations. In other words, you must be able to perform and compensate for individual operations without regard to the effect of other operations, all the while leaving the affected database entities in a consistent state.

Not all database operations are compensatable. In fact, very few are. However, you can design applications so that they perform primarily compensatable operations. Consider the two operations that make up the self-service registration application's distributed transaction:

- *Enrollment operation*—The application inserts a row into the ENROLLMENTS table for every class for which a student registers. This is a compensatable operation since the application can just as easily delete the same rows.

- *Roster operation*—The application decrements the number of open seats for every class for which a student registers. This is a compensatable operation since the application can increment the number of open seats for the same set of classes if it needs to.

Compensating Transaction describes a generalized scheme for managing transactional semantics that involve exclusively compensatable operations. If an error occurs while an application is committing operations that make up a Compensating Transaction, the application cycles through the same operations in reverse order, compensating for each one. This has the effect of rolling back any committed operations.

APPLICABILITY

Use the Compensating Transaction pattern when:

- Your application carries out logical units of work whose operations involve multiple data sources.

- No distributed transaction manager is available in your application environment.

- One or more of the data sources involved in your applications' logical units of work do not support participation in a distributed transaction.

- You can define compensating operations for the entire contents of a logical unit of work.

STRUCTURE

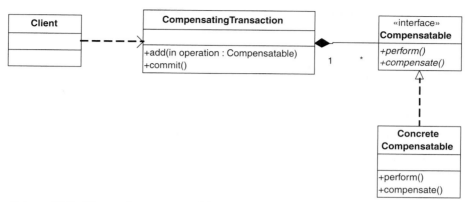

FIGURE 25.2: The static structure of the Compensating Transaction pattern.

Figure 25.2 illustrates the static structure of the Compensating Transaction pattern. The Compensatable interface defines primitives for performing and compensating for one or more database operations. Applications define a ConcreteCompensatable class that implements these primitives for each operation that participates in a compensating transaction.

CompensatingTransaction maintains an ordered list of Compensatable instances. This list represents the set of operations that makes up a single unit of work.

INTERACTIONS

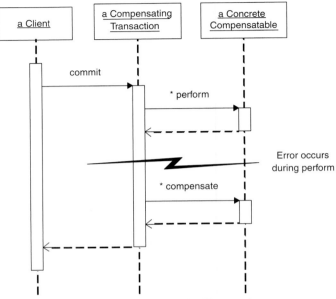

FIGURE 25.3: A client commits a CompensatingTransaction.

Client code instantiates and adds Compensatable instances to a CompensatingTransaction, but it does not invoke their primitives directly. Figure 25.3 portrays what happens when a client commits a CompensatingTransaction. In the normal course of events, the CompensatingTransaction simply iterates through each of its Compensatable operation instances, performing each one in turn.

If any of these operations throws an exception or otherwise indicates an error, the CompensatingTransaction reverses the direction of its iteration and invokes the compensate primitive for each Compensatable operation that it has already performed.

CONSEQUENCES

The Compensating Transaction pattern has the following consequences:

Benefit

- *Consistent semantics for distributed units of work*—Distributed transaction support is common, but not pervasive. Application control of distributed transactions is sometimes necessary, and this pattern defines a consistent strategy that can be employed within multiple applications.

Drawbacks

- *Many operations are not explicitly compensatable*—Compensatable operations typically involve a delta update to specific values or a relative change to a table's state and can be performed and compensated for in isolation of other, similar database operations. In practice, most application database operations do not meet these criteria.

- *No recourse when errors occur during compensation*—Application-controlled compensating transactions are not as robust as those implemented at the database level. Specifically, there is no defined recovery when errors occur during compensate operations. This fact can compromise a unit of work's atomicity.

- *Transaction properties are not maintained on a distributed scale*—While it is feasible to maintain atomicity, consistency, isolation, and durability on the local scale for each operation, it is quite difficult to enforce these properties on a distributed scale without implementing a full transaction management system in cooperation with database-level support.

STRATEGIES

Only a small subset of an application's database operations are compensatable. This fact restricts this pattern's applicability. These are some characteristics of explicitly compensatable database operations:

- *Delta operations*—Operations that update data in terms of increments or decrements are usually compensatable, since any operation that decrements values can be compensated by incrementing values by the same amount. Delta operations work in isolation of other updates to the same data and work particularly well for quantities such as university class sizes or on-hand inventories.

- *Create or delete operations*—Operations that create or delete database entities or whole rows of data are usually compensatable since their opposite compensating operation is straightforward to define.

On the contrary, update operations that change data without regard to its previous value or state are usually not compensatable. An example of an operation that is not compensatable is changing a student's mailing address. This operation does not depend on the student's previous address. It is not safe to define compensation as simply changing the address back to its old value since this may result in missing updates when a student makes multiple address change requests and the order of these requests is unclear.

Each compensatable operation can include multiple database operations that apply to the same data source. It is still beneficial to execute these operations within a local transaction. If an error occurs with any individual database operation, you can roll back the local transaction and reissue the error to the client. Despite the potential for inconsistencies on the distributed transaction scale, data integrity remains intact within each data source.

SAMPLE CODE

This is a sample definition for the Compensatable interface:

```
public interface Compensatable {

    /**
    Performs the operation.
    **/
    void perform() throws SQLException;

    /**
    Compensates for the operation.
    This has the opposite effect of perform.
    **/
    void compensate() throws SQLException;
}
```

The CompensatingTransaction class maintains an ordered list of Compensatable operation instances. Its commit operation defines the iteration through this list and the semantics for calling each Compensatable instance's perform and compensate primitives.

```
public class CompensatingTransaction {

    private List contents = new LinkedList();

    /**
    Adds an operation to this transaction.
    */
    public synchronized void add(Compensatable operation) {
        contents.add(operation);
    }

    /**
    Performs operations in this transaction.
    @throws SQLException If a compensation error occurs.
    */
    public synchronized void commit()
        throws SQLException {

        List performedOperations = new LinkedList();
        try {
            for(Iterator i = contents.iterator();
                i.hasNext(); ) {
                Compensatable operation
                    = (Compensatable)i.next();
                operation.perform();
                performedOperations.add(0, operation);
            }
        }

        // If an error occurs, back up through each
        // operation that has already been performed
        // and compensate in reverse order.
        catch(SQLException e) {
            for(Iterator i = performedOperations.iterator();
                i.hasNext(); ) {
                Compensatable operation
                    = (Compensatable)i.next();
                operation.compensate();
            }
        }
    }
}
```

The next two classes define Compensatable operation implementations for the self-service registration application example that the "Context" section described. EnrollmentsOperation represents the addition of rows to the ENROLLMENTS table for each class in which a particular student enrolls. Its perform primitive inserts these rows and its compensate primitive deletes them.

Notice that a single EnrollmentsOperation instance includes multiple physical database operations. Both the perform and compensate primitives execute them in terms of a local transaction.

```java
public class EnrollmentsOperation
implements Compensatable {

    private Connection connection;
    private int studentID;
    private int[] classIDs;

    public EnrollmentsOperation(
        Connection connection,
        int studentID,
        int[] classIDs)  {

        this.connection = connection;
        this.studentID = studentID;
        this.classIDs = classIDs;
    }

    /**
    Inserts enrollment information for each class.
    */
    public void perform() throws SQLException {
        try {
            StringBuffer buffer = new StringBuffer();
            buffer.append("INSERT INTO ENROLLMENTS ");
            buffer.append(" (STUDENT_ID, CLASS_ID) ");
            buffer.append("VALUES (?, ?)");

            PreparedStatement ps
                = connection.prepareStatement(
                buffer.toString());

            ps.setInt(1, studentID);
            for(int i = 0; i < classIDs.length; ++i) {
                ps.setInt(2, classIDs[i]);
                ps.executeUpdate();
            }
            ps.close();
```

```
            connection.commit();
        }
        catch(SQLException e) {
            connection.rollback();
            throw e;
        }
    }

    /**
    Deletes enrollment information for each class.
    */
    public void compensate() throws SQLException {
        try {
            StringBuffer buffer = new StringBuffer();
            buffer.append("DELETE FROM ENROLLMENTS ");
            buffer.append("WHERE STUDENT_ID = ? ");
            buffer.append("AND CLASS_ID = ?");

            PreparedStatement ps
                = connection.prepareStatement(
                buffer.toString());

            ps.setInt(1, studentID);
            for(int i = 0; i < classIDs.length; ++i) {
                ps.setInt(2, classIDs[i]);
                ps.executeUpdate();
            }
            ps.close();

            connection.commit();
        }
        catch(SQLException e) {
            connection.rollback();
            throw e;
        }
    }
}
```

RosterOperation defines the update operation for the ROSTER table. Its perform primitive decrements the number of open seats for each class in which the student enrolls by one. Similarly, its compensate primitive increments the number of open seats for the same class by one. Since a single RosterOperation's primitives involve multiple physical database operations, it runs them within the scope of a local transaction.

```java
public class RosterOperation
implements Compensatable {

    private Connection connection;
    private int[] classIDs;

    public RosterOperation(
        Connection connection,
        int[] classIDs) {
        this.connection = connection;
        this.classIDs = classIDs;
    }

    /**
    Decrements the number of open seats in each class.
    */
    public void perform() throws SQLException {
        updateOpenSeats(-1);
    }

    /**
    Increments the number of open seats in each class.
    */
    public void compensate() throws SQLException {
        updateOpenSeats(1);
    }

    /**
    Updates the number of open seats in each class.
    */
    private void updateOpenSeats(int openSeatsDelta)
        throws SQLException {
        try {
            StringBuffer buffer = new StringBuffer();
            buffer.append("SELECT CLASS_ID, OPEN_SEATS ");
            buffer.append("FROM ROSTERS ");
            buffer.append("WHERE CLASS_ID = ?");

            PreparedStatement ps
                = connection.prepareStatement(
                buffer.toString(),
                ResultSet.TYPE_FORWARD_ONLY,
                ResultSet.CONCUR_UPDATABLE);

            try {
                for(int i = 0; i < classIDs.length; ++i) {
                    ps.setInt(1, classIDs[i]);
                    ResultSet rs = ps.executeQuery();
```

```
                    try {
                        if (rs.next()) {
                            int openSeats = rs.getInt(2);
                            openSeats += openSeatsDelta;

                            // If the number of open seats
                            // ducks below zero, then flag
                            // an error—the student cannot
                            // enroll.
                            if (openSeats < 0) {
                                throw new SQLException(
                                "There are no seats available"
                                + " in class " + classIDs[i]
                                + ".");
                            }

                            rs.updateInt(2, openSeats);
                            rs.updateRow();
                        }
                    }
                    finally {
                        rs.close();
                    }
                }
            }
            finally {
                ps.close();
            }

            connection.commit();
        }
        catch(SQLException e)  {
            connection.rollback();
            throw e;
        }
    }
}
```

This client code defines a single logical unit of work within the self-service registration application. It instantiates an EnrollmentsOperation and a RosterOperation, adds them to a CompensatingTransaction, and commits.

```
Compensatable enrollmentsOperation
    = new EnrollmentsOperation(
            enrollmentsConnection,
            studentID,
            classIDs);
```

```
Compensatable rosterOperation
    = new RosterOperation(
            rosterConnection,
            classIDs);

CompensatingTransaction transaction
    = new CompensatingTransaction();
transaction.add(enrollmentsOperation);
transaction.add(rosterOperation);
transaction.commit();
```

RELATED PATTERNS AND TECHNOLOGY

- Transaction (379) provides a more robust solution and is usually preferred to Compensating Transaction when native distributed transaction support is available.

Afterword

My first exposure to design patterns came in 1995 during an OOPSLA conference tutorial on framework design. It was the first time I had considered a software abstraction at a higher level than a class library. Before that tutorial, I had concentrated on writing reusable code, but I had repeatedly struggled with the fact that similar applications still duplicated a lot of control and program flow logic. The tutorial introduced me to how well-designed frameworks refactor and reuse control logic and can be customized through subclassing and assembling granular components.

When I got back to my office the following Monday, I tried to design a simple framework for a software build system. I found that many approaches I took resulted in multiple subclasses with redundant code, or worse, defect-prone glue code that patched together components that did not fit snugly into the framework.

Just before I relegated the advantages of frameworks to the theoretical realm, I stumbled across *Design Patterns: Elements of Reusable Object-Oriented Software*

[Gamma 1995]. It is no coincidence that this book was co-authored by Ralph Johnson, the instructor of the OOPSLA framework tutorial I attended. I solved many of the problems I faced while designing my first frameworks by applying a few of the patterns that [Gamma 1995] describes. Patterns like Visitor, Composite, and Bridge fit precisely, and I gradually increased my understanding and appreciation for the role that design patterns play in application design.

Today, I regularly incorporate patterns into the software I design. I keep several of my favorite design pattern books close at hand and apply their contents when they make sense. Localized patterns like Singleton and Composite show up quite frequently in my code, and I have built entire architectures around Decorator and Chain of Responsibility. I have found that using these patterns enables me to elegantly decouple orthogonal concepts, avoid circular dependencies, and significantly increase the degree to which the code I write is maintainable and reusable.

When I apply a pattern in practice today, I make sure to document it clearly and emphatically. A design pattern does not always present the most straightforward solution. I have found that I frequently have to teach and defend my application of a particular pattern to colleagues. Using the pattern's well-known name in code and design documentation as well as accurately referring to its sources alleviates this reaction to some degree. For example, simply indicating that a class is an instance of the Session Facade pattern [Alur 2001] effectively attaches the pattern's documentation along with it.

The second time I need to document or explain an effective but not necessarily intuitive structure or object interaction, I try to invest time in documenting it as a pattern. Even if it is not widely applicable or a design pattern in the strict sense, I find significant value in documenting it as if it was. This documentation enables me to refer to it briefly within inline code commentary and saves me from having to include a detailed explanation in multiple code blocks and design documents. Thinking of concepts as patterns also enables me to define naming and packaging conventions that enhance the consistency of the software I create.

I appreciate the elegance of simple and clean software designs. I also benefit regularly from code that is easier to debug and enhance. I have personally applied the patterns in this book to the data access problems I face daily in the course of my programming and software design work. I encourage you to apply these patterns when it makes sense. I also hope that this book inspires you to identify, document, and share your own patterns.

Glossary

accessor
A software entity that encapsulates data access.

access plan
An internal database structure that describes the most efficient strategy for executing a database operation.

application domain
The specific concepts and processes that an application models.

atomicity
A characteristic of transactions that dictates that all operations within a unit of work are carried out logically as a single, atomic operation.

bean-managed persistence (BMP)
A characteristic of an Enterprise JavaBean (EJB) that takes on the responsibility for its own domain object mapping and physical data access.

buffer
An unstructured block of memory that is allocated from the primary storage heap.

cache
An entity that stores data for fast, repeated access. Data caches usually reside in primary storage.

cache coherency
A property of multiple caches whose contents reflect consistent data.

cache collection strategy

A set of rules for identifying and removing expired cache entries.

cache transparency

The visibility of a cache to applications and middleware code.

caching

A strategy that enables applications to avoid issuing multiple database read operations for the same data. After an application reads data for the first time, it stores it in a cache that enables fast access to its contents.

commit

A primitive that instructs the database to commit all of a transaction's operations.

compensating operation

A database operation that has the opposite or reverse effect of another, committed database operation.

connection

A database resource that serves as a handle to a database manager or server and implements fundamental database operations.

connection pool

An entity that stores pre-initialized database connection objects intended for repeated use. Connection pools help to reduce the performance and concurrency overhead that stems from connection initialization.

consistency

A property of transactions stating that the system is left in a consistent state when a unit of work is complete.

container-managed persistence (CMP)

A characteristic of an Enterprise JavaBean (EJB) that relies on its container to implement its domain object mapping and physical data access.

current statistics

A representation of cache or pool statistics that immediately reflects changes.

cursor

An entity that points to the current position within a result set.

daemon thread

An independent task that runs concurrently with other program logic and services requests or handles periodic housekeeping in the background.

data access

A application's dynamic mechanism for reading and writing data.

data access pattern

A solution to a common data access problem described for general applicability.

database driver

A middleware entity that mediates interactions between an application and its physical data.

database metadata

A collection of information that describes the support levels and contents of a database in generic terms.

database uniform resource locator (URL)

A string that designates a JDBC data source's location, type, and connection properties.

data model

The static structure of an application's data. This includes tables and any associated indices, views, triggers, and referential integrity features. This term also refers to an application's understanding of the static structure of its data.

declarative transaction

A facility that enables you to associate a transaction attribute with each application module. The application environment uses transaction attributes to issue transaction primitives on the modules' behalf.

decorator

A software entity that attaches additional behavior to an existing object with minimal disruption to application code. A decorator extends another object's functionality without subclassing or changing its implementation.

demarcating

The process of indicating where transactions begin and end to group database operations into units of work.

design pattern

A solution to a common software design problem described for general applicability.

dirty read

A condition that occurs when one application instance depends on a working copy that is based on tentative, uncommitted data.

disconnected result set

A result set that stores an entire collection of query results in local storage and does not require an active database connection.

distributed transaction

A transaction whose operations span multiple data sources.

domain object

An object that directly models an application or business concept.

domain object mapping

A translation between domain objects and relational data.

durability

A characteristic of transactions that states that the effect of completed units of work remains intact once they are committed.

Enterprise JavaBean (EJB)

A domain object or process model that runs within a managed container in a Java 2 Enterprise Edition (J2EE) environment.

entity bean

An Enterprise JavaBean (EJB) that represents application domain data.

expired cache entry

A cache entry whose presence in a cache no longer provides any performance benefit to applications.

factory

A software entity whose primary responsibility is creating new objects.

file handle

A software entity that encapsulates physical file access.

foreign key

A combination of one or more table columns whose values can be matched with a primary key in another table.

garbage collection

A feature of some application environments in which memory and other resources are automatically freed or closed when applications are finished using them.

hardwiring

Implementing a detail in a way that is configurable only by changing and recompiling code.

identity object

An object that uses domain concepts to precisely identify the relational data set that corresponds to one or more domain objects.

inactive resource

A resource whose operations have not been invoked for a particular period of time.

inactivity threshold

The interval that a resource timer waits before automatically cleaning up inactive resources.

isolation

A characteristic of transactions that dictates that each unit of work must run independently of other concurrent units of work.

isolation level

The degree to which units of work are isolated from each other.

Java Database Connectivity (JDBC)

The common call-level programming interfaces that are part of the Java 2 Standard Edition (J2SE). Java programs use JDBC for managing database resources and issuing Structured Query Language (SQL) operations.

Java Data Objects (JDO)

A common interface specification that defines semantic operations that enable Java programs to read and write objects to persistent storage.

join

A query that forms rows by matching the contents of related columns across multiple tables.

layer

A set of components that implements a software abstraction in terms of less abstract entities.

local transaction

A transaction whose operations are confined to a single data source.

lock

A software or database entity that indicates when one or more processes have exclusive access rights to a particular data set.

metadata

Data that describes characteristics of other data.

middleware

A software layer that intermediates between application and system code. Middleware is sometimes referred to as "plumbing."

missing update

A condition that occurs when two application instances update precisely the same data concurrently. The second instance overwrites changes made by the first, and the first instance's changes appear to be missing.

non-repeatable read

A condition that occurs when multiple, identical read operations return inconsistent results within the same unit of work. This usually happens when a second process issues an update operation that involves data the first process is reading.

object/relational map

A translation between domain objects and relational data.

Open Database Connectivity (ODBC)

A common call-level programming interface that C programs use for managing database resources and issuing Structured Query Language (SQL) operations.

optimistic locking

A concurrency strategy that involves comparing a working copy's version with that in the physical database to ensure that update operations remain consistent.

orphan lock

A condition that occurs when an application locks a database entity and neglects to release it.

orthogonality

A relationship between software components or features that address completely disjointed issues. You can assemble orthogonal components in any combination to build an overall solution.

pessimistic locking

A concurrency strategy that requires applications to lock affected data throughout the duration of a corresponding logical unit of work.

phantom read

A condition that occurs when results change within a single unit of work because one application instance queries a particular table at the same time that another instance inserts data into it.

physical data

Data that is stored in a database, in contrast to a software representation that an application manipulates in memory.

placeholder entry

A cache entry that represents corresponding physical data that does not exist.

pool

An entity that stores pre-initialized objects intended for repeated use.

pooled resource

A resource that is managed by a resource pool.

prepared statement

An optimized statement handle that stores compiled database instructions and parameter values so that an application can efficiently execute it multiple times.

primary key

A combination of one or more table columns whose values uniquely identify its rows.

replicated cache

A cache instance that notifies others when its contents change.

replicated cache notification

A mechanism that caches use to replicate changes. Notification can take the form of system events, messages sent across the network, or through a reliable, distributed queuing mechanism.

replicated cache topology

A layout that describes how replicated caches connect with and notify each other.

resource

An entity that represents and enables access to storage, a server, or a device. Examples of database resources are connections, statement handles, result sets, and transactions.

resource leak

A problem that arises when an application opens or allocates a resource but neglects to close or free it. As an offending application gradually consumes more resources, the supply available for other applications similarly depletes.

resource pool

An entity that manages a set of active resources that is recycled for repeated use.

result set

A database resource that encapsulates database query results.

rollback

A primitive that instructs the database to roll back, or undo, all of a transaction's operations.

savepoint

An intermediate step within a transaction that represents the transaction's state at a particular instant.

search sequence

A series of related cache read operations. A search sequence ends when one of its operations finds the cache entry that an application requested.

selection

An entity or expression that applications pass to database drivers to precisely specify a data set on which to operate.

shortcut entry

A placeholder cache entry that optimizes future read operations or search sequences.

snapshot statistics

A representation of cache or pool statistics that records its state at one particular instant.

socket

A network connection handle to another application or server.

software abstraction

The processes of defining a solution to a specific problem so that it is useful in a broader scope.

stale connection

A database connection whose socket has been inadvertently closed as a result of an underlying system administration policy, network problem, or hardware defect.

statement cache

A software entity that stores prepared statement handles intended for repeated use. Statement caches help to reduce the performance overhead that stems from repeatedly parsing and compiling the same database instructions.

statement handle

A database resource that stores contextual and state information for one thread or module's database operations.

statement morphing

The process of replacing literal values in database operations with parameter markers. This improves the chances for reusability in conjunction with a statement cache.

Structured Query Language (SQL)

A standard language for concisely expressing simple and complex database operations. SQL is the most prevalent mechanism for implementing dynamic interactions between applications and relational databases.

stub

A trivial class or method implementation that exists as a temporary placeholder for missing implementation details.

transaction

An entity that groups a unit of work's database operations so that either all or none of the operations get committed to the database.

transaction attribute

An indicator of how an application server issues transaction primitives on behalf of an application module.

trigger

A software module that databases invoke automatically before or after carrying out specific operations on a particular table.

two-phase commit

A common protocol that transaction managers use for committing distributed transactions.

Unified Modeling Language (UML)

A common object-oriented modeling language. This book uses UML to illustrate pattern structures and object interactions.

unit of work

A group of related database operations that forms a logical operation from an application's perspective.

unmapped attribute

A domain object attribute that does not map directly to a single relational data item.

updatable cursor

A cursor that locks subsets of query result data. Applications use updatable cursors to issue operations that modify query results.

working copy

A software representation of physical data. Applications often interact with working copies rather than directly manipulating physical data.

Bibliography

Alur, D., J. Crupi, and D. Malks, *Core J2EE*^{TM} *Patterns: Best Practices and Design Strategies*, Prentice Hall PTR, 2001.

Arnold, K., J. Gosling, and D. Holmes, *The Java*^{TM} *Programming Language, Third Edition*, Addison-Wesley, 2000.

Binder, R., *Testing Object-Oriented Systems: Models, Patterns, and Tools*, Addison-Wesley, 1999.

Bloch, J., *Effective Java*^{TM}: *Programming Language Guide*, Addison-Wesley, 2001.

Booch, G., *Object-Oriented Analysis and Design with Applications, Second Edition*, Benjamin/Cummings, 1994.

Buschmann, F., R. Meunier, H. Rohnert, P. Sommerlad, and M. Stal, *Pattern-Oriented Software Architecture, Volume 1: A System Of Patterns*, John Wiley & Sons, 1996.

Carey, J., B. Carlson, and T. Graser, *SanFrancisco*^{TM} *Design Patterns: Blueprints for Business Software*, Addison-Wesley, 2000.

Fowler, M., D. Rice, M. Foemmel, E. Hieatt, R. Mee, and R. Stafford, *Patterns of Enterprise Application Architecture*, Addison-Wesley, 2002.

441

Fowler, M. and K. Scott, *UML Distilled: A Brief Guide to the Standard Object Modeling Language, Second Edition*, Addison-Wesley, 1999.

Gamma, E., R. Helm, R. Johnson, and J. Vlissides, *Design Patterns: Elements of Reusable Object-Oriented Software*, Addison-Wesley, 1995.

Groff, J. and P. Weinberg, *SQL: The Complete Reference*, McGraw-Hill/Osborne, 1999.

Haggar, P., *Practical Java*™*: Programming Language Guide*, Addison-Wesley, 2000.

IBM Corporation, *IBM Toolbox for Java: Programmer's Guide, V5R2*, IBM, 2002.

The Jakarta Project, *Object/Relational Bridge (OJB), Version 0.9.5*, Apache Software Foundation, 2002.

Kassem, N. and the Enterprise Team, *Designing Enterprise Applications with the Java*™ *2 Platform, Enterprise Edition*, Addison-Wesley, 2000.

Lea, D., *Concurrent Programming in Java*™*: Design Principles and Patterns, Second Edition*, Addison-Wesley, 1999.

Marinescu, F., *EJB*™ *Design Patterns: Advanced Patterns, Processes, and Idioms*, John Wiley & Sons, 2002.

Matena, V., S. Krishnan, B. Stearns, and P. Nardi, *Applying Enterprise JavaBeans*™ *2.1: Component-Based Development for the J2EE*™ *Platform, Second Edition*, Addison-Wesley, 2003.

Monday, P., J. Carey, and M. Dangler, *SanFrancisco*™ *Component Framework: An Introduction*, Addison-Wesley, 2000.

Monday, P. and W. Connor, *The Jiro*™ *Technology Programmer's Guide and Federated Management Architecture*, Addison-Wesley, 2001.

Noble, J. and C. Weir, *Small Memory Software: Patterns for Systems with Limited Memory*, Addison-Wesley, 2001.

Object Management Group, *Transaction Service Specification, Version 1.2*, Object Management Group Standard, 2001.

The Open Group, *Distributed Transaction Processing: The XA Standard*, Open Group Technical Standard, 1992.

Pont, M., *Patterns for Time-Triggered Embedded Systems: Building Reliable Applications with the 8051 Family of Microcontrollers*, Addison-Wesley, 2001.

Schmidt, D., M. Stal, H. Rohnert, and F. Buschmann, *Pattern-Oriented Software Architecture, Volume 2: Patterns for Concurrent and Networked Objects*, John Wiley & Sons, 2000.

Sharma, R., B. Stearns, and T. Ng, *J2EE*™ *Connector Architecture and Enterprise Application Integration*, Addison-Wesley, 2001.

Sun Microsystems, *Enterprise JavaBeans*™ *Specification, Version 2.1*, 2002.

Sun Microsystems, *Java*™ *Blueprints, J2EE*™ *Patterns*, 2002.

Sun Microsystems, *Java*™ *Data Objects, Version 1.0*, 2002.

Sun Microsystems, *Java*™ *Transaction API, Version 1.0.1*, 1999.

Sun Microsystems, *Java*™ *Transaction Service, Version 1.0*, 1999.

Thomas, T., *Java*™ *Data Access: JDBC*™, *JNDI, and JAXP*, John Wiley & Sons, 2001.

Vermeulen, A., S. Ambler, G. Bumgardner, E. Metz, A. Vermeulen, T. Misfeldt, J. Shur, and P. Thompson, *The Elements Of Java*™ *Style*, Cambridge University Press, 1999.

Vlissides, J., *Pattern Hatching: Design Patterns Applied*, Addison-Wesley, 1998.

White, S., M. Fisher, R. Cattell, G. Hamilton, and M. Hapner, *JDBC*™ *API Tutorial and Reference: Universal Data Access for the Java*™ *2 Platform, Second Edition*, Addison-Wesley, 1999.

Index

Other Patterns Resources from Addison-Wesley

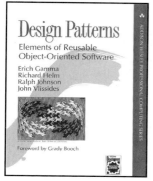

0-201-63361-2

0-201-18462-1

0-201-43293-5

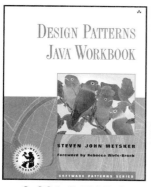

0-201-74397-3

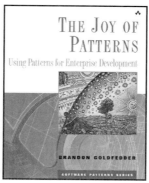

0-201-65759-7

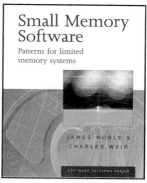

0-201-59607-5

0-201-71594-5

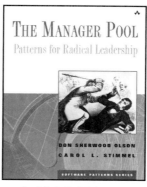

0-201-72583-5

0-13-140157-2

informIT

YOUR GUIDE TO IT REFERENCE

Articles

Keep your edge with thousands of free articles, in-depth features, interviews, and IT reference recommendations – all written by experts you know and trust.

Online Books

Answers in an instant from **InformIT Online Book's** 600+ fully searchable on line books. For a limited time, you can get your first 14 days **free**.

POWERED BY
Safari®
TECH BOOKS ONLINE®

Catalog

Review online sample chapters, author biographies and customer rankings and choose exactly the right book from a selection of over 5,000 titles.

Register
Your Book

at www.awprofessional.com/register

You may be eligible to receive:

- Advance notice of forthcoming editions of the book
- Related book recommendations
- Chapter excerpts and supplements of forthcoming titles
- Information about special contests and promotions throughout the year
- Notices and reminders about author appearances, tradeshows, and online chats with special guests

Contact us

If you are interested in writing a book or reviewing manuscripts prior to publication, please write to us at:

Editorial Department
Addison-Wesley Professional
75 Arlington Street, Suite 300
Boston, MA 02116 USA
Email: AWPro@aw.com

Addison-Wesley

Visit us on the Web: http://www.awprofessional.com